The Pedagog,

The Pedagogy of Lifelong Learning aims to bring together a selection of contemporary international research related to pedagogical matters in the field of lifelong learning and teaching. It builds on two previous research-based volumes on themes within the domain of lifelong learning.

There has been a long-standing interest in the role of educational institutions in shaping identities and cultures, in particular within the field of higher education. More recently, the relationship between identity and learning and the way in which individuals pursue a career as learners has become a concern in other sectors of post-compulsory education, within the non-formal sector and in informal learning sites.

In examining these issues, the book covers three key areas:

- Learning careers and identities
- Pedagogy and learning cultures
- Learning beyond institutions

This book seeks to examine empirically, methodologically and theoretically contemporary research in teaching and learning in diverse contexts. It will be of interest to all of those interested in teaching and learning in post-compulsory education, especially teachers and lecturers, researchers and policy-makers. The collection includes contributions from a number of well-known researchers concerned with pedagogy and lifelong learning including Richard Edwards, John Field, Sheila Riddell, Nicky Solomon, John Stevenson and Miriam Zukas.

Michael Osborne is Professor of Lifelong Education and Co-Director of the Centre for Research in Lifelong Learning, University of Stirling, UK.

Muir Houston is Research Fellow at the Institute of Education and CRLL, University of Stirling, UK.

Nuala Toman is Research Fellow at CRLL, Glasgow Caledonian University, UK.

The Pedagogy of Lifelong Learning

Understanding effective teaching and learning in diverse contexts

Edited by
Michael Osborne, Muir Houston
and Nuala Toman

Routledge
Taylor & Francis Group

LONDON AND NEW YORK

First published 2007
By Routledge
2 Park Square, Milton Park, Abingdon, Oxon OX14 4RN

Simultaneously published in the USA and Canada
by Routledge
270 Madison Ave, New York, NY 10016

Routledge is an imprint of the Taylor & Francis Group, an informa business

Typeset in Times New Roman by
Keystroke, 28 High Street, Tettenhall, Wolverhampton
Printed and bound in Great Britain by
TJ International Ltd, Padstow, Cornwall

British Library Cataloguing in Publication Data
A catalogue record for this book is available from the British Library

Library of Congress Cataloging in Publication Data
A catalog record has been requested for this book

ISBN10: 0–415–42494–1 (hbk)
ISBN10: 0–415–42495–x (pbk)
ISBN10: 0–203–94529–8 (ebk)

ISBN13: 978–0–415–42494–3 (hbk)
ISBN13: 978–0–415–42495–0 (pbk)
ISBN13: 978–0–203–94529–2 (ebk)

Contents

Figures

Tables

Contributors

James Carmichael is Lecturer in the Social Sciences at Anniesland College, Glasgow. He acted as College-based Research Co-ordinator for the LfLFE project team at Anniesland, researching literacy practices in Modern Studies, Business Studies, Multi-Media and Child Care.

Lucila Carvalho is an educational psychologist and a PhD student, based at the Key Centre of Design Computing and Cognition, at the University of Sydney, Australia. Her research interests encompass informal learning, sociology of education, computer-supported learning and design. Presently, her research investigates perceptions of achievement and membership within the design field, and how those who are new to design may learn about this specialised knowledge within an informal environment. The research also involves the development, implementation and evaluation of an informal eLearning environment to experience design in a technology museum.

Dianne Conrad is currently the Director of the Centre for Learning Accreditation at Athabasca University (AU), where she is responsible for the management of AU's university-wide system of prior learning assessment and recognition. A practising adult educator for 25 years, she also has experience in distance, professional, continuing and online education and is actively engaged in both PLAR research and eLearning research that focuses on the development of community among online learners and the positioning of eLearning as a societal phenomenon.

Nicolas Dedek is a Reference Services Co-ordinator with the Literacy Foundation in Montreal. The Literacy Foundation is a non-profit organisation whose aim is to ensure all adults have access to basic training in reading and writing. He is responsible for delivering reference services allowing poorly educated or lesser literate individuals to obtain the necessary information to enable a return to training.

Dr Darryl Dymock works as an educational researcher, writer and lecturer. He is a part-time Principal Research Fellow in the Centre for Learning Research at Griffith University, Brisbane, Australia, where he also teaches the Adult and

Vocational Education programme. In 2005–6 and 2007 he has been working on research funded by the National Centre for Vocational Education Research. Since 2000, Darryl has been editor of the respected international peer-reviewed periodical, the *Journal of Workplace Learning*.

Rob Edmunds is a Research Fellow at the Open University working on an ESRC-funded project entitled, What is Learned at University: The Social and Organisational Mediation of University Learning (SOMUL). His general area of interest is cognitive psychology, with a specific focus on skill acquisition and information reduction strategies following the work of Haider and Frensch. Before completing his PhD at the Open University in 2006, he studied for an MSc in Cognitive Science and a BSc in Psychology, both at the University of Wales, Cardiff. Before undertaking his PhD, he worked for Unilever Research situated in Bedford.

Professor Richard Edwards is Professor of Education at the University of Stirling and was Co-Director of the Literacies for Learning in Further Education (LfLFE) project. He is the author of a number of books, including R. Edwards and R. Usher (2007) *Globalisation and Pedagogy* (London: Routledge).

Professor John Field is a Professor in the Institute of Education, University of Stirling, where he also served as Deputy Principal (Research) between 2002 and 2007. He has written widely on aspects of lifelong learning, as well as on theories of social capital. He is an Honorary Professor at Birkbeck, University of London. In 2006, he was awarded an honorary doctorate by the Open University.

Dr Brian Findsen has worked in the field of adult and continuing education for over 20 years, primarily in his home country of New Zealand. In 2004, he took up an academic position in the Department of Adult and Continuing Education at the University of Glasgow where he has been Head of Department since 2006. The area of older adults and learning has been the major focus of Brian's recent research. His other interests include the sociology of adult education, social equity issues, international adult education and the education of adult educators. Amid his various publications, he co-authored a significant book on New Zealand adult and community education, *The Fourth Sector* (1996), and recently Krieger in Florida published his new book, *Learning Later* (2005), a blend of social gerontology and adult learning.

Dr Anna-Lena Göransson works as an editor at the Swedish Rescue Services Agency. She is a Doctor of Philosophy in the theory and practice of teaching and learning Swedish, and her research interests centre on language use and the question of how to use language as a tool that can unite theory and practice in various forms of vocational training.

Dr Sotiria-Grek has recently completed her doctoral thesis on adult education in the cultural sector. She worked at the State Museum of Contemporary Art in

Thessaloniki, Greece, as assistant curator and education officer (1998–2002). Currently she is working as a Research Fellow for the Centre for Educational Sociology at the University of Edinburgh on a collaborative project on the impact of quality assurance and evaluation on education governance. Her research interests include museum studies, education policy and governance, education and European integration, and political economy of education.

Rita Kop is Lecturer in the Department of Adult Continuing Education, University of Wales, Swansea, and developed the MA in Lifelong Learning programme on which she currently teaches. She started work in the department in 1998 after a career in Dutch primary education, and has a wide experience in developing access to higher education. Her main activities have been in the area of providing access routes and new learning opportunities for previously excluded groups. She is interested in the potential of online learning to develop and deliver innovative learning opportunities and her research interests are in online communications, learning and teaching in online environments, widening participation and institutional change.

Irene Malcolm is a Lecturer in Lifelong Learning at the University of Stirling. She researches and writes about learning in changing workplaces, related to globalisation, technology and emotional labour. Recent research includes work on the ESRC project, *Learning Lives*, studying learning, identity and agency in the working lives of adults

Dr Janice Malcolm is a Senior Lecturer at the University of Kent, UK. She has researched and published on the construction of academic, disciplinary and pedagogic identity for several years in collaboration with Miriam Zukas. She is a teacher educator working principally on programmes for university lecturers.

Isabelle Medeiros is a graduate of the University of Montreal in psycho-education. She is currently completing a Master's degree in Education at the University of Quebec at Montreal (UQAM), as well as a graduate studies diploma in Management at HEC Montreal. Her focus is on the relations between social–professional and educational paths.

Dr Kate Miller is a Researcher in the School of Education and Social Work, University of Dundee. Previously she was a university-based researcher on the LfLFE project, with specific responsibility for data collection and analysis at Perth College.

Professeure Chantal Ouellet is a professor in the Department of Education and Specialized Training at the University of Quebec at Montreal (UQAM) in the school–society adaptation section. She is interested in the relations between literacy and work; her doctoral thesis focused on this topic. Her research projects also deal with reading and writing difficulties of adolescents and adults, as well as with intervention programmes.

Albert Renkema is a Researcher at the Department of Educational Sciences of the University of Groningen. He has been engaged in the evaluation of experiments with Individual Learning Accounts issued by the Dutch government.

Professor Sheila Riddell is Director of the Centre for Research in Education Inclusion and Diversity at the Moray House School of Education, University of Edinburgh. Her research interests are in the broad field of equality and social inclusion, with particular reference to gender, social class and disability in the fields of education, training, employment and social care. Sheila has published extensively in these areas and sits on policy advisory committees on disability and equal rights.

June Smith is a PhD student at the University of Stirling. Previously she was a university-based researcher on the LfLFE project, with specific responsibility for data collection and analysis at Anniesland College, following many years teaching in further education in Scotland.

Professor Nicky Solomon is Professor of Education and Lifelong Learning at City University, London. Her research and teaching work focus on pedagogical practices and the production of knowledge in a changing world, with particular attention to changes in work practices, work identities, as well as changes in the relationships between education institutions, workplaces and communities. Her research is informed by writers who draw on social theories and in particular those writers who foreground language and discourse as productive of meaning (and not just reflecting it).

Professor John Stevenson is currently Deputy Dean Research for the Faculty of Education, and is the foundation appointment to the Chair of Post-Compulsory Education and Training at Griffith University, Queensland, Australia. He established and led the Centre for Skill Formation Research and Development, as well as the Centre for Learning Research at Griffith University, and has been head of various academic schools there. His research interests are in the ways in which people come to learn and make sense in new ways, especially how they connect different ways of understanding.

Dr Ruth Watkins is a Lecturer and Co-ordinator of Student Learning Services in the Institute of Education, University of Stirling. Her current research interests include research ethics in the social sciences and student learning and choice in higher education. She is an associate researcher on the SOMUL project.

Dr Elisabet Weedon is Deputy Director in the Centre for Research in Education Inclusion and Diversity at the Moray House School of Education, University of Edinburgh. Her main research interests are in the area of adult learning. She is currently working on a number of projects within the centre, including disabled students' learning experiences in higher education, lifelong learning in Europe and learning in the workplace and has published research in this area.

Leesa Wheelahan is a Senior Lecturer in Adult and Vocational Education at Griffith University, Australia. Her research interests include lifelong learning, tertiary education policy, recognition of prior learning, credit-transfer and student articulation between the sectors of post-compulsory education and training, and cross-sectoral relations between Australia's vocational education and training and higher education sectors. Her current research is on the intersection between policy and learning theory, and the role of knowledge in the curriculum, drawing on the theories of Basil Bernstein and the philosophy of critical realism.

Professor Miriam Zukas is Professor of Adult Education at the University of Leeds, UK. She has researched and published on the construction of academic, disciplinary and pedagogic identity for several years in collaboration with Janice Malcolm. She teaches a wide range of professionals on postgraduate programmes.

Chapter 1

Introduction

Michael Osborne, Muir Houston and Nuala Toman

This book brings together a selection of contemporary international research related to pedagogical matters in the field of lifelong learning and teaching. It builds on two previous research-based volumes (on widening participation (Osborne et al. 2003) and learning outside the academy (Edwards et al. 2005)) on themes within the domain of lifelong learning. Specifically, the book draws upon and develops presentations made at the third international Centre for Research in Lifelong Learning (CRLL)[1] conference in June 2005. The conference was inspired by the fact that CRLL itself hosts a number of research projects with the UK's Teaching and Learning Research Programme (TLRP), funded by the Economic and Social Research Council (ESRC) and the Scottish Executive. These projects focus on lifelong learning, higher education, community-based learning, and literacy practices in further education, and in themselves have strong international dimensions. Using this work as an inspiration, the conference sought to review more widely emerging issues from researching teaching and learning in different post-school contexts, an issue which has grown in research importance around the world in recent years, with the concern both to widen participation and improve student attainment. This book seeks to examine empirically, methodologically and theoretically contemporary research in teaching and learning in diverse contexts. It focuses on three main areas: learning careers and identities; pedagogy and learning cultures; and learning beyond institutions.

The chapters in first section of the book concentrate on the long-standing interest amongst researchers in the role of educational context in shaping identities and cultures (e.g. Becker et al. 1968; Dubet 1994). This has been emphasised in particular within the field of higher education and in so doing such work has extended our notions of learning outcomes to areas such as attitudes, values, confidence, personal autonomy, self-esteem and moral development (Pascarella and Terenzini 1991, 2005). More recently the relationship between identity and learning, and the way in which individuals pursue a career as learners, has become a concern in other sectors of post-compulsory education, within the non-formal sector and in informal learning sites, with the work of Bloomer and Hodkinson (2000) in particular popularising these concepts. The related notion of learning trajectory has also become a common theoretical base for studies of teaching and learning in post-compulsory settings, including in vocational education (see Crossan et al. 2003), and refers to the aggregate of an individual's learning experiences across the life span, determined by social capital, contextual factors, and individual choices that reflect learner identity (Gorard 2002). Thus in this part of the collection the chapters deal with questions of learning identity, learning careers and trajectories in a range of different locational contexts, and pays particular attention to the experiences of diverse learners, including those with low attainment and in both formal and informal contexts. The opening chapter in this section, by Janice Malcolm and Miriam Zukas, is the first of two chapters which deal specifically with the higher education context. However, whilst for Malcolm and Zukas the focus is on academic staff, Elisabet Weedon and Sheila Riddell consider a specific sub-group of students.

Within an overall context of academic identity formation, Malcolm and Zukas examine in terms of structural differences the separation between teaching and research within UK higher education. They suggest that this division is continued and conditioned by reasons of policy and culture. In terms of policy, they suggest that differential rewards are offered to universities in terms of funding for the purposes of teaching and research activities; while in terms of culture they argue that individual promotion and institutional kudos are more readily awarded in relation to research rather than teaching. Despite this apparent separation, much research (e.g. Hattie and Marsh 1996, 2002) has suggested some form of 'nexus' between the research and teaching functions of universities and, indeed, academics themselves often claim that a dialectical relationship exists between the two. However, Malcolm and Zukas (2000) suggest that pedagogy has been somewhat neglected in analyses of the epistemological and social characteristics of academic identities which tend to emphasise research as the focus of academic work. Through a series of vignettes the authors examine the ways in which the practice of knowledge production is experienced by academics through their teaching (Becher and Trowler 2001). This is followed by an examination of what they term artificial dichotomies between: research and teaching; and disciplinary and pedagogic identities. Finally, a rationale for the demise of these dichotomies is presented (Zukas and Malcolm 2007).

In Weedon and Riddell's chapter, the object of analysis is the differential experience of dyslexic students in higher education. To examine similarities and differences in student populations and perceptions they present survey data from four universities. They provide an overview of dyslexia research and note difficulties of definition and diagnosis (e.g. Hatcher et al. 2002; McLaughlin 2004). However they note that dyslexic students now constitute the largest single group of disabled students in UK higher education and argue that the rise in the number of dyslexic students is attributable to three main factors: earlier identification in school; the Disabled Students' Allowance; and an increase in mature students. The institutions comprise two pre-1992 and two post-1992 institutions, and differences in terms of location, size and the composition of the student population are reported. The main findings from the survey research deal with the evidence for inclusive practices in relation to support services focused on disabled and specifically dyslexic students. Issues examined include: students' perceptions of inclusive practices in relation to, for example, taking notes, reading materials and completing assignments on time; the range and flexibility of the assessment regime, with a focus on the specific difficulties dyslexic students face in relation to particular assessment instruments; and perceptions of academic support. While differences appear between the four institutions, Weedon and Riddell also note differences in access to support *within* institutions. Overall, while noting that progress is being made in the provision of support and assistance to dyslexic students the picture from this chapter suggests that much has yet to be done.

John Stevenson's chapter shifts the contextual focus to the workplace, in an attempt to provide an answer to the question of 'meaning' and how it is 'made' through reference to two main theoretical perspectives. Drawing on both Piagetian and Vygotskian perspectives, Stevenson explores how 'meaning' is acquired. In the first part of the chapter, findings about values, literacy, use of technology and problem solving within the context of motel front offices are reported. Drawing on a range of perspectives, including Engeström's (1987, 1999, 2001) conceptualisation of an activity system, Beven's 'situated cognition lens' (2002), and the cognitive theory of Middleton (2002), Stevenson finds that for each of the activities under investigation the making of meaning is highly contextualised. Stevenson's purpose is two-fold: firstly, to understand how abstracted concepts can be translated into everyday settings; and secondly, how the concepts can be meaningfully applied in new situations. For Stevenson, this is akin to the Piagetian concept of accommodation and similar to the interaction of spontaneous and scientific concepts developed by Vygotsky. However, Stevenson recognises that this transition is not without struggle and illustrates the apprehension and dis-comfort individuals can experience when this transformation of meaning takes place. However, Stevenson also reports feelings of empowerment when new meanings are made. In both the studies in this section, Stevenson reports evidence of a struggle to render existing meaning in new ways. In concluding, Stevenson suggests that the making of meaning and the role of accommodation are important for the development of a pedagogy for lifelong learning where the role of the educator or trainer is to involve learners in activities which are accessible and meaningful but must be applied in diverse contexts.

The focus for Brian Findsen and Lucilla Carvalho is on older adults' learn-ing patterns and what this means in terms of trajectory and changes to identity. They examine formal, informal and non-formal learning and the influence of group membership on learning trajectories and changes in learners' self-conceptualisation. Specifically, they wish to discover if motivation for learning changes from an instrumental approach allied to a vocational outcome to an expressive approach associated with greater leisure time. Drawing on a qualitative methodology, the research focuses on existing groups of older learners in two different locations in New Zealand. Their sample were mostly in the 65–74 age range; tended to be from a middle-class background; had a relatively high level of previous educational experience; and were generally in good health. In report-ing the findings, a range of motives for connecting with lifelong learning are proposed which include the pervasiveness of learning; its potential to provide new insights; the positive health benefits; and, even in later life, the positive influence of role models. In relation to context, Findsen and Carvalho examine how differences in context mirror differences in the purpose and nature of study. One impression gained was that the active theory of retirement (Laslett 1989) is sup-ported for these third age learners and that learning whether in formal, informal or non-formal contexts is important for many in developing new social relationships, particularly as existing ones tied to previous employment become less important or possible. Overall, Findsen and Carvalho suggest that the dichotomy proposed by Glendinning (2000) in relation to instrumental versus expressive motivation is largely redundant and in addition participants do not adhere to gender stereotypes where males exhibit instrumental motives and females exhibit expressive motives for learning. Finally, they suggest that the rule rather than the exception is for older adults to maximise life chances not only for personal growth but also for the benefit of the wider community.

The final chapter in this section, by John Field and Irene Malcolm, also utilises age as a factor in changing attitudes and behaviours in adult learning. Using a concept of time that incorporates both historical and generational aspects, Field and Malcolm through adoption of a life-history approach seek to understand how this can impact on people's orientation towards learning. Firstly, they exam-ine debates which suggest ways in which age interacts with learning and report that survey findings consistently show that participation in learning declines by age (e.g. O'Donnell and Chapman 2006; Sargant and Aldridge 2002). For Field and Malcolm, increasing interest in age inequalities in educational participation is primarily driven by two separate but related developments. The first is the increasing interest in the social and policy implications of ageing (Tuckett and MacAulay 2005); while the second is the development of social models of ageing which investigate not only the way age and old age are socially constructed, but also the ways in which older people shape their lives (Phillipson 1998). However, despite recognising existing research they point to some notable limitations, at least in the British context. They introduce the concept of generation as developed by Mannheim (1952) to investigate relationships between age, values and behav-iour, and also take note of studies which supplement this through reference to the work of Bourdieu (1993). The framework outlined above is then operation-alised through a life history approach to consider the shifts in trajectories and identities of two different subjects. What is of interest in these case stories is the different role that generational and historical time plays in each.

The second section focuses on the role of pedagogy in developing learning culture and the ways in which cultures of organisations and communities facilitate, prescribe and determine learning, and once again considers these issues within different sites of post-compulsory learning. On the one hand, learning in formal settings may be contingent on particular sets of disciplinary power, regulations and time/space relationships, with students exerting little by way of agency, as in Nespor's (1994) classic study of higher education. By contrast, other sites of learning provide much greater opportunity for collaborative learning and negotiation between teacher and learner, as exemplified in much recent work in the domain of communities of practice. In this section, sites from which research is presented include vocational education institutions, workplaces, higher education and community settings.

Darryl Dymock's chapter is broadly located within domains, variously referred to as 'the learning region/city' and 'learning communities', that can be traced back to the pioneering work of the OECD (1973, 2001a) and which has attracted considerable attention in recent years, particularly in Europe (see Longworth 2006; Sankey and Osborne 2006). Here he is concerned with sparsely-populated rural Australian communities, in particular an area of some 4,500 people, with around 1,850 of these resident in the largest town. The research was undertaken in conjunction with a local council, and its purpose was to identify learning needs, opportunities and barriers, and to make recommendations that might help the area develop its learning capability. It considers the development of learning communities in a rural context and mechanisms of knowledge development that extend beyond formal approaches. There are questions, however, as to the extent to which small rural towns without an existing vision for learning and with limited local government and community resources can provide the learning support necessary to develop a learning culture. This can include people resources associated with sharing tasks required in vocational education and training. There are also issues about adults' motivations to learn, participation in adult education and the extent of purposive but often unacknowledged learning. The development of a learning culture is also part of the concept of a learning community, and has been explored internationally in recent years in Canada, the United States, Europe and the United Kingdom, as well as Australia (Faris and Wheeler 2006). The chapter addresses: the differing conceptions of learning amongst people in a small rural community and the implications for pedagogy therein; the extent to which small town learning needs differ from metropolitan areas; the identification of realistic responses to learning needs for more isolated communities, including the extent to which individual needs can be catered for; the value and practicality of utilising local skills and knowledge; and mechanisms through which to best promote learning opportunities and support learning in small rural communities.

Carmichael and colleagues present research from a TLRP project involving two universities and four UK further education (FE) colleges. The research draws on existing work concerned with literacy practices engaged in by individuals in schools, higher education and the community, and seeks to extend the insights gained from these studies into FE. It aims to explore the literacy practices of students and those practices developed in different parts of the curriculum and develops pedagogic interventions to support students' learning more effectively. The work involves examining literacy across the many domains of people's experiences, the ways in which these practices are mobilised and realised within these different domains, and their capacity to be mobilised and recontextualised elsewhere to support learning. One of the premises for the project is that literacy practices of institutions are not always fashioned around the resources that students bring to college life – indeed college staff may be unaware of these potential resources. The intention of the research is to achieve a critical understanding of the movement and flows of literacy practices in people's lives. It seeks to determine how literacy practices are ordered and re-ordered, networked or overlapped across domains, across social roles in students' lives and what objects might mediate such mobilisations. The research raises many theoretical, methodological and practical challenges, not least in ensuring validity across four curriculum areas in four sites, drawing upon the collaboration of 16 practitioner researchers. Drawing on the analysis of initial empirical data, the chapter examines staff assumptions about students' learning and their consequences in terms of the texts they use in their teaching and the literacy practices expected of students.

Anna-Lena Göranssen considers how a group of firefighters, who consistently maintain that they are 'practitioners and not theorists', relate to various forms of language-based knowledge and 'knowledging' in their problem-based vocational learning. The study considers how learning can take place with the aid of words and actions, and how the verbal manners and attitudes towards language and language use of teachers and students might impact upon or even prevent learning. In this context the significance of how we communicate, read, write and learn is considered. The chapter considers how despite their intentions, teaching methods can sometimes fail to stimulate reading or writing, formal classroom interaction, abstract thinking or generalisation. It presents examples in which firefighters have built strong bonds of trust and respect with each other, but may distrust teachers' knowledge and their pedagogical skills; study questions formulated by teachers often failed to stimulate critical and analytical knowledge searching. In this sense, approaches to 'knowledging' can become instrumental and consist of strategic or ritualistic actions. The firefighters in this study formed a collective of more or less experienced firefighters and the workplace's unwritten and written rules and power structures appear to follow them into the learning space and influence their learning. The chapter points towards how practical activities and language can stimulate firefighters and create a dynamic learning environment. This work suggests the importance of learning methods and approaches in the development of the learning space.

There is significant interest internationally in learning at work, much of it driven by the rhetoric of economic competitiveness in a global economy (see EC 2001a; OECD 2001b). Billet (2001), amongst others, argues that the workplace is the only viable place for individuals to learn and develop their vocational practice, and the integration of work and learning is seen as essential in work environments and increasingly in educational institutions. In many workplaces it is now taken for granted that while working we learn, and arguably it could be said that employment and the production of workers are central to much of secondary and post-compulsory education. Terms such as 'new vocationalism', 'employability', 'generic skills' and graduate attributes are now part of the rhetoric that argues the need for educational institutions to integrate the business of work and employment with the outcomes of teaching and learning programmes. This connection between work and learning is often discussed in the literature as a blurring of boundaries between education and work, between the real world and education, between education and training, and between worker and learner. Recent trends to bring work into classrooms and to make learning 'real' has encouraged interest in the kinds of pedagogical practices that operate in these arenas. Nicky Solomon's chapter draws upon the findings of an Australian research study and focuses upon the pedagogical complexities that are emerging as the world of work is increasingly brought into our classrooms. The context is a vocational level school operating as a hotel, with students shifting between different work roles, such as receptionist, housekeeper and waiter. The simulation is all-encompassing in an attempt to create a 'realistic work environment' and in this sense it is not teacher-designed but generated through 'normal' work. The focus of the study is pedagogy as identity, and explores how new work requirements and worker identities are understood and enacted in the classroom. This leads to a consideration of how the 'real' and 'authentic' world of work is played out, and how the intersection of the two domains of practice-work and education are managed.

What kind of curriculum, pedagogy and qualifications do we need for an uncertain future? Leesa Wheelahan seeks to answer these questions by engaging with the influential ideas of Ronald Barnett (2004a, 2004b), who has called for an 'ontological turn' in curriculum and pedagogy away from a primary focus on knowledge and skills to 'pedagogy for human being', which seeks to develop the human qualities and dispositions needed to thrive in an uncertain future. Barnett counter-poses his approach with the 'generic skills' approach, arguing that the latter is a *cul-de-sac*, because it is premised on certain knowable skills to navigate an uncertain world. While agreeing with Barnett that generic skills are a dead-end, the chapter argues that a 'pedagogy for human being' must be contextualised by a vocation. Wheelahan argues that unless the notion of vocation is used to ground Barnett's 'ontological turn' in the curriculum, there is a danger that the attributes and dispositions he seeks will result in disconnected and fragmented identities. These find expression in market-oriented capacities and patterns of consumption, rather than an intrinsic inner calling, or (as sought by Barnett) an authentic self. The author uses critical realism to critique Barnett's analysis, draws on Bernstein (2000) to argue against decontextualised notions of 'trainability', offers Dewey's (1966) notion of vocation as an alternative, and Young (2003) to argue for an alternative model of qualifications and curriculum. She concludes that Barnett's call for an ontological turn is useful because it forces us to consider the outcomes we seek from education. However, it requires an anchor in the notion of vocation.

The final chapter, by Ruth Watkins et al., in this section presents an overview of another ESRC TRLP project that explores how the social and organisational aspects of the university experience may mediate student learning. The research particularly focuses on how variations in the social and organisational mediation of institutional and disciplinary environments may impact on what students in UK higher education perceive that they learn. The nature of the research design means that a range of theoretical perspectives have been deployed and attempts are made to integrate aspects of these into a coherent, multidisciplinary framework, employing a multi-method approach to data collection and analysis. The chapter reports on an investigation of three conceptions of learning outcomes derived from the three academic literatures, namely learning as cognitive development (cf Richardson 2001), as academic and professional identity (cf Maassen 1996) and as personal identity and conception of self (Becker et al. 1968; Dubet 1994), and in three distinct disciplines. It measures these outcomes through analysis of the experiences and views of students and graduates at various points in their academic careers and beyond. The chapter focuses upon improving understanding of what the formal and learning outcomes actually are for a student within higher education in the UK and the significant factors which may impact upon these outcomes.

The third section develops the theme of sites of learning, and focuses specifically on pedagogies of lifelong learning beyond traditional face-to-face teaching in institutional settings. These chapters present research concerned with learning at work, in a museum and in virtual environments.

Since the majority of workers are located in small and medium-sized enterprises (SMEs) considerable attention has been given to the role of this part of the corporate sector in learning. However, in general authors report on the difficulties in both engaging employers and workers in SMEs, where often operational demands of the business and the economic 'bottom-line' (see Brink et al. 2002) compete with both individual and organisational opportunities to learn. The chapter by Albert Renkema is based on a quasi-experimental study on the impact of Individual Learning Accounts (ILAs) on learning intention and learning culture on the workfloor in the Netherlands. It focuses on the impact on older employees in two sectors of employment: the elderly care sector and SMEs in the technological installation sector using Ajzen's (1991) *Theory of Planned Behaviour* to measure impact. He presents differences in the effect of ILAs on learning intention and learning culture between both sectors. Whilst in technological installation companies ILAs were most effective with regard to the learning intentions of older employees, in the elderly care organisations, they had most effect on the informal learning culture amongst employees. These differences relate to factors such as gender, organisation size, organisation structure and strategic training policy, and the study aims to clarify the way in which these factors operate.

Chantal Ouellet and colleagues from Québec argue that the globalising economy has weakened demand for less qualified workers across a range of economic sectors and that as a consequence there are good reasons to be concerned about the prospects of less educated individuals. They point to both Canadian (Statistics Canada and HRDC 2001) and international studies (OECD 2002, 2003) that show that participation rates in training are a function of levels of higher education, and that this pattern is further accentuated in the context of employer-sponsored training, given difficulties of access to essential skills training. The research presented in this chapter relates to disparities amongst workforce sectoral committees in Québec in relation to their efforts in raising awareness about training and in creating contexts for the delivery of essential skills. The chapter presents results from documentary analysis and semi-directed interviews with sectoral committee directors and reveal that whilst all committees have a training mandate, essential skills training figures among the activities of only half of the sample interviewed. Perceptions of essential skills training by managers, trainers and workers diverge significantly from how they engage in it, and this has an impact on corporate actions. Moreover, in this study it appears that the context of such training appears to be closely linked to these differing perceptions, visions or 'representations' by those in sectoral committees. The authors argue that understanding the representations of the various actors involved would allow for a better appreciation of their perceptions of, and modes of participation in, essential skills training, and enable the development of relevant awareness strategies aimed both at managers and at workers.

The museum as a site of informal learning has a rich history and, as Knutson and Crowley (2005) from the University of Pittsburg have recently reported, has called upon a range of learning theories in its practices, including behaviourism (Melton 1935), post-Piagetian constructivism (Gelman et al. 1991; Hein 1995), multiple-intelligences (Davis 1993) and socio-cultural theory (Matusov and Rogoff 1995). In her chapter here, Sotoria Grek explores methodological issues relating to conducting research in the field of museum and gallery education, building on a critical theory approach and within a methodological framework of critical ethnography and critical discourse analysis. The aim of her research is to examine adult education in museums and galleries; it seeks to investigate the significance, reasons and impacts behind the shift from museums' more traditional educational practices to a new learning discourse. It examines the possibilities of such a shift unfolding in the urban context of Dundee in Scotland, a city of many galleries, a long history of adult education and a vibrant community life. The study is rooted in a very specific theoretical framework, and utilises critical ethnographic research tools, which take into account the historically given circumstances within which the subjects are acting. The chapter also explores critical discourse analysis as a research tool for investigating ideologies and power through the systematic examination of semiotic data, be they written, spoken or visual. Thereby the chapter examines how commercial, political and pedagogical interventions influence the learning of adults in museums, and how critical discourse analysis could be utilised in order to reveal both hegemonic and oppressed discourses.

The final two chapters in this section of the book concern virtual sites of learning. Rita Kop's chapter is contextualised within arguments that the expansion of the internet and the opportunities presented by new and ever more powerful forms of Information and Communication Technology (ICT) will change our communities forever. In an educational context, technological change has been a major driver for a new flexibility in lifelong learning, namely to meet the learning needs of students at times, places and paces of their own choosing (see EC 2001b). The growth in the use of the internet has been a factor in the emergence of new ways of applying existing theories of learning and knowledge and to an extent has led to the emergence of new models signalling that ICT may fundamentally change the way in which we all learn and teach. Much of the theory underpinning the design of virtual learning environments has emerged from the application of principles that have emerged from situated cognition and the work of Vygotsky (1978) and the creation of virtual communities of practice (Lave and Wenger 1991). Hung and Chen's (2001) principles of design for e-learning, which are based around design principles of *commonality*, *situatedness*, *interdependency* and *infrastructure*, draw heavily on these theories and present a good overview of dominant thinking.

There has been much discussion about the changed position of educational institutions such as universities due to these virtual developments. The changed sense of space and place has been lamented as a loss, as universities were seen as places where people came together, where minds met and where new ideas were conceived as nowhere else in society. Proponents of the internet argue that new online phenomena such as *wikis* and *blogs* can fulfil exactly this same role, as the openness of these media and the willingness of people to share in such experiences encourages a similar discussion of ideas and a collaborative development of thoughts and knowledge. The added advantage of the online tools would lie in their globally positioned discussion forums, which provide immediate responses on a scale unimaginable in the traditional university with its huge lecture theatres and much slower publication rates. This chapter explores the role of these two recent innovations in our virtual world, *wikis* (virtual sites that invite co-construction of knowledge) and *blogs* (interactive online diaries), as informal online learning tools. It then examines how these forms could play a part in mean-ingful knowledge acquisition, investigating in particular the nature and validation of knowledge acquired, or whether these media form part of a new internet 'hype' that has only limited value in an educational setting.

Online environments raise fundamental questions about who we are and who we purport to be. Identity is a complex phenomenon in virtual worlds, where it is perhaps easier to withhold certain aspects of one's characteristics and to purport others that mislead and deceive (see Timms 2007). In the penultimate chapter of this collection, Diane Conrad considers the way in which increasing numbers of online learners are engaging in interactive activities through intimate 'revela-tions of self' – acts similar in nature to the act of confession. This chapter positions the phenomenon of confession as an emergent trend in online pedagogy, draw-ing upon the literatures of adult, lifelong, and online learning, communication theory, and communities of practice in raising pedagogical issues around online participation, motivation, assessment and effective instructional strategies.

In conclusion, in this collection we draw the links between research that focuses upon the three concepts of learning careers and identities, pedagogy and learning cultures and learning beyond formal institutions, drawing upon work within an international domain. We return to these themes in the concluding chapter.

Note

1   See http://crll.gcal.ac.uk for further details.

References

Ajzen, I. (1991) 'The Theory of Planned Behavior', *Organizational Behavior and Human Decision Processes*, 50: 179–211.

Barnett, R. (2004a) 'Learning for an unknown future', *Higher Education Research & Development*, 23(3): 247–260.

Barnett, R. (2004b) 'The purposes of higher education and the changing face of academia', *London Review of Education*, 2(1): 61–73.

Becher, T. and Trowler, P. (2001) *Academic Tribes and Territories*, 2nd edition, Buckingham: SRHE/Open University.

Becker, H.S., Geer, B. and Hughes, E.C. (1968) *Making the Grade: The Academic Side College Life*, New York: Wiley.

Bernstein, B. (2000) *Pedagogy, Symbolic Control and Identity*, 2nd edition, Oxford: Rowman & Littlefield Publishers.

Beven, F. (2002) 'The knowledge required for database use', *International Journal of Educational Research*, 37: 43–65.

Billett, S. (2001) 'Participation and continuity at work: a critique of current workplace learning discourses. Context, power and perspective: confronting the challenges to improving attainment in learning at work'. *Joint Network/SKOPE/TRLP international workshop*, 8–10 November, Sunley Management Centre, University College of Northampton, at: http://www.infed.org/archives/e-texts/billett_workplace_learning.htm.

Bloomer, M. and Hodkinson, P. (2000) 'Learning careers: continuity and change in young people's dispositions to learning', *British Educational Research Journal*, 26(5): 583–597.

Bourdieu, P. (1993) *Sociology in Question*, London: Sage.

Brink, B., Munro, J. and Osborne, M. (2002) 'Using online learning technology in an SME work-based setting', *Educational Technology & Society*, at: http://ifets.ieee.org/periodical/vol_2_2002/v_2_2002.html.

Crossan, B., Field, J., Gallacher, J. and Merrill, B. (2003) 'Understanding participation in learning for non-traditional adult learners: learning careers and the construction of learning identities', *British Journal of Sociology of Education*, 24(1): 55–67.

Davis, J. (1993) *Games for Museum-goers to Play* (Technical Report #38), Cambridge, MA: Project Zero, Harvard Graduate School of Education.

Dewey, J. (1966) *Democracy and Education: An Introduction to the Philosophy of Education*, New York: Free Press (first published in 1916).

Dubet, F. (1994) 'Dimensions et figures de l'expérience étudiante dans l'université de masse' (Dimensions and representations on student experience in mass university), *Revue Française de Sociologie*, XXXV(4): 511–532.

Edwards, R., Gallacher, J. and Whittaker, S. (2006) *Researching Experiental and Community-based Learning*, London: Routledge.

Engeström, Y. (1987) *Learning by Expanding: An Activity–Theoretical Approach to Developmental Research*, Helsinki: Orienta-Konsultit.

Engeström, Y. (1999) 'Expansive visibilization of work: an activity-theoretical perspective', *Computer Supported Cooperative Work*, 8: 63–93.

Engeström, Y. (2001) 'Expansive learning at work: toward an activity-theoretical reconceptualization', *Journal of Education and Work*, 14(1): 133–156.

European Commission (2001a) *Making the Lifelong Learning Area a Reality*, Brussels: European Commission.

European Commission (2001b) *The Memorandum on Lifelong Learning*, Brussels: European Commission.

Faris, R. and Wheeler, L. (2006) 'Learning communities of place: situating learning towns within a nested concept of social learning environments', paper presented at Australian Learning Communities Network (ALCN) National Conference 2006, *Learning Communities*, 25–27 September, Brisbane.

Gelman, R., Massey, C.M. and McManus, M. (1991) 'Characterizing supporting environments for cognitive development: lessons from children in a museum', in L. Resnick and J. Levine (eds) *Perspectives on Socially Shared Cognition*, Washington, DC: American Psychology Society, pp. 226–256.

Glendenning, F. (ed.) (2000) *Teaching and Learning in Later Life: Theoretical Implications*, Aldershot: Ashgate.

Gorard, S. (2002) *Lifelong Learning Trajectories in Wales: Results of the NIACE Adult Learners' Survey*, at: http://www.cf.ac.uk/socsi/ict/niacewales.doc.

Hatcher, J., Snowling, M. and Griffiths, Y. (2002) 'Cognitive assessment of dyslexic students in higher education', *British Journal of Educational Psychology*, 72: 119–133.

Hattie, H.W. and Marsh, J. (1996) 'The relationship between research and teaching – a meta-analysis', *Review of Educational Research*, 66(4): 507–542.

Hattie, H.W. and Marsh, J. (2002) 'The relation between research productivity and teaching effectiveness: complementary, antagonistic or independent constructs?', *Journal of Higher Education*, 73(5): 603–641.

Hein, G.E. (1995) 'The constructivist museum', *Journal of Education in Museums*, 16: 21–23.

Hung, D.W.L. and Chen, D. (2001) 'Situated cognition, vygotskian thought and learning from the communities of practice perspective: Implications for the design of web-based e-learning', *Educational Media International*, 38(1): 3–12.

Knutson, K. and Crowley, K. (2005) 'Museum as learning laboratory: Developing and using a practical theory of informal learning', *Hand to Hand*, 18(4): 4–5.

Laslett, P. (1989) *A Fresh Map of Life: The Emergence of the Third Age*, London: Weidenfeld and Nicholson.

Lave, J. and Wenger, E. (1991) *Situated Learning: Legitimate Peripheral Participation*, Cambridge: Cambridge University Press.

Longworth, N. (2006) *Learning Cities, Learning Regions, Learning Communities: Lifelong Learning and Local Government*, London: Routledge.

Maassen, P. (1996) *Government Steering and the Academic Culture: The Intangibility of the Human Factor in Dutch and German Universities*, Maarsen: De Tijdstroom.

Malcolm, J. and Zukas, M. (2000) 'Becoming an educator: communities of practice in higher education', in I. McNay (ed.) *Higher Education and its Communities*, Buckingham: SRHE/Open University.

Mannheim, K. (1952) *Essays on the Sociology of Knowledge*, London: Routledge and Kegan Paul.

Matusov, E. and Rogoff, B. (1995) 'Evidence of development from people's participation in communities of learners', in J. H. Falk and L. D. Dierking (eds) *Public Institutions for Personal Learning: Establishing a Research Agenda*, Washington, DC: American Association of Museums, pp. 97–104.

McLaughlin, D. (2004) 'Dyslexia in the workplace – policy for an inclusive society', in G. Reid and A. Fawcett (eds) *Dyslexia in Context: Research, Policy and Practice*, London: Whurr.

Melton, A.W. (1935) *Problems of Installation in Museums of Art*, New Series, number 14, Washington, DC: American Association of Museums.

Middleton, H.E. (2002) 'Complex problem solving in a workplace setting', *International Journal of Educational Research*, 37: 67–84.

Nespor, J. (1994) *Knowledge in Motion: Space, Time and Curriculum in Undergraduate Physics and Management*, Brighton: Falmer.

O'Donnell, K. and Chapman, C. (2006) *Adult Education Participation in 2004/05*, Washington: National Center for Education Statistics.

Organisation for Economic Cooperation and Development (OECD) (1973) *Recurrent Education: A Strategy for Lifelong Learning*, Paris: OECD/CERI.

OECD (2001a) *The Well-being of Nations: The Role of Human and Social Capital*, Paris: OECD.

OECD (2001b) *Economics and Finance of Lifelong Learning*, Paris: OECD.

OECD (2002) *Regards sur l'Éducation. Les indicateurs de l'OCDE 2002*, Paris: OECD.

OECD (2003) *Au-delà du discours. Politiques et pratiques de formation d'adultes*, Paris: OECD.

Osborne, M., Gallacher, J. and Crossan, B. (eds) *Researching Widening Access*, London: Routledge.

Pascarella, E.T. and Terenzini, P.T. (1991) *How College Affects Students: Findings and Insights from Twenty Years of Research*, San Francisco, CA: Jossey-Bass.

Pascarella, E.T. and Terenzini, P.T. (2005) *How College Affects Students. Volume 2: A Third Decade of Research*, San Francisco, CA: Jossey-Bass.

Phillipson, C. (1998) *Reconstructing Old Age*, London: Sage.

Richardson, J.T.E. (2001) *Researching Student Learning: Approaches to Studying in Campus-based and Distance Education*, Buckingham: SRHE/Open University Press.

Sankey, K. and Osborne, M. (2006) 'Lifelong learning reaching regions where other learning doesn't reach', in R. Edwards et al. (eds) *Researching Learning Outside the Academy*, London: Routledge.

Sargant, N. and Aldridge, F. (2002) *Adult Learning and Social Division: A Persistent Pattern. Volume 1*, Leicester: National Institute of Adult Continuing Education.

Statistics Canada and HRDC (2001) *Un rapport sur l'éducation et la formation des adultes au Canada. Apprentissage et réussite*, Ottawa: Statistics Canada and HRDC.

Timms, D. (2007) 'Identity, local community and the internet', in M. Osborne, K. Sankey and B. Wilson (eds) *Social Capital, Lifelong Learning and the Management of Place: An International Perspective*, London: Routledge.

Tuckett, A. and McAulay, A. (eds) (2005) *Demography and Older Learners: Approaches to a New Policy Challenge*, Leicester: National Institute of Adult Continuing Education.

Vygotsky, L.S. (1978) *Mind in Society: The Development of Higher Psychological Processes*, Cambridge, MA: Harvard University Press.

Young, M. (2003) 'Comparing approaches to the role of qualifications in the promotion of lifelong learning', *European Journal of Education*, 38(2): 199–211.

Zukas, M. and Malcolm, J. (2007) 'Teaching, discipline, net-work', in A. Skelton (ed.) *International Perspectives on Teaching Excellence in Higher Education*, London: Routledge.

Chapter 2

Poor relations

Exploring discipline, research and pedagogy in academic identity

Janice Malcolm and Miriam Zukas

Metaphors of knowledge production

Within UK higher education, and to some extent elsewhere, teaching and research are increasingly organised within separate academic structures, and subjected to discrete quality assurance procedures and funding arrangements. The divisions between research and teaching continue both for policy reasons (differential rewards are offered to universities for teaching and research), and for cultural reasons (individual promotion and institutional kudos come more readily from research than from teaching). Universities are often anxious to reject any suggestion that they might focus solely on teaching, claiming instead to be 'research-led' or 'research-intensive' and thus engaged in 'research-led teaching'. These claims seem only to confirm perceptions of the differential status of research and teaching, and their meaning remains unclear. What is clear in much policy and institutional discourse is the assumption that research and teaching are fundamentally separate and distinctive activities between which a relationship of some kind may or may not exist. Numerous research studies, meta-analyses and reviews address the nature of this relationship in terms of 'links', 'nexus', 'interaction', 'influence' and 'impacts' (e.g. Brew and Boud 1995; Hattie and Marsh 1996; Brew 1999; Zubrick et al. 2001; Jenkins 2004). Attempts are made to produce statistical correlations between Teaching Quality Assessment (TQA) scores and the Research Assessment Exercise (RAE) (Drennan 1999), or other measures of research 'productivity' and teaching 'effectiveness' (Hattie and Marsh 2002). Unsurprisingly, many of these studies exhibit fundamental methodological flaws arising from the quantitative assessment of teaching and research 'quality' using indicators of doubtful validity or usefulness. Epistemological questions, and the consequent ways in which the complex activities of teaching and research are understood, are rarely explored in any detail in discussions of the research/teaching 'nexus' (Brew 1999: 293), giving many of the studies the rather fragile and rickety air of a complex but insubstantial house of cards.

Anna Sfard observed that two kinds of metaphor dominate discussions of learning – those of acquisition (learning as the acquisition of something) and participation (learning as a process of becoming a member of a community).

Within the acquisition metaphor, teachers are conceptualised as possessors, providers, facilitators and mediators of some property, possession or commodity (knowledge and concepts). Within the participation metaphor, teachers are expert participants, preservers of practices, discourses and activities (their knowledge) who engage learners (peripheral participants) in a community of practice in which they may ultimately participate as full members. Both policy discourse and studies of the 'nexus' tend to employ the acquisition metaphor, which implies a clear distinction between teaching and research: research is essentially about getting, discovering or even creating knowledge, whilst teaching is about transmitting it to learners. Coaldrake and Stedman, for example, refer to 'the generation of new knowledge' and 'the transmission of knowledge' (1999: 17). Boyer's much-cited four types of scholarship also divide teaching from the research activities of discovery, integration and application (1990). Yet, as many contributors to the debate have noted, academics themselves often claim that research and teaching not only inform and influence each other, but are integral aspects of their disciplinary work and lifeworld.

From the perspective of acquisition, then, teaching is separated from research or knowledge production: knowledge is what is acquired by learners from teachers who already possess it. Teachers mediate or facilitate knowledge through their actions; but it is pre-existing and separate from learning. The use of the metaphor assumes a clear separation between teaching/learning and the production of knowledge, or research.

Pedagogy, as we have argued elsewhere (Malcolm and Zukas 2000), has often been neglected in analyses of the epistemological and social characteristics of academic disciplines and their impact upon higher education structures and practices, which have tended to emphasise research as the focus of academic work (e.g. Lodahl and Gordon 1972; Biglan 1973; Becher 1989). However, the way in which discipline constructs particular versions of the relationships between research and teaching in the academic workplace – the bringing together of these two strands of analysis – is now being addressed more explicitly. Burton (1999), for example, considers the common process of learning enacted by research-active mathematicians and their learners, echoing Brew and Boud's analysis of research and teaching as forms of learning (1995). Geirsdottir (2004) undertakes a Bernsteinian comparative analysis of the ways in which teachers in different academic disciplines conceptualise the curriculum and their role in creating and practising it. Most notably, Nespor (1994) explores the ways in which different disciplines work to enrol students in disciplinary practices through the embodiment of those practices in curriculum, organisation and technology. In all of these examples, the question of epistemology and its role in both research and teaching, as forms of knowledge production, is brought strongly to the fore.

If we employ Sfard's alternative metaphor (1998), learning is participation; teachers and learners are *producers* of knowledge as participants in a disciplinary or practice community. This is already well understood, and indeed taken for granted, in relation to research. For example, as part of research work, people go to conferences, read journals, review articles, etc.; these activities themselves contribute to the production of knowledge. We understand teaching and learning to be equally and inextricably situated in social practice within the disciplinary community (Lave 1996). Teachers' pedagogic identities involve the negotiation of meaning, with learners, as members of a disciplinary community of pedagogic practice, just as research identities involve the negotiation of meaning with other disciplinary actors. As with research, this negotiation can take place across a range of academic activities, in a range of different settings and at different times. The participation metaphor integrates these apparently dichotomous aspects of knowledge production and recognises that researchers, teachers and learners are all engaged in producing knowledge as members of the disciplinary community of practice.

Knowledge production in practice

In this section the ways in which the practice of knowledge production is experienced by academics through their teaching is explored. The material is drawn from a series of 15 extended and semi-structured interviews with teachers in post-compulsory education, of whom nine worked in the UK and six in Australia. It is part of a larger ongoing project on pedagogic identity in post-compulsory education – in our usage, this is understood as the lived identity of teachers, rather than as the more student-focused 'positioning' favoured by Bernstein (2000: 66). The examples used here share a number of characteristics: the teachers are all adult educators in higher education and work in humanities and social science disciplines. We are currently exploring the extent to which the perceptions and understandings described are shared by academics in other disciplines and pedagogic contexts. However, here, we consider this problem in the context of contemporary academic work and the ways in which the academic workplace co-constructs identity: in short, how discipline, research and teaching are played out in the lived experience of academics at work, and the impact they have on identity construction. As Becher and Trowler argue (2001: 16–17), the fact that academic work has perforce become more fragmented, intense and stratified does not in itself diminish the agency of academics themselves in interpreting and responding to these changes.

As an example of agency in practice, Sarah describes how she develops from a position in which she understands pedagogy as the process of knowledge acquisition and transmission:

> . . . I had this image of the teacher as a knower when I started and in order to be an authentic teacher I had to know a lot – and I nearly killed myself trying to know a lot about the fourteen different subject areas that we taught across in that associate diploma – and I was really embarrassed if I had to say 'look I don't know – I haven't got to that bit in the book yet [laughs] or whatever it was'.

In addition to her understanding of pedagogy as the transmission of knowledge, in this extract Sarah also shows how, in common with most new teachers, she believed that her identity as a teacher was constructed through knowing more than the students about what she was teaching; and this knowing was supposed to arise through learning that took place at a spatial and temporal distance from the students, so that its prior existence was a prerequisite for pedagogy. However, through her engagement in both teaching and research, she comes to an understanding of pedagogy as a collective engagement with learners in knowledge production:

> And slowly but surely I realised that I was never going to be able to do that but it was actually okay to say, 'No, I don't know, let's find out' and the more I now think I probably know the more I know I don't know, but the more okay I am with that. So I have changed. And I've also – because of that understanding about how complex and how multiple people are, they're knowers in so many other domains and yet they can be positioned in the academy as not knowers so easily – so part of – the theory and practice and what I do in the teaching and learning environment is all tied up – so I go over that too about how they are knowers in all these other ways – what makes them think they know nothing when they're over here? So we practise being knowers and not knowers. So I give myself permission in front of them to not know things and to incorporate them as knowers – and they give themselves permission to be learners too without feeling as though they're being diminished – so hopefully that happens. But of course it's more complex than that.

Here, Sarah's view of what it means to be a teacher has undergone a radical change. She has moved from a conception of pedagogy as the transmission of knowledge to a more complex understanding of pedagogy as the co-production of knowledge through social practice – 'we practise being knowers and not knowers'. This transformation is based on her understanding that, first, to know is to know that you don't know; second, that her learners are simultaneously knowers and not knowers – an important political issue in her teaching; and, third, that teachers' not knowing – as well as knowing – is a critical part of both teachers' identity and pedagogy. Sarah's account highlights the importance of knowledge production in both teacher identity and pedagogic practice, raising significant challenges for the dichotomy between research and teaching.

Artificial dichotomies 1: research and teaching

We use three examples to show how academics insist upon the relations between teaching and research in practice. The first of these is Ron, a philosophy lecturer, who makes an even stronger case for the relations between research and teaching as forms of knowledge production than Sarah does. He finds it difficult to extricate his disciplinary research activity from his production of materials for students:

> With philosophy, even when you're writing for students, you're never just presenting ready-made materials. A philosophy textbook will always reflect the writer's own perspective and the writer's own philosophical position and judgments, so even writing something for students is a way of working through what I think . . .

Like Sarah, Ron is not simply teaching what he knows but, instead, his activities as a teacher – his preparation of materials, his writing for students – are ways of engaging afresh with ideas; in other words, of researching. He also feels that his work is linked over far distant time to early philosophers such as Plato and Socrates through a kind of disciplinary 'apostolic succession':

> But I think . . ., I mean in very grandiose terms I think of myself as part of a historical tradition I suppose. I think of myself as doing something that people have been doing for two thousand five hundred years – a part of that.

So whether giving a lecture, or writing a scholarly paper, he is mobilising the ideas of others, re-working his own and his students' understanding of them in his explanations and, crucially, engaging in the historical process of philosophical knowledge production – in other words, his teaching itself produces knowledge.

A second example comes from the work of Jan Nespor (1994), who cites an example of the way in which a physics professor came to an understanding of core physics concepts through teaching the same subject again and again:

> . . . in my own experience as a student I recall I didn't really feel comfortable with classical mechanics even after receiving my PhD and I was horrified to learn that my first teaching assignment was classical mechanics at the introductory and intermediate levels. It wasn't until I had several years of teaching at those levels that I found myself comfortable with mechanics.
>
> (Nespor 1994: 53)

Once again teaching is a form of knowledge production, not entirely differentiable from research. Here, it is the teacher who is engaged in the 'spiral curriculum' in which he revisits basic concepts repeatedly over a number of years, each year understanding more and more of the 'formal apparatus' that goes with them (Bruner 1960: 13). In both examples, time emerges as a significant issue: time reaching back, iterations over time, time working through what one thinks in order to teach students. Time unifies academic practices, even if those practices are kept separate through a variety of management and accounting devices.

So, if academics themselves find it difficult to distinguish between the practices of research and pedagogy, how do research and teaching come to be named as such strongly dichotomous activities? In our final example in this section, Natalie explores some of the complex relations between the ways in which her identity is constructed by her university and its workload model, and the ways in which she talks about herself outside the academic workplace:

> There's always institutional constructions of who I am and what I am and what I do. And they're very powerful, right? Whether or not I always take them up or not . . . varies, but I'll say explicitly the institution's effect on how I understand myself. And I would say that the institutional position's as a researcher, right? And that's because half of my job – or more than half, in workload terms, is as a researcher. And even my PhD work isn't considered to be proper teaching. . . . So I'm located as a researcher. And when people outside the institution say 'What do you do?' I say I'm a teacher. Because it's . . . especially in educational research, it's so hard to explain and talk about and people understand research to be a certain thing, and I'm not any of those things. So I just settle with the teacher business. And . . . they've immediately got some image of lecturing or lecturer or something like that. Just something – but that's not [how] I primarily see myself now, which is . . . contextually . . . as a researcher. . . . And when I'm with students, they only see me as a teacher. So it's that constant flipping flopping between those . . . .

Natalie's description of 'flipping flopping' between particular kinds of research and pedagogic identities as constructed by her institution, her students and those outside the institution shows firstly how difficult it can be to keep apart these supposedly separate kinds of academic work. Natalie is defined by her organisation as a researcher, but within this definition she is engaged in what she regards as pedagogic work in relation to her PhD students, even if this is not defined as 'proper teaching'. Her students see her as a teacher – as do those outside the institution. Secondly, Natalie has to deal with issues arising out of what it means to be a teacher or researcher within the context of her own discipline. She is concerned that people understand research to be 'a certain thing', but she does not consider herself to be 'any of those things' as an educational researcher. And when she describes herself as a teacher, she also rejects the notion of teaching as 'lecturing or lecturer or something like that'.

Natalie sometimes wants to stop teaching altogether to take up her 'researcher' identity full time (an opportunity some academics might envy), but will not do this because of the complementary relationship, as she sees it, between research and teaching:

> And like sometimes I think I don't care if I never enter another classroom again [laughs]. These two things co-exist of 'Oh, let me out of here, honestly, really' . . . part of me thinks if I never went into another classroom again [laughs] it would be okay. But . . . I actually think it's a good place to be. Like

> I think research is good and blah, blah, blah but there is something else that complements it in teaching.

So, despite Natalie not appearing to be enamoured of teaching, and the fact that she has the opportunity to be a full-time researcher, she still believes that she 'ought' to teach because teaching complements research. It is precisely this insistence that research and teaching both inform and influence each other that we noted earlier. Thus academics argue, without prompting, that research and teaching are somehow related to each other through the working up of ideas, through the co-production of knowledge, through pedagogical practices, and through time.

Artificial dichotomies 2: disciplinary and pedagogic identities

We turn now to a second artificial dichotomy: the separation of discipline and pedagogy. Our research participants work in higher education within the broad context of the study of adult education. However, they come to it with their own disciplinary backgrounds, and these, in turn, are inextricably linked with their pedagogic identities, as we suggested earlier.

Peter has been teaching adults for most of his 30-year career in teaching, and at the time of the interview worked in a range of settings with adult students. His first degree and doctorate are in sociology. He suggests that this disciplinary training and an awareness of learners as 'persons in the world' are part of his pedagogic identity:

> I do teach across disciplines but I do like to think that I teach sociologically, whatever I teach – so I teach from a particular discipline unless I'm consciously taking an interdisciplinary approach – trying to give a balanced view and become more philosophical. But the contrast at the moment is teaching a more vocational course and teaching, if you like, a course for personal development and personal awareness. In both cases I teach things which are very close to their [the students'] experience – it's never remote.

Peter's statement that he teaches sociologically concerns both his pedagogy in general and the specific content of his teaching. He would like his students to have a sociological understanding of the world and of their own teaching but, like Sarah, he is concerned that, regardless of curriculum, he needs to make connections with students' lives, first and foremost. In addition, Peter sees teaching as a creative act in which students get involved in producing knowledge of their own, be it the deconstruction of a television programme or participation in an exercise:

> I think a lot of the creativity in teaching cultural study subjects is to get them involved in that – get them to think about how they would construct – and to

do that you need to get them to deconstruct first. So you take a programme and break it down into its bits – and say decisions were made – this isn't an accident it was like this – why was that ten minutes? So that they could put in adverts because it's going to be for commercial TV and it had to end there. And similarly . . . I still need to get people to think about their own teaching whatever they're reading, all these things about philosophy and history and politics – it's got to be made relevant to them. They read it for its own sake but they won't know what it's got to do with them – and that for me is the creativity of making that leap – of designing an exercise of some kind – of getting them to say 'oh yeah – that's what's happening to me'.

Peter's students participate in the disciplinary practices appropriate to the subject they are studying: they deconstruct television programmes if they are studying cultural studies; they consider the impact of philosophy, history and politics on teaching if they are training as teachers. Peter is concerned that they make 'that leap' to make sense of the world around them. He and his students are engaged, through Peter's pedagogic interventions, in the production of disciplinary knowledge as members of the disciplinary community of practice.

Natalie is also concerned with the relations between discipline and pedagogy. Natalie began her career being trained for secondary education and then began teaching English to speakers of other languages by chance, but felt that she had no disciplinary basis:

Again, I didn't know how to teach English. I mean there was kind of the assumption in those days that if you can speak English you can teach English. And if you're a teacher, therefore you know how to teach. And I actually don't believe that at all . . . I guess it relates to that other issue I have, about one's pedagogy related to the disciplinary theme, is that I felt my experience itself wasn't enough to give me the necessary understanding about language.

After many years teaching ESOL in a number of different contexts, Natalie went back to take a Masters in Applied Linguistics. Despite her criticisms of what she learnt, she found that this transformed her pedagogic practice:

I mean I completely question the tools now, and I – but at the time, oh it was like – it was like seeing the light. I mean and this was after ten years of doing it. It gave me a language for what I was working with anyway, and I felt in classrooms it was actually useful to give them a language to talk about it.

Her participation in the community of Applied Linguistics enabled her to work with her own students as disciplinary apprentices ('it was actually useful to give them a language to talk about it') despite the rather different aims of her own

Masters and the English language courses she was teaching. For Natalie, this strengthened her views about the relationships between discipline and pedagogy:

> I think the kind of, if you like, discipline area actually affects a lot how you teach. I mean at some level . . . it almost becomes an intuitive sense of how to connect to people in relation to oneself, and in relation to them, and in relation to what it is that is being taught, or learnt, or whatever. But that actually comes through experience, right?

Natalie's view that there must be a link between discipline and how one teaches is one which is shared by many academics, and often creates serious challenges for those who design and teach on teaching development programmes for new academics. Whilst the doctorate has become an essential element of the academic apprenticeship, in most universities, preparation for teaching is limited to a generic introductory course. Teaching within the discipline has not become an integral part of the disciplinary apprenticeship. For both new and experienced academics, there remains a pressing need to explore the relations between disciplinary epistemologies, research and pedagogy and their complex interrelationships within knowledge production.

Failing dichotomies?

We have argued here that the distinctions which exist within contemporary policy and educational discourse rely on artificial dichotomies: between teaching and research and between disciplinary and pedagogic identity. Whilst we believe that policy discourse and interventions do affect academic work, and our existing empirical data supports this argument, we have also begun to develop a theoretical perspective using actor-network theory as a resource to show how these discursive and managerial manoeuvres are only partially and temporarily successful (Malcolm and Zukas in preparation; Zukas and Malcolm 2007). We therefore wish to explore in more detail, first, the relations between such manoeuvres and the actor networks of a sub-set of disciplines, particularly with regard to research and teaching; second, the ways in which different pedagogic contexts construct different knowledge production practices in time and space; and third, the extent to which epistemological and ontological variations across disciplines modify the relations between teaching, research and knowledge production. The disciplinary turn within the current policy context provides a welcome opportunity to re-ignite the debate through which disciplinary communities can come to 'own' pedagogy as an integral aspect of knowledge production, just as they do with research. The official dichotomies outlined above are, it seems, destined for failure.

References

Becher, T. (1989) *Academic Tribes and Territories*, Buckingham: SRHE/Open University Press.

Becher, T. and Trowler, P. (2001) *Academic Tribes and Territories*, 2nd edition, Buckingham: SRHE/Open University Press.

Bernstein, B. (2000) *Pedagogy, Symbolic Control and Identity: Theory, Research, Critique* (revised edition), Lanham, MD: Rowman and Littlefield.

Biglan, A. (1973) 'Relationships between subject matter characteristics and the structure and output of university departments', *Journal of Applied Psychology*, 57(3): 204–213.

Boyer, E.L. (1990) *Scholarship Reconsidered*, Princeton, NJ: Carnegie Foundation for the Advancement of Teaching.

Brew, A. (1999) 'Research and teaching: changing relationships in a changing context', *Studies in Higher Education*, 24(3): 291–301.

Brew, A. and Boud, D. (1995) 'Teaching and research: establishing the vital link with learning', *Higher Education*, 29(2): 261–273.

Bruner, J. (1960) *The Process of Education*, Cambridge, MA: Harvard University Press.

Burton, L. (1999) 'Epistemology, philosophy and pedagogy of mathematics', *Philosophy of Mathematics Education Journal*, 12, November, at: http://www.people.ex.ac.uk/PErnest/pome12/article1.htm.

Coaldrake, P. and Stedman, L. (1999) *Academic Work in the Twenty First Century: Changing Roles and Policies*, occasional paper, Higher Education, Canberra: Department of Education, Training and Youth Affairs.

Drennan, L. (1999) 'Teaching Quality Assessment scores and their influences – the Scottish experience', paper presented at the 2nd International Conference on Evidence-based Policies and Indicator Systems, University of Durham, 11–14 July.

Geirsdottir, G. (2004) 'Academics' disciplinary conceptions of the curriculum', paper presented at Society for Research in Higher Education Annual Conference, *Whose Higher Education? Public and Private Values and the Knowledge Economy*, University of Bristol, 14–16 December.

Hattie, H.W. and Marsh, J. (1996) 'The relationship between research and teaching – a meta-analysis', *Review of Educational Research*, 66(4): 507–542.

Hattie, H.W. and Marsh, J. (2002) 'The relation between research productivity and teaching effectiveness: complementary, antagonistic or independent constructs?', *Journal of Higher Education*, 73(5): 603–641.

Jenkins, A. (2004) *A Guide to the Research Evidence on Teaching–Research Relations*, York: Higher Education Academy.

Lave, J. (1996) 'Teaching, as learning, in practice', *Mind, Culture and Activity*, 3(3): 149–164.

Lodahl, J.B. and Gordon, G. (1972) 'The structure of scientific fields and the functioning of university graduate departments', *American Sociological Review*, 37(February): 57–72.

Malcolm, J. and Zukas, M. (2000) 'Becoming an educator: communities of practice in higher education', in I. McNay (ed.) *Higher Education and its Communities*, Buckingham: SRHE/Open University Press.

Malcolm, J. and Zukas, M. (in preparation) 'Discipline, teaching and research: making a mess of academic work'.

Nespor, J. (1994) *Knowledge in Motion: Space, Time and Curriculum in Undergraduate Physics and Management*, London: Falmer Press.

Sfard, A. (1998) 'On two metaphors for learning and the dangers of choosing just one', *Educational Researcher*, 27(2): 4–13.

Zubrick, A., Reid, I. and Rossiter, P. (2001) *Strengthening the Nexus between Teaching and Research*, Canberra: Department of Education, Training and Youth Affairs.

Zukas, M. and Malcolm, J. (2007) 'Teaching, discipline, net-work', in A. Skelton (ed.) *International Perspectives on Teaching Excellence in Higher Education*, London: Routledge.

Chapter 3

To those that have shall be given?

Differing expectations of support among dyslexic students

Elisabet Weedon and Sheila Riddell

Introduction

This chapter explores the learning experiences of dyslexic students in four different universities. It examines similarities and differences between the four institutions, both in terms of student populations and students' perceptions, using data from a survey of 602 students. The way in which students' learning careers may develop differently and their expectations vary is considered in relation to the characteristics of the student populations. It is suggested that the variation between the students cannot be explained solely in terms of an individualistic perspective; rather, the variation needs to take into account the context the students are in and their previous background. Socio-cultural factors, it is suggested, are as likely to impact on the students' views of their experiences as are the actual difficulties that individual students face in relation to their dyslexia. In addition to this, dyslexia, along with other specific learning difficulties, is not a well-defined construct. This lack of clear definition allows for a range of interpretations which are likely to be linked to social as well as psychological factors and also to impact on who acquires the label of dyslexia. The chapter starts by providing an overview of changes in higher education with special focus on issues around supporting students with dyslexia and the rising numbers of this group of students. It then explains the context and the findings from the survey. The conclusion summarises key points, with particular emphasis on the impact of student background on expectations of academic support.

Background

Dyslexic students now form the largest single group of disabled students in higher education, and supporting this group of students poses particular challenges for universities. In addition, higher education in the UK has undergone changes over the past two decades. The new public management of institutions is evident through a range of ways in which institutions have to demonstrate accountability (Deakin 1994; Clarke and Newman 1997). New legislation in relation to equal opportunities also impacts on universities; of particular importance here is the Disability Discrimination Act, Part 4, which came into effect in September 2002. This legislation, based on the social model of disability (Oliver 1990; Barnes 1991), argues that disability is caused by societal barriers that exclude disabled people from full participation in society. It downplays individual characteristics as it attempts to move from a model based on individual deficit to one of social and cultural barriers as an explanation of disability. One aspect of the legislation links to the new management of universities, as it requires institutions to monitor the implementation of this Act and to return statistics on students who have disclosed a disability to the Higher Education Statistics Agency (HESA). The legislation has considerable implications for institutions as they are expected to make 'reasonable' adjustments in all aspects of their delivery of the curriculum. However, the legislation recognises that there are a range of factors that impact on the extent to which institutions can make adjustments – including health and safety, cost, maintenance of academic standards and the needs of other students. Case law has not yet established what constitutes a 'reasonable' adjustment. Clearly, then, students' and lecturers' perceptions of what constitutes reasonable adjustments may vary both within and between institutions. For an unseen and contested disability such as dyslexia, this may be even more so than for a physical impairment.

Whilst there is agreement amongst dyslexia researchers that the phenomenon exists, its causes and manifestations are not necessarily agreed upon. Miles (2001) notes the considerable diversity in concerns of those exploring what the term 'dyslexia' entails. The British Psychological Society (1999) definition states that: '*Dyslexia is evident when accurate and fluent word reading and/or spelling develops incompletely or with great difficulty.*' This definition was aimed at providing an inclusive working definition; however, it has been criticised by both researchers and practitioners as being too broad and unworkable.

Narrow definitions of dyslexia focus on language processing difficulties, usually emphasising phonological difficulties (see Hatcher et al. 2002; Farmer et al. 2002). According to Stein (2001), the brains of dyslexics are different from those of non-dyslexics. Rice, with Brooks (2004) agree that these differences exist; however, they argue that evidence does not necessarily support that this difference is innate. Rather, they suggest the plasticity of the developing brain may mean that the difference arises out of a complex interaction between the developing brain and particular environmental events. McLaughlin (2004) also criticises the focus on reading and literacy skills and proposes a wider definition, as follows:

Dyslexia is a deficiency in the cognitive processes that underlie effective performance in conventional educational and workplace settings. It has a particular impact on written and verbal communication, as well as organisation, planning and adaptation to change.

(McLauglin 2004: 179)

The implementation of DDA Part 4 and the advent of the Disabled Students' Allowance (DSA) stress the need for accurate identification; however, the problematic nature of what constitutes dyslexia creates difficulties in its identification. Proctor and Prevatt (2003) examine the difficulties of using discrepancy models which employ different criteria in measuring discrepancies. They tested four models with a group of 170 students and found that identification of learning disability (the US term corresponding to dyslexia) in this group varied from 24.7 per cent to 46.5 per cent.

Clearly, then, the lack of consensus of definition, the associated problems with identification and the considerable rise in incidence of dyslexia pose challenges to both the individual student and educational institutions. However, it is worth noting that inherent in the discussion above is that dyslexia is an impairment that resides within the individual and that it can be 'diagnosed' through some form of measurement or test. This medical approach has been challenged both by those who argue that this increasingly 'pathologises' everyday experiences (Furedi 2004) and also by others who see the creation of a particular identity as socially constructed. Swedish researchers Hjörne and Säljö (2004) have adopted a socio-cultural approach in exploring the considerable rise in attention deficit hyperactivity disorder (ADHD) in the school population. This approach focuses on the impact the diagnosis of a particular category of disability can have on the development of a student's learning career. The socio-cultural approach thus emphasises that any medically diagnosed condition is interpreted by those involved using the social and cultural values in society; whilst dyslexia is not identified by medics, it is 'diagnosed' by experts using a range of measurements and its diagnosis could be compared to that of ADHD. Given the lack of consensus over the definition of dyslexia, a socio-cultural approach offers a framework for exploring the variation in student experiences in our survey.

The incidence of dyslexia and the considerable increase in the number of dyslexic students will be considered before an examination of the survey data.

Disabled students in higher education

Table 3.1 shows that an overall increase in student numbers has been accompanied by a rise in disabled students. The statistics in Tables 3.1 and 3.2 are based on data available from HESA (2004). The composition of the group has also changed, with a considerable rise in the number of students with dyslexia now entering higher education (Table 3.2). In 1994/95, 15 per cent of first degree disabled students were known to be dyslexic; in 2004/05, the proportion had risen to 50 per cent; over the same period of time, those in the category 'unseen disability' decreased considerably (see Table 3.2); if only full-time students are included, this figure rises to 54 per cent. These changes are attributed to three main factors: earlier identification in the school population, support through the Disabled Students' Allowance (DSA) and the increase in mature students through wider access policies (National Working Party on Dyslexia in Higher Education 1999).

Table 3.1 A comparison of total numbers of students in higher education and those with
a known disability (first degree programmes)

Year	Number of students (in brackets FT)		Number of disabled students		(%)
1994–95	32,3011	(273,586)	11,162	(9,719)	3.5
2004–05	37,9150	(320,865)	26,085	(22,890)	7

Table 3.2 Categories of disability used by HESA and percentages of first degree disabled
undergraduates as a percentage of total numbers of disabled students
1994–95 and 2004–05

Type of disability	1994–95: First degree (in brackets FT only) (%)		2004–05 First degree (in brackets FT only) (%)	
Dyslexia	15	(16)	50	(54)
Blind/partially sighted	4	(4)	2.4	(2.4)
Deaf/hard of hearing	6	(6)	4	(3.7)
Wheelchair/mobility difficulties	6	(4)	2.8	(2.5)
Personal care support	0.1	(0.2)	0.1	(0.1)
Mental health difficulties	2	(1.2)	4.6	(4)
An unseen disability	53	(57)	17	(17)
Multiple disabilities	5	(3.3)	7.5	(4.8)
Other disability	10	(9)	10.5	(10)
Autistic spectrum disorder	–		0.7	(0.8)

Having demonstrated a nationwide increase in dyslexic students in higher
education, the survey data will now be examined to explore its incidence in our
four institutions.

The survey

The survey forms Stage 1 of a Phase 3, ESRC TLRP project entitled: 'Enhancing
the learning experiences and outcomes for disabled students in higher education'.
Stage 1 consisted of a survey of all disabled undergraduate students in four
universities. The data to be included here will focus on the responses of dyslexic
students and provides a quantitative analysis of the experiences of students with
dyslexia.

The questionnaire was developed specifically for the survey, although it drew
on already developed learning, teaching and assessment questionnaires. The
changes were made in order to capture experiences relevant to disabled students.
The composition of the four participating institutions is shown in Table 3.3. The

Table 3.3 Key characteristics of the four institutions

Institution	Type of institution	No of undergraduate entrants		Student population					
		All	Young	% from state schools	% low participation neighbourhood	% from social class IIIM, IV and V	% in receipt of DSA	% disclosed disability 2003–04*
A	Post-92	1,835	1,365 74.3%	94.2	12.5	31.1	3.2	10
B	Post-92	4,920	3,140 63.8%	96.6	19.2	36.2	3.2	4.3 2002–03
C	Pre-92	2,355	1,365 73.2%	90.7	10.2	19.0	2.1	5.3
D	Pre-92	3,785	3,340 88.3%	65.7	8.9	17.8	2.8	6*

* Based on the institutions' own figures.

survey was carried out during spring 2004, included 602 dyslexic students and the overall survey return rate was 36 per cent.

Institution A is located in an affluent part of the country, in contrast with institution B, which is situated in an industrialised area. Both of these institutions have emerged out of earlier educational establishments; institution A has a long tradition in teacher training and institution B is a former polytechnic. The student populations differ in size, with institution A having a total of just over 7,000 undergraduate students, of which a quarter are part time. Institution B has a total of 25,500 undergraduates, with 40 per cent of these being part-timers. The large number of part-timers may be a reflection of a high proportion of mature students. Institution C is a 1960s institution developed on a green field site a short distance from the nearest town. The two pre-92 institutions (C and D) differ from institutions A and B as they have fewer students from state schools and from low participation neighbourhoods. However, institution C is still closer to the post-92 institutions in terms of students from state schools compared to institution D. Institution D, situated in the centre of a city with a dispersed campus, has the largest number of students. The institutions can be split into two groups based on a pre- and post-92 criterion; however, as can be seen there are other important variables on which the institutions differ and social class is one important factor.

The two new institutions have the largest number of students in receipt of DSA but the differences between the four institutions are not great, with institution C having the smallest number. Possibly the most noteworthy difference is that institution A has a higher number of students disclosing disabilities than the other three institutions and above the national average. Statistics (HESA) for session 2002–03, covering the whole sector, show that around 6 per cent of students have disclosed a disability. Institutions C and D are thus closest to that figure, though the data from these institutions come from data gathered a year later. Institution B is slightly below but its figures are based on the same period as the HESA statistics. Care should be taken when interpreting these figures – HESA warns that differences between institutions in recording the data may mean that the figures do not fully reflect the number of students with disclosed disabilities. However, the figures do allow for trends to be noted in terms of the number of students with particular impairments and how these differ between the institutions. The focus in this paper is on dyslexic students and in 2002–03 HESA reported that first degree students with dyslexia constituted nearly half of all students with a disclosed disability (see Table 3.4).

As can be seen, the highest number of dyslexic students are to be found in institution D, followed by institution A, and the lowest number are in institution B. These are noteworthy differences, as earlier research has noted that disabled higher education students are more likely to be found in higher social classes (Riddell et al. 2006). However, there is also the possibility that those in higher social classes have easier access to a diagnosis of dyslexia due to costs of assessment. All HE institutions require an assessment that is carried out by an

Table 3.4 Number of students who have disclosed a disability to the institution (2003–04)

Impairment/learning disability	Institution A		Institution B 2002–03		Institution C		Institution D	
Dyslexia	351	49%	467	42%	196*	46%	657	52%
Wheelchair/ mobility impaired	22	3%	71	6%	16	4%	28	2%
Unseen impairment (e.g. asthma)	195	27%	120	11%	62	14%	271	21%
Other impairment (specified)	65	9%	224	20%	0		168	13%
Blind/partially sighted	17	2%	33	3%	21	5%	29	2%
Personal care	1	0.1%	3	0.3%	5	1%	0	
Multiple impairments	15	2%	81	7%	23	5%	28	2%
Deaf/hard of hearing	30	4%	81	7%	16	4%	53	4%
Mental health difficulty	18	3%	28	3%	7	2%	35	3%
A disability not listed below/ no details/ not known	5	1%			83	19%		
Total disabled	719	10%	1108	4.3**	429	5.3%	1269	6%

* Students classified as having learning difficulties and dyslexia; ** Calculated as a percentage of the number of all undergraduate students, including part-time students.

educational psychologist or equivalent and there are differences in the extent to which institutions pay for such assessments.

All of the institutions provide specialised disability support; however, only two of the institutions – C and D – specifically mentioned dyslexia tutors (see Table 3.5).

Findings from the survey

The questionnaire covered a range of questions which aimed to capture the experiences of students with different disabilities. In this analysis there will be a focus on those aspects that are particularly pertinent to dyslexic students. This includes their perceptions of difficulties that impact on learning, practices that help make their course more inclusive and experiences of academic support within their course. Chi-square tests are used for the statistical analysis.

Table 3.5 Institutional support for disabled students

Institution	Type of support
A	Disability Office, 2 full-time advisers, part-time administrator
B	Disability Service Office, 5 part-time advisors, 2 with responsibility for the deaf and mental health
C	Support network includes Disability Service with specialist dyslexia support
D	Disability Office, with 6 members of staff, one administrator, includes 2 dyslexia specialists

Evidence for inclusive practices

The majority of students (more than 70 per cent in all institutions) felt that they were offered good support by disability advisors and there were no statistically significant differences between the students in the different institutions. As anticipated, most also stated that they had literacy difficulties and that they had a range of difficulties that were linked to the literacy difficulties such as taking notes, reading materials and completing assignments on time. Statistical analysis reveals no significant differences between the students in the different institutions. However, when it came to their perceptions of inclusive practices there were some differences. The students were asked about the extent to which they had experienced the following:

- a scribe or someone to check spelling or grammar
- lecture notes made available in advance
- key resources available on the internet of intranet
- permission to tape lectures
- additional time to complete assignments or in exams
- clear and understandable assessment criteria.

Students in the new universities (A and B) were significantly ($p < 0.01$) more likely to have a scribe/someone to check spelling and grammar. Although these students had greater access to this type of support, only around one-third in institution A and about a quarter in institution B stated they had such support. In the older institution around 15 per cent of students were supported in this manner. Key informant interviews carried out for this project indicate that senior managers in institution D put greater emphasis on literacy skills than senior managers in A. The level of support may thus indicate the extent to which the institution sees this as appropriate support for graduate students. In addition, interview data from institution D shows that some students have equivalent support through adapted software and may not require scribes/proofreaders.

However, when it came to support such as online materials (see Figure 3.1), making lecture notes available in advance (see Figure 3.2) and additional time in

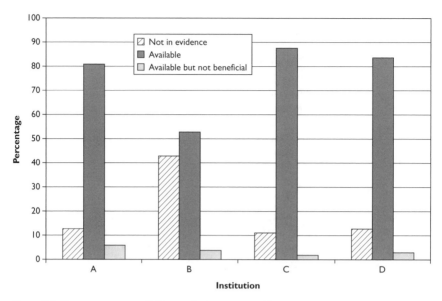

Figure 3.1 Key resources available on the internet and intranet.

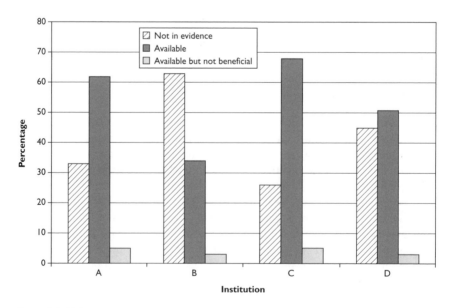

Figure 3.2 Making lecture notes available in advance.

exams, there were marked differences between institution B and the rest. Students in institution C are most likely to have lecture notes in advance, followed by those in A and D. In relation to provision of additional time in exams or for completion of assignments students, in institution D were most likely to have such provision. These differences were statistically significant (p < 0.01).

There were no significant differences between the institutions in relation to taping of lectures or seminars, although availability of flexibility in assessment type was significant at the 5 per cent level. Students in institution A were most likely, followed by institutions C and B, to have flexible assessments. However, even in institution A, only around one-third of the students indicated that this practice was in evidence. This reflects findings from other research, such Rust (2002). He notes that there is greater variety in assessment practice nowadays but this is unevenly distributed across the university sector.

It seems, then, that institutions are making adjustments, reflecting a social model approach to disability in terms of allowing extra time, especially in exams. However, there is limited change in terms of variety of assessments. This lack of flexibility was most evident in the most traditional institution. This lack of, and need for, alternative modes of assessment was also noted by the National Working Party on Dyslexia in Higher Education (1999) and Fuller et al. (2004). They stated that students, particularly those with dyslexia, found written coursework problematic. The lack of change is likely to reflect the concern over maintaining standards (for a fuller debate, see Tinklin et al. 2004).

These findings do indicate that there are some differences in the way that institutions are dealing with implementing inclusive practices but there seems to be little evidence that one single institution offers overall better support than the other institutions. The data do indicate that students in institution B have generally less support (except in terms of scribes and note-takers). In terms of their attitudes to lecturers and the support provided by the lecturers, one could expect them to be the least satisfied. This is indeed the case when asked about unco-operative lecturing staff, as can be seen in Figure 3.3. However, there was a different picture in relation to the following questions:

- lecturers' helpfulness in relation to disability related barriers
- lecturers' attempts to understand a student's (disability related) difficulties (see Figure 3.4)
- lecturers providing useful comments on work
- lecturers giving helpful feedback
- lecturers making an effort to understand a student's difficulty with their work.

In the case of all of these questions, it was the students in institution D who were the least satisfied. The differences between D and the other institutions for the last three questions was statistically significant (p < 0.01). Overall, then, students in institution B seem to fare less well in terms of support that helps remove barriers; in addition, students in this institution come from less advantaged

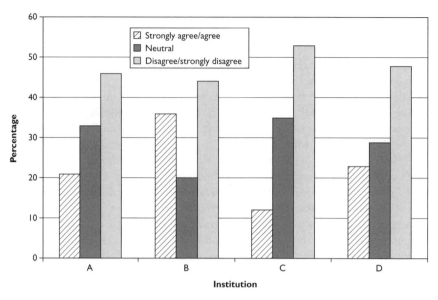

Figure 3.3 I have difficulties with unco-operative lecturing staff.

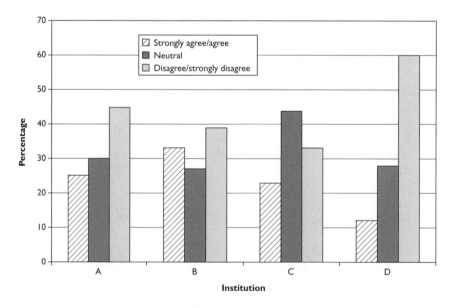

Figure 3.4 My lecturers make a real effort to understand my difficulties.

backgrounds (see Table 3.3). This is in contrast to the students from institution D, who generally come from a more advantaged background and seem to be well supported within the institution. However when it comes to satisfaction with academic support, the students in institution D seem least satisfied. This could be a reflection of poorer academic support; however, it is unlikely to be the only explanation for these differences. Other possible explanations will be explored in the section below.

Summary and conclusion

Dyslexic students in these four institutions indicated that they were generally satisfied with the disability support provided and also that they all experienced similar types of literacy-related difficulties. The two older institutions emphasised dyslexia support to a greater extent (as evidenced in their organisation of the disability support (see Table 3.5). The responses also indicated differences within the institutions, as well as between the institutions. Within-institution differences are likely to reflect the relative autonomy that departments have had in the past. However, there is an indication that certain types of support are becoming main-streamed across the institutions (e.g. extra time in exams) and that management of disability support could be seen to be part of the new managerialist agenda. Whilst the aim of this agenda is to provide the same kind of support to all students in higher education irrespective of individual institutions, the manner in which the legislation is translated into practice has been shown to differ (see Riddell et al. 2006). The findings also demonstrate that in all institutions there remain barriers. This reflects earlier research by Tinklin et al. (2004), who noted problems with provision of lecture notes and also that assessment changes were seen as potentially compromising academic standards.

What is of particular note, though, are the differences in students' perceptions of the support they are being offered. Students in institution B seem to have had generally less access to some of the support considered of particular importance to dyslexic students, such as lecture notes available in advance. These students did indicate that they felt that lecturers were at time unco-operative. However, it was students in institution D that were the most critical of the support they were given by lecturers in spite of the fact that aspects of their general level support seemed to be greater than those in institution B. Perhaps the responses of students in institution D could be interpreted as an accurate reflection of the academic support provided, as the lecturers may actually be less supportive. It could, for example, be argued that academics in old institutions focus more on research to the detriment of teaching. However, such a simplistic response is unlikely to recognise the interactive nature of teaching and learning and the way that students' and academic staff's expectations in different institutions shape the way that the learning is presented.

It does seem that other explanations are also required. The survey highlighted a considerable difference between the institutions in the percentage of dyslexic students (see Table 3.4). Institution D had, at the time of the survey, 52 per cent of disabled students that were classed as dyslexic. This is around the national average. Institution B, however, had only 42 per cent in this category, which is below the national average. As already noted, there are social class differences between the students in these two institutions – with those in institution B more likely to come from a lower social class than those in A, and more likely to come from state schools. A number of social and cultural differences could therefore be considered in relation to the ways in which these students have in the first instance been identified as dyslexic and how this then affects their expectations of support in higher education. Acquiring a label of dyslexia is not straight-forward and the assessment is costly. This could explain the initial differences between these two institutions in terms of numbers of dyslexic students. Students from higher social classes are potentially also more likely to have parental support and encouragement to achieve in early education and are more likely to have attended independent schools. This was clearly the case for a sizeable propor-tion of students in institution D (see Table 3.3). The level of academic support offered to students in independent schools tends to be greater than that in state schools and this could impact on expectations of the level of support when entering higher education. This factor was emphasised by one of the students in the longitudinal part of the study in institution D, who describes his school experience as:

> I had an extra English class from [when I was] quite young . . . the classes were very small, never more than 20 . . . it was a very small [specialist dyslexia] school [and] you also had a tutor.

This type of experience, it could be argued, raises expectations of what is the 'norm' and thus may have impacted to some extent on the way that students in institution D related to the academic support they were offered. The learning careers of students diagnosed as dyslexic may thus develop differently depend-ing on their background and also on the institution that they attend. They are also likely to emerge out of different sets of expectations, which depend on past educational experience and possibly parental support. Explanations that include social and cultural factors therefore seem to be necessary when exploring the differences in perceptions between the students that participated in this survey.

A survey of this nature does not provide enough data to explore these aspects in depth. However, it does suggest that a simplistic interpretation focusing on individual differences is not likely to provide a sufficient explanation of the way in which the students in the different institutions perceived the support that they were offered by the academics within their individual institutions. As has been shown here the students in the institution with well-developed support, and who have perhaps experienced a high level of support from home and school, have higher expectations of the support provided than those that had not experienced this level of support. This would suggest that those from a more advantaged social and educational background expect and also receive more support than those from a less privileged background.

Acknowledgements

The survey forms part of a longitudinal study, 'Enhancing the learning experiences and outcomes for disabled students in higher education', funded by ESRC TLRP Phase III – reference RES-139-25-0135. Special thanks to Andrew Bradley, Mary Fuller and Mick Healey for developing the questionnaire and analysing it and to the rest of the team for gathering the data.

References

Barnes, C. (1991) *Disabled People in Britain and Discrimination*, London: Hurst & Co.
British Psychological Society (1999) *Dyslexia, Literacy and Psychological Assessment* (Report of a working party of the division of educational and child psychology), Leicester: BPS.
Clarke, J. and Newman, J. (1997) *The Managerial State*, London: Sage.
Deakin, N. (1994) *The Politics of Welfare: Continuities and Change*, London: Harvester Wheatsheaf.
Farmer, M., Riddick, B. and Sterling, C. (2002) *Dyslexia and Inclusion: Assessment and Support in Higher Education*, London: Whurr.
Fuller, M., Healey, M., Bradley, A. and Hall, T. (2004) 'Barriers to learning: a systematic study of the experience of disabled students in one university', *Studies in Higher Education*, 29(3): 303–318.
Furedi, F. (2004) *Therapy Culture: Cultivating Vulnerability in an Uncertain Age*, London: Routledge.
Hatcher, J., Snowling, M. and Griffiths, Y. (2002) 'Cognitive assessment of dyslexic students in higher education', *British Journal of Educational Psychology*, 72: 119–133.
HESA (2004) Student tables, at: www.hesa.ac.uk/holisdocs/pubinfo/stud.htm.
Hjörne, E. and Säljö, R. (2004) '"There is something about Julia": symptoms, categories and the process of invoking Attention Deficit Hyperactivity Disorder in the Swedish school: a case study', *Journal of Language, Identity and Society*, 3(1): 1–24.
McLaughlin, D. (2004) 'Dyslexia in the workplace – policy for an inclusive society', in G. Reid and A. Fawcett (eds) *Dyslexia in Context: Research, Policy and Practice*, London: Whurr.
Miles, T.R. (2001) 'Editorial: reflections on policy', *Dyslexia*, 7(1): 1–2.
National Working Party on Dyslexia in Higher Education (1999) *Dyslexia in Higher Education: Policy, Provision and Practice*, Hull: University of Hull.
Oliver, M. (1990) *The Politics of Disablement*, London: Macmillan.
Proctor, B. and Prevatt, F. (2003) 'Agreement among four models used for diagnosing learning disabilities', *Journal of Learning Disabilities*, 36(5): 459–466.
Rice, M., with Brooks, G. (2004) *Developmental Dyslexia in Adults: A Research Review*, at: www.nrdc.org.uk/uploads/documents/doc_166.pdf.
Riddell, S., Weedon, E., Fuller, M., Healey, M., Hurst, A., Kelly, K. and Piggot, L. (2006) 'Managerialism and equalities: tensions within widening access policy and practice for

disabled students in UK universities', at: http://www.springerlink.com/content/1573-174X/?k=Riddell.

Rust, C. (2002) 'The impact of assessment on student learning: how can the research literature practically help to inform the development of departmental assessment strategies and learner-centred assessment practices?', *Active Learning in Higher Education*, 3(2): 145–158.

Stein, J. (2001) 'The magnocellular theory of developmental dyslexia', *Dyslexia*, 7(1): 12–36.

Tinklin, T., Riddell, S. and Wilson, A. (2004) 'Policy and provision for disabled students in higher education in Scotland and England: the current state of play', *Studies in Higher Education*, 29(5): 637–657.

Chapter 4

Making meaning in workplace settings

John Stevenson

In most fields of learning and research, there are theoretical positions on the making of meaning. The most fundamental are those of Piaget (1936) and Vygotsky (1934). Drawing upon these traditions, in this chapter the making of meaning is conceptualised in terms of 'making' and in terms of 'meaning' through an analysis of what constitutes meaning from several theoretical viewpoints, and through exploring what is powerful about 'making' in the apprehension of meaning in workplace settings. The chapter draws upon key concepts from Piaget and Vygotsky, even though each criticised the work of the other. So the focus of the chapter is on how meaning is made in the workplace settings that are investigated, rather than on the debate about the relationships between the works of Piaget and Vygotsky as a whole (e.g. see Tryphon and Vonéche 1996).

Piaget (1936: 307) coined the phrase 'accommodation' and discussed the struggle that accommodation involves as a child overcomes the problems of using existing schemata to come to terms with realities. Using Piaget's concepts, one finds it easier to go through life assimilating – seeing things in the same ways as we always have, with the same mental apparatus – until we encounter novelties that do not fit. Then, it becomes necessary to find a new equilibrium between seeing new experience in terms of our existing schemata or changing the schemata themselves through accommodation.

Even with more contemporary theories about learning at later stages in life, or learning for vocational or professional purposes, or learning throughout a life-long journey, Piaget's concepts are still explanatory. For instance, our readiness to learn, as we undergo significant life events (Brookfield 1987), indicates that we are ready for accommodation – i.e. we are ready to take the risks involved because of what is at stake. Similarly, from a critical theory perspective (Mezirow 1981), as learners are empowered to move beyond repetitive training that is designed to meet the needs of others, to the kind of learning that enables them to see how they are socially and politically constituted and to take action, this involves a considerable amount of accommodation.

Further, it is the significance of experiences that carries the motivation and mechanism for making new meaning through accommodation. For Dewey (1916), significant experiences such as those of vocations are an important source of meaning-making because of the ways in which they afford significance to mental acts:

> A vocation means nothing but such a direction of life activities as renders them perceptibly significant to a person, because of the consequences they accomplish, and also useful to his [*sic*] associates.
>
> (Dewey 1916: 307)

The second major tradition in understanding the making of meaning stems from the work of Vygotsky. Vygotsky (1934: 148) differentiated 'spontaneous' (everyday, personal, experiential) and 'scientific' (culturally developed) concepts. He examined the interaction between spontaneous and scientific concepts in depth, e.g.:

> we are concerned to show that systematicity and consciousness do not come from the outside, displacing the child's spontaneous concepts, but that, on the contrary, they presuppose the existence of rich and relatively mature representations. Without the latter, the child would have nothing to systematize. Systematic reasoning, being initially acquired in the sphere of scientific concepts, later transfers its structural organization into spontaneous concepts, remodeling them 'from above'. The interdependence between spontaneous and scientific concepts stems from the special relations existing between the scientific concept and the object. In the scientific concepts that the child acquires in school, the relation to an object is mediated from the start by some other concept. Thus the very notion of scientific concept implies a certain position in relation to other concepts, i.e. a place within a system of concepts. It is our contention that the rudiments of systematization first enter the child's mind by way of his contact with scientific concepts and are transferred to everyday concepts, changing their psychological structure from the top down.
>
> (Vygotsky 1934: 172–173)

Similarly, this idea of purpose in activity, and the centrality of the concreteness of experience, are central to Leontiev's (1959) conception of meaning. For Leontiev it is the object of collective activity that provides the meaning for individual actions directed at that overall purpose. Engeström (1987, 1999, 2001) has elaborated this idea into his conception of an activity system where the making of sense and collective meaning for individual actions is mediated by the artifacts in the setting. In this cultural-historical activity theoretical conception of meaning, artifacts in the setting not only mediate meaning-making, but also carry historically-made meanings.

More recently, Beach (1999: 114) labeled the deliberate engagement of learners across socially different kinds of experiences consequential transitions, because of the ways in which they contribute to the development of knowledge, identity and skills. Using Piaget's terms, one could also say that individuals' schemata develop from the experiences of such activity in such a way that they have utility in achieving the collective purposes of the activity.

In order to explore how meanings are made through accommodation in workplaces, the following section outlines recent findings about values, literacy, use of technology (databases) and problem-solving in motel front offices. Then, two studies of the teaching of different kinds of meaning are reviewed. Finally, conclusions are advanced about understanding the making of meaning, and the implications for a pedagogy of lifelong learning.

Making meaning at work

Recent studies (Stevenson 2002a) have examined workplace activities in terms of reading, problem-solving, uses of technology and values in the work of front office motel staff. The research involved videotaping and analysing transactions between workers and customers over a continuous period, in different companies, and in different locations.

The goal was to explore the idea that knowledge could be taught or acquired generically – i.e. in a form that could be ticked off on a checklist, recognised as a competence, and re-applied unproblematically whenever needed in new situations. In this research, values, together with the Australian Key Competencies (Mayer 1992), were examined to test the idea of generic knowledge, teaching and learning. For Key Competencies to be generic, one would expect practitioners' work to be captured by such competence descriptions, and that they would be common across like-occupations.

However, as outlined below, workers were found to make their meanings in the activities that they were undertaking. Certainly artifacts and the culture of the practice helped them, and certainly some of these artifacts and values could be found in other places. But the meanings that were made were local: they had meaning for immediate purposes, for the immediate context and as mediated by the immediate artifacts. But because the purposes, contexts and artifacts were not the same (did not contribute in the same way to meaning-making) in different settings, the meanings were not the same across settings. The studies are outlined in the following sub-sections.

Values

To ascertain the values that guided work, transcripts were analysed in terms of the norms that appeared to be involved in the activity (Stevenson 2002b). Each transcript was read to identify any stated norms (e.g. 'be polite and friendly to guests') or any norms that could be inferred from the activity (e.g. 'Have a nice day, Sir') itself. The list became larger as the researcher moved through the transcripts adding norms as they were identified. The transcripts were then read a second time against the entire list of norms to ensure completeness. Utterances were coded as instances of various norms.

Using Engeström's (1987, 1999, 2001) conceptualisation of an activity system, the identified norms were examined for relationships among them, in order to speculate on the collective motive (object) of the activity systems and the particular normative actions directed at this object. According to Engeström, all individual actions in an activity system are directed at a collective object that gives meaning to the actions. The object provides the (normative) motive for the actions. Hence the coded utterances were separated into those that appeared to be actions and those that appeared to represent the object (or more disaggregated facets of the object that may or may not have already become separated from the object as distinct goals for action). Actions were then clustered according to the various facets of the object (Table 4.1).

One might have expected the object of the activity system to be related to such a motive as *successful business*. However, such an object was never explicit. Rather, 'business success' appeared to have been substituted by three other more immediate purposes: *profit*, *return trade* and *accountability* (and even more specific aspects of these, such as customer satisfaction and professional appearances for *return trade*, and efficiency and funds for *profit*), as indicated in Table 4.1. That is, the object (presumably of a successful business) was being operationalised in activity where the explicit or implicit motive was at a more disaggregated level, related more directly to the task and instruments at hand and their immediate meanings, rather than some abstracted overall meaning for the business as a whole. That is, the individual actions were directed at normative goals at a much more disaggregated level, e.g. be persistent, be friendly, be courteous, keep the cash right, meet the audit requirements, keep others informed, make sure the account is paid; and took their form from such concrete aspects of the setting as the equipment being used. This meaningfulness of actions was also most accessible at the disaggregated level of actions – it was these actions that the respondents appeared to understand, and which they felt that others working in their setting would need to know or learn.

The extent to which these kinds of actions, which constituted the workplace activity, could be learned in a generic way is problematic. For instance, one cannot assume that competence at being friendly in one setting, or, at a more abstract level, appearing professional, transfers directly to other settings. That is, one cannot ignore the role of concrete and less visible aspects of the setting in effecting transfer. Moreover the observed competence in different settings would be meaningful to the individual person in one setting in a different way to how it would be meaningful to another person in a different setting. Further, individuals would each have different ways of resolving tensions in the objects towards which their actions were directed, e.g. appeasing a guest and making a profit; being friendly, but laying down the rules. Still further, the clustering of normative actions as given in Table 4.1 is somewhat arbitrary: there would be different groupings when clustering in terms of the imputed facets of the object, more proximal 'goals' or apparent conceptual similarity.

Table 4.1 Normative actions and imputed facets of the object in motel front offices

Inferred normative actions	Intuitive labels for goals of clusters of actions	Possible facets of the collective object
Be friendly Be courteous Be helpful Resolve complaints	Customer satisfaction	Return trade
Inform guests Assert but appease Keep front office staffed Find out and clarify Do more than one thing at time	Professional appearances	Return trade
Refer matters to the boss Keep back-up records Assign responsibility Meet audit requirements Keep back-up procedures Direct responsibility to guest or others Lay down rules Check up on others Keep others honest Keep cash/charges right		Accountability
Reconcile anomalies Use own judgement Ensure do everything Keep others informed Be accurate Be persistent Intervene	Efficiency	Profit
Realise all charges Ensure account paid	Funds (payments, costs)	Profit

Reading

Using a context-text model of language-in-use approach, Searle (2002) found that spoken language, reading and writing were highly contextualised, i.e. situated within the specific discourses of the individual workplaces. She contrasted generic kinds of statements with the specific task or skill that the individuals engaged in. For example, compare the generic reading skill of *Locating information: indexes, alphabetical order, skim, scan*, with the transcription of how information was being located in a booking:

> I will just put in the first three letters and ask the system to look through all those related . . . to find out what the actual charge was . . .

Similarly, compare the generic skills of *Cross-referencing information in tables, charts, computer screen*, with the transcription of recording payments:

> If I put a cheque in and I received cash I would have to swap it around because I have received the wrong code.

These examples illustrate, as Searle concluded, that the construction of 'labelling' and 'assessing' as sets of decontextualised literacy skills in competencies statements overlooks the way in which work practices are generated, sustained and learned. Moreover, these abstracted renditions would not be automatically meaningful to the workers. Again, meaning was accessible at a highly disaggregated level, in direct relation with the artifacts being used in the setting and in relation to goals of the action, rather than the overall motive of the organisation. The meaning would be less accessible through the generic skills descriptions and may not even be understood in such terms by the persons undertaking the work.

Using databases

Using a situated cognition lens, Beven (2002) found that, for data work, operators in different motel front offices used different sequences of keystrokes to reach the check-in screen. The screens were set up in different ways, through different ideas of what was 'functional'. For instance in one workplace, the Reservations screen was organised in terms of numbered *Functions* and *Inquiries*, where numbered *Functions* included Check in, Group Check in, Reservations, Guest Information and Cancellations. The operator needed to navigate by numbers. In another site the Reservations screen was organised by Function Keys referring to categories of information about the guest. In a third site, Function Keys could be used to access functional aspects of the work organised as Housekeeping, Registration, Operator Assistance, In-house Financial Summary and so on.

While an observer could construct conceptual labels to describe similarities in some of the ways in which databases were constructed and used, these similarities were not apparent at the functional level, when operators were interacting with customers or directly with the databases. That is, one could conceivably label actions in terms of navigation, entering data, manipulating data, making enquires or reporting, but these descriptions are of actions that are understood in different ways. That is, the knowledge utilised in these activities was not known in terms of the various abstract labels that could be constructed on it by observers, software designers or curriculum developers. Moreover, if it were known in such terms, it would be inadequate for functional effectiveness.

Solving complex problems

Using cognitive theory, Middleton (2002) found that the complex problems encountered in these various workplaces could be conceptualised as similar at only a superficial (non-functional) level. He devised the following labels to communicate the kinds of problems that were thought important in five different motels in different locations: problem staff (two businesses), problem guests, prioritising tasks under pressure, marketing (two businesses), competition, government regulations, work overload, isolation (two businesses), communication, weather, complex bookings, architectural constraints, wild animals, national park, floods, loss of experienced staff, locating problems (one business in each case). As can be seen, the problems were of different kinds, and a particular concept of 'problem-solving' or particular approaches to problem-solving would not be universally applicable across them. Moreover, the kinds of 'staff problems' or 'competition' would be different and amenable to different kinds of problem-solving and solutions in the different sites. That is, the problems were understood (meaningful) in terms of their contexts and their impacts on the particular kinds of businesses and their objects. Solutions would be forged utilising different kinds of mediating artifacts, with different involvements and contributions from various people, each taking different responsibilities for different parts of the problem.

That is, the problems were 'found' (conceptualised for solution) by the workers and strategies used for generating solutions to these complex problems were also site-dependent. Further, the solutions would be dependent on the elements of activity systems identified by Engeström (1987, 1999, 2001): rules, mediating artifacts and divisions of labour.

Understanding the making of meaning

In these studies, the following conclusions can be drawn:

- Meaning was made through accommodation in purposeful, functional, situated, normative activity that was culturally mediated.
- It did not come ready-made in some conceptual label – it was made when engaging in real activity, and it was mediated by instruments and other elements in the setting. The meanings had been apprehended through accommodation to the demands of experience.
- Particulars were important for meaning-making; they weren't noise or background – they were central to accommodation.
- Meaning was being made directly – it was not understood as literacy or problem-solving or navigation through a website or some abstract value, but as action as part of object-directed activity.

It is conceivable that individuals could make further connections between the meanings that they made in real activity and the culturally transmitted concepts that are shared orally and in writing, such as in textbooks. This Vygotskian process would, however, require further accommodation, and so it is problematic to assume that the meanings we witness in activity and can check off as competence are those same concepts; and we cannot assume that those concepts on their own can be unproblematically, directly and meaningfully applied (transferred) to new situations. Research work on the teaching and learning challenges involved in this inter-connection of meanings across different communities of practice is outlined in the following section.

Learning new meanings

In the work reviewed above, it is not intended to suggest that there is no place in learning for the concepts, theories and methods derived from centuries of human scholarship and found in the academy. Rather, the teaching and learning challenge is to bring such abstracted concepts into dialogue with the ways in which meaning is made in everyday settings, so that Piaget's accommodation can take place. Put another way, the challenge is for Vygotsky's (1934) spontaneous concepts to meet with, and to become controlled by, scientific concepts. Two studies are outlined below: one on connecting the meanings of part-time work with those of the academy, and one of how acting tutors seek to express the goals for the learning of new meanings in drama schools.

Learning to connect work and other meanings

A recent study has examined an attempt at forging accommodation (in Piaget's terms) or development of scientific concepts (in Vygotsky's terms). It examined how humanities students forged relationships between existing spontaneous understandings of part-time work (usually in a fast-food outlet), ideas of generic skills (adopted by educational institutions) and the content of their university studies (which has developed from an academic tradition). These students were pressed into reflecting upon their part-time work experiences in order to identify 'generic skills' that they had acquired at work and how they related to their humanities studies (Stevenson and Yashin-Shaw 2004).

One interesting finding was the apprehension, discomfort and struggle for respondents when engaging in these reflective experiences, as indicated in the following extracts. These exemplify Piaget's view that accommodation and assimilation are oppositional, and that struggles are involved in accommodation; and Vygotsky's view that direct interaction between scientific and spontaneous concepts is effortful.

> Like after starting this subject and having to – like at first it was sort of like ohhhhhh, I don't know how I can change this abstract to this practical. At first it was kind of a stretch to think like that.
>
> (AAAA, 22–24)

... whereas before when you first started asking me questions in this course, I was sort of sitting there going ooooh, I don't know if there's any links. I can't – I'm sitting going oh no, this is going to be horrible because I, I don't think I have anything that I'll be able to apply in this course and then you sort of worked it out of us which was really, really good.

(BBBB, 389–399)

I found it quite difficult because – in my assignment to actually – I sat down and I looked at it and I couldn't start at the reflection side of things so I went straight down to the part where I wanted to put my research in and then slowly after a while, worked up to the reflection side.

(CCCC, 250)

A second interesting finding was how the transformations in meanings (the triumph of accommodation over assimilation) and scientific concepts over spontaneous ones increased confidence, self-esteem, and the value placed on experiences.

The confidence boost was in the fact that the realisation of the diversity of skills that I do have and that I don't have to learn because they're already there and . . .

(DDDD, 195–197)

. . . and I looked back over the last ten years when I was 17 and I hadn't even left home and I looked at all the little things that I'd accomplished and all the things I'd learnt and all the people I've met and the conversations I've had, and I sort of systematically went through all the little things and then stood back from it, and in the big picture I just went WOW! It was uplifting to think about all those – you look at something really specifically and then you stand back from it and then you just sort of appreciate what you have experienced.

(EEEE, 490–503)

I'm very good at you know, um, analytical thinking. You sort of make us prove it and, um, I guess it gets you thinking a lot more and a lot more confident with saying that like that I'm able to initiate and lead enterprises.

(FFFF, 345–354)

At SSSS. Yep. I'm a kitchen hand. Um, absolutely. Before coming to this course I thought SSSS was pocket money. Something to do and something quite embarrassing to put on my resume, like to say that I've been a kitchen hand for five years and no employer will ever want anything to do with my skills there. I handed in a resume this week actually and I proudly put kitchen hand.

(GGGG, 55–59)

Thus, learners struggled to find the connections between differently contextualised meanings. In the process, there appeared to be more holistic accommodation taking place, with the development of greater control over spontaneous concepts. The findings are taken as evidence of learners engaging in consequential transitions (Beach 1999), where they made new meanings by inter-connecting existing particularised meanings (van Oers 1998).

Setting goals for drama education

The struggle to communicate new meanings and to assist learners in the process of accommodation towards new meaning is nowhere more apparent than in practical and creative education, where the expression of new meanings and the capacity to make new meanings is often rendered in physical ways. For example, Prior (2005) examined the objectives of acting tutors in Australian and English drama schools, as they explained their approach to drama and drama education. He found that the goals that tutors had for actor training were difficult to communicate. For instance, in his interviews with the tutors, the meanings of their teaching goals were expressed metaphorically, e.g. broaden the acting muscle; make interesting people; train creative, imaginative, brave, independent artists; liberate; inspire ideals; create a poet; learn about themselves; power of ensemble.

That is, the meanings that the tutors had constructed on acting and on the teaching of acting were difficult to communicate in conventional ways. Prior explains these difficult-to-convey meanings as developing in the acting school 'community of practice' (Lave and Wenger 1991), over time, as a result of the different experiential histories of people who work in these schools. Some of the respondents in Prior's study, had come from careers in acting, some had worked in the theatre industry more broadly and most had a training background, coming from drama schools. It is possible that their differences in constructing meaning may have been due to differences in their historically derived frameworks or contexts against which they constructed meaning – different 'knowledge(s)-with' (Bransford and Schwartz 1999). Prior suggests that, as a result, there had developed a shared 'craft-based way of knowing' of what acting is and how actor training should proceed.

As the tutors had a variety of backgrounds that presumably shaped their meanings, Prior refers to a trajectory (Lave and Wenger 1991) towards a 'craft-based way of knowing', reflected in the common metaphors that developed over time, in the community of practice. What is evident here is that the meanings were being made and re-shaped through practice, interaction and accommodation into somewhat forced verbal renditions.

Central aspects of learning new meanings

In both of these studies of challenges in teaching new meanings, there is evidence of a struggle to render existing meanings in new ways: using new words (e.g.

generic skills), or expressing understanding in verbal ways (using metaphors to try to capture the meanings). The success of mastering the accommodation led to feelings of empowerment and satisfaction, not because of the abstracted or generalised scientific concepts themselves, but because of the new ways in which concrete particulars could be understood. That is, the learning of new meanings should not replace older meanings; rather, it should operate to bring together and articulate with older meanings and afford greater control over understanding (Vygotsky 1934).

Conclusions

In this chapter, it has been argued that the process of accommodation that leads to new meaning is one where meanings are made and re-made through activity that is collective, purposeful and culturally mediated. Examples have been given from situations as diverse as front office work in motels, drama tutoring and the study of humanities. In all of these cases, meaning was not given or directly transferred. Rather, it was made and re-made in relation to the object of the immediate activity. This making of meaning involved struggle and was sometimes resisted, echoing Piaget's concepts of assimilation and accommodation, where reaching equilibrium often requires the making of new meaning, through developing new schemata.

This kind of analysis supports the view that generalisation of meaning occurs through re-contextualisation (van Oers 1998). That is, because making occurs in context, Piaget's idea of accommodation can be viewed in terms of van Oer's (1998) contention that context provides for 'two essential processes: it supports the *particularisation of meanings* by constraining the cognitive process of meaning construction, and by eliminating ambiguities or concurrent meanings that do not seem to be adequate at a given moment; on the other hand, context also prevents this particularised meaning from being isolated as it *brings about coherence* with a larger whole (van Oers 1998: 475). This description also provides an explanation of the processes of interaction between Vygotsky's scientific and spontaneous concepts as they move in opposite directions in the development of an individual's thinking.

The implications for a pedagogy of lifelong learning are plural. Learners come with different ways of knowing and will not automatically perceive the meaningfulness of other ways of knowing. In a lifespan approach to pedagogy, different ways of knowing should therefore not be viewed as hierarchical, as each contributes in important ways to the particularisation of meaning and its coherence with larger wholes. Hence, the role of the educator/facilitator/trainer, at any point in lifelong learning, is to involve learners in activities that are accessible and meaningful; but which press them into accommodation through the interconnection of different ways of knowing appropriate and significant at that point in their life journey (see also Stevenson 2003).

As the studies of humanities students has demonstrated, it is not automatic that learners will perceive the relationships among different ways of knowing, e.g.

workplace competence, generic skills and academic thinking. When pressed into making inter-connections, learners find it stressful and a struggle; and, in the process, undergo significant personal change. As indicated in that research, learning experiences are more powerful if they include explicit attention to operating upon such different ways of knowing. Thus, learners should be encouraged to provide different kinds of renditions of meaning, transform one kind of rendition into another, explore their inter-connections and evaluate their utility in different kinds of activity, rather than have academic (scientific) concepts transmitted to them.

As most of these examples have demonstrated, meaning does not reside in an abstract concept on its own. For it to come alive, it needs to be utilised in activity and rub up against other ways of engaging in activity. Its contribution to activity needs to be evaluated. Thus, educators across the lifespan should provide for the evaluation of the utility of concepts in different kinds of meaningful (significant) activities.

Finally, it needs to be acknowledged that experiential knowledge or action procedures are not meaningful on their own. This has particular implications for the relationships among formal, non-formal and informal learning. Particularised, experiential, spontaneous meanings, often developed in adult, community, workplace and vocational educational settings, need to be afforded legitimacy; but equally need to be brought into coherence with each other and with the larger whole.

References

Beach, K. (1999) 'Consequential transitions: a socio-cultural expedition beyond transfer in education', in A. Iran-Nejad and P. D. Pearson (eds) *Review of Research in Education*, 24: 101–140.

Beven, F. (2002) 'The knowledge required for database use', *International Journal of Educational Research*, 37: 43–65.

Bransford, J.D. and Schwartz, D.L. (1999) 'Rethinking transfer: a simple proposal with multiple implications', in A. Iran-Nejad and P. D. Pearson (eds) *Review of Research in Education*, 24: 61–100.

Brookfield, S. (1987) 'Significant personal learning', in D. Boud and V. Griffin (eds) *Appreciating Adult Learning: Learning from the Learners' Perspective*, London: Kogan Page.

Dewey, J. (1916) *Democracy and Education*, Toronto: Collier-Macmillan (reprinted in 1966).

Engeström, Y. (1987) *Learning by Expanding: An Activity-theoretical Approach to Developmental Research*, Helsinki: Orienta-Konsultit.

Engeström, Y. (1999) 'Expansive visibilization of work: an activity-theoretical perspective', *Computer Supported Cooperative Work*, 8: 63–93.

Engeström, Y. (2001) 'Expansive learning at work: toward an activity theoretical reconceptualization', *Journal of Education and Work*, 14(1): 133–156

Lave, J. and Wenger, E. (1991) *Situated Learning: Legitimate Peripheral Participation*, Cambridge: Cambridge University Press.

Leontiev, A.N. (1959) *Problems of the Development of the Mind*, Moscow: Progress Publishers (reprinted in 1981).

Mayer, E. (Chair) (1992) Key competencies. Report of the committee to advise the Australian Education Council and Ministers of Vocational Education, Employment and Training on employment-related key competencies for postcompulsory education and training, Canberra: Australian Education Council and Ministers of Vocational Education, Employment and Training.

Mezirow, J. (1981) 'A critical theory of adult learning and education', *Adult Education*, 32(1): 3–24.

Middleton, H.E. (2002) 'Complex problem solving in a workplace setting', *International Journal of Educational Research*, 37: 67–84.

van Oers, B. (1998) 'From context to contextualisation', *Learning and Instruction*, 8(6): 473–488.

Piaget, J. (1936) *The Origins of Intelligence in Children*, translated by Margaret Cook, Harmondsworth: Penguin (reprinted 1977).

Prior, R. (2005) 'Characterising actor trainers': understanding of their practice in Australian and English drama schools', unpublished PhD dissertation, Griffith University.

Searle, J. (2002) 'Situated literacies at work', *International Journal of Educational Research*, 37: 17–28.

Stevenson, J.C. (2002a) 'Concepts of workplace knowledge', *International Journal of Educational Research*, 37: 1–15.

Stevenson, J.C. (2002b) 'Normative nature of workplace activity and knowledge', *International Journal of Educational Research*, 37: 85–106.

Stevenson, J.C. (ed.) (2003) *Developing Vocational Expertise*, Sydney: Allen & Unwin.

Stevenson, J.C. and Yashin-Shaw, I.V. (2004) 'Towards an instructional approach to linking humanities studies and part-time work', *Journal of Vocational Education and Training*, 56(3): 449–462.

Tryphon, A. and Vonéche, J. (1996) *Piaget-Vygotsky: The Social Genesis of Thought*, Hove: Psychology Press.

Vygotsky, L. (1934) *Thought and Language*, translated and edited by A. Kozulin, Cambridge: MIT Press (reprinted in 1986).

Chapter 5

Older adults' learning patterns

Trajectories and changing identities?

Brian Findsen and Lucila Carvalho

Introduction

This chapter reports on a participatory research project based in Auckland, New Zealand. This research was seeking to understand further what kind of learning older adults engage in, for what purposes, under which conditions, and with what kind of outcomes for individuals, for groups in which they have membership and for the wider community.

In this research, older adults have been arbitrarily defined as 55 years or older. This age demarcation assists in educators' understanding of the important life transition from full-time worker to retiree (including emergent identities as community volunteer, grandparent, sage, mentor and elder).

Key questions addressed in this chapter are: What is the character of older adults' learning (informal; non-formal; formal)? What influence does group membership have on learning trajectories and self-concepts as learners? Does learning move from a largely instrumental path (allied to vocational purpose) to an expressive one (associated with greater leisure time)?

Research design

The primary research question for this study was: 'What are the learning patterns of older adults in Auckland?' The methodology chosen for this research has been participatory and qualitative. It has been participatory in the sense that older adults have been active agents doing research as much as they are the objects of research. Several existing groups in two different locations of Auckland (North Shore, an urban context; Pukekohe, largely a satellite town on the southern boundary) were collaborators in this study; they offered people to be trained as researchers as well as subjects to be interviewed. In total, 75 useable transcripts have been collated as the basis for further analysis, much of which has been completed and selected aspects of which are reported in this chapter. The qualitative aspect of the research has related to the exploratory nature of the design in which in-depth face-to-face interviews have provided the backbone of the data (Merriam 1998; Taylor and Bogdan 1998).

The research team used a questionnaire as the primary instrument in the semi-structured interviews delving into older people's lives in a holistic manner in which the following areas were addressed: family background; early years of schooling; friendships and networks; group membership; cultural activities; work (paid and voluntary); retirement; community involvement; leisure and hobbies; religion and spirituality; lifestyle changes; and emergent learning opportunities. In each case, some preliminary biographical data were collected prior to the interview. The intention of the interviewing was to elicit from participants' their material and social realities from which learning arises (Findsen and Carvalho 2004).

Characteristics of the sample

Six institutions whose membership focuses on or includes older adults were selected, providing unintentionally a predominantly middle-class intake. Seventy-five per cent of the sample were women (reflecting the bias towards female participation in these institutions) (Arber and Ginn 1995). The age range was broad, from eight 'younger' older adults through to four over the age of 85. The bulk of the respondents were distributed in the 65–74 age range.

Participants were asked to choose with which ethnicity they identify themselves. Most of the interviewees considered themselves as Pakeha (European), being 95 per cent of our sample. Hence, the study did not address the learning patterns of other significant ethnic groups such as Maori, Pasifika Peoples or Asians. As researchers we acknowledge the bias of the sample – the study largely presents a portrayal of Pakeha New Zealanders, the majority of whom are middle-class (further studies are recommended to investigate the learning patterns of minority groups).

Participants revealed high levels of prior formal education; 23 of the respondents having completed secondary school, while 55 had attended tertiary education. In terms of health, on a self-assessment scale, the vast majority identified themselves as either in excellent health (10) or very good health (41).

Participants were asked to identify their relationship with other people in their household. Our findings show that 43 per cent of the interviewees live alone, while 51 per cent are living with someone else (a son, daughter, mother or partner).

They were also requested to determine their own asset level by estimation after considering home ownership, car, shares and others. The spread of assets shows that the majority of participants' assets are situated below 500,000 dollars. Regarding work arrangements, 42 per cent declared they get involved in some sort of paid work, although this often would be seasonal, such as work during university exams. Fifty-eight per cent are not involved in any paid work.

In summary, the sample points to a predominantly white middle-class female clientele, but this portrayal hides considerable diversity within this categorisation.

This chapter focuses on those emergent themes addressing what constitutes a learning career for older adults and maps changes in their identities as older adult learners.

The character of older adult learning

Different contexts are described as providing a space and opportunity to learn. Older adults are able to explore and get a sense of learning in formal settings (e.g. university courses), but the vast majority of learning settings are non-formal or informal, such as University of the Third Age (U3A), a model of self-help adult education provision amid seniors of a largely professional class, community classes, Probus,[1] book clubs and specific training courses (in general, work related – paid work or volunteer).

Non-formal settings for learning can occur when working as a volunteer, and informal settings are encountered in contacts with other cultures, from media exposure, by exchanging ideas with others, informal meetings with friends or family, intergenerational learning and in situations of self-directed learning (Findsen 2005). A summary of these learning settings is presented in Table 5.1.

In the next section, older adults' learning in formal, non-formal and informal contexts are discussed (Jarvis 1985).

Table 5.1 Learning contexts

Formal settings	Non-formal settings	Informal settings
Universities	U3A	Voluntary work
Polytechnics	Probus	Cultural exposure
	Community classes	Self-directed learning
	Book clubs	Inter-generational learning
	Work-related training sessions	Exchanging ideas with others
		Media/news programmes and articles

Connecting themselves with lifelong learning

While it would be an exaggeration to assert that most of these respondents saw themselves as lifelong learners, there were many who did consciously make the connection between themselves as learners and the groups and activities in which they engaged.

One woman, whose view is shared by several others, points to the all-pervasiveness of learning and its potential for new insight:

> I don't have any idea that because I'm 70 I can't, I don't want to learn, I can't learn. I was thinking about it the other day and I don't find that it's, I don't think it's any harder to learn now than it used to be. Whether I am fooling myself or not, I don't know. People say it takes you longer to learn and you

can't teach an old dog new tricks and all that sort of thing but I don't think I learn any less easily than I did when I was 12.

(OAL 035)

The perceived relationship between learning and health is made explicit by one respondent:

The only thing I'd like to add is that I do think it's terribly important for one, well through life to keep learning and to be aware that you've got to keep your body physically fit and your brain fit, you've got to use it.

(OAL 029)

While an advocate for lifelong learning/education suggests:

Education does not end when you leave school. Education is for life and that's the sort of thing I'd like to tell other people and I've always said I never want to stop having something to learn and something to do and if I got to the stage where I had no concern and nothing to do, well, I might as well pop off.

(OAL 055)

The inspiration that some older adults gain from observing others, modelling the kind of life they want to follow, should not be under-estimated, as witnessed by this observer:

I think of myself as young elderly, you know, and then I look at people like my neighbour who is still travelling at 81 and people who are a decade older than I am who are, you know, still playing bridge, still learning history, literature, art and no, I think, that's been really significant, finding that there are so many active people in the community who are older.

(OAL 010)

Hence, the identities of older adults as learners are continually evolving but the data from this study suggest that more seniors have an alert consciousness of themselves as learners than most people give them credit for (Biggs 1993).

Learning in formal contexts

Formal settings for learning are those where education is hierarchically-structured, expert driven and usually graded for credit. Such learning entails mainly structured situations where the main objective is to acquire some specific sort of learning and/or develop particular skills bestowed by an authority as in university or polytechnic classes.

Universities constitute one possible context for older adults' learning. These settings offer the opportunity to acquire a great sense of achievement by obtaining a formal degree.

> And then in about 1987 I'd heard about this New Start course and I thought to myself, 'I know I haven't got the ability to do a university degree and I suppose it's absolutely cheeky of me to even think that I just might try this New Start course.' So I did, I did do it, and I was absolutely amazed to get through, to be told now you're eligible for a nod at university, and from then on I went ahead.
>
> (OAL 029)

However, the environment might sometimes be hard for older adults, who can find themselves having to re-assess old acquired values or habitual behaviours. These courses may challenge older adults' sometimes conservatively held beliefs. In addition, the relatively high cost of such education is mentioned as reducing older adults' access to these settings (Merriam and Caffarella 1999).

> Sociology I found a little more difficult because a lot of the stuff I learned at university really was a challenge to what . . . you know I'd lived in a very conservative background, my original family and then the school I went to and the training college I went to when I was 18. All very conservative, and so I was having a lot of the things that I'd grown up with challenged completely. So yes, I really had to do a lot of thinking when I was at university. So I graduated in 1996, finished my . . . and then I carried on doing two more papers, just for the fun of it and then decided it was too expensive and had to give it up.
>
> (OAL 029)

For older adults to feel comfortable with university contexts, there needs to be an intermeshing of their political, cultural and economic interests with the academic culture of the institution (Findsen 2001).

Learning in non-formal contexts

Non-formal learning contexts are those where structured environments shape the direction of learning but where older adults tend to have greater control of content. The importance of the social dimensions of learning (Illeris 2002) is captured in the following remark:

> You can do so much yourself, if you just do it . . . you can do so much yourself. I mean you can read, you can look at videos and so on but er . . . it has an important social aspect to it but you're sharing the learning with like-minded people and there's a degree of stimulation that you don't get when you're doing it on your own.
>
> (OAL 002)

As an exemplar, U3A offers a setting for non-formal learning for older adults in the sense that this is a structured environment where people continue to learn.

Learning in U3A is available in different formats. In the more formal monthly meeting, a speaker is invited to talk on a specific subject. This is usually followed by general discussion and then a social time. Members are encouraged to belong to study groups meeting twice a month. Here, more active participation is encouraged. Members choose an aspect of the overall theme to research and present to the group. In general, a wide array of structural activities are open to members. However, through the participants' comments it is obvious that each U3A group is different, where they set their own rules dictated by each idiosyncratic learning group of older adults.

> We're a bit light-hearted and casual about it. It's a lot of fun. We aren't as specific as that, we sort of take a topic and then people look up what they can and we have a meeting for about two hours; everyone seems to have plenty to say.
>
> (OAL 047)

Probus has some similar characteristics to U3As. These organisations sometimes provide sessions with speakers but have a stronger focus on opportunities for older adults to socialise. They also offer opportunities to travel with a group of others similar in age and in interests. The vast majority of members have previously undertaken professional and business roles before retirement.

Community classes in high schools also offer a structured and affordable environment for learning. Courses of continuing education offered at universities are generally much more expensive and this factor, accompanied by others, can prevent them from engaging in these courses.

Book clubs offer a non-formal setting for learning, in the sense that older adults get together to discuss or read about specific themes. Although these study groups are outside formal learning institutions, they are still organised around a structured task of discussing a specific subject.

Non-formal learning settings provide fairly systematic opportunities for personal renewal but just as importantly, informal learning provides unexpected benefits for older adults.

Informal learning contexts

Informal learning occurs in daily life, where individuals learn in minimally structured environments, quite often vicariously. The intention to learn is often submerged. This kind of awareness of the informal nature of much learning is recognised by the following respondent:

> Well, again, I think learning is really informal in that you learn off the organisation you are involved in; mainly you learn about the human nature more than . . . it's not a formal learning and it gives you great satisfaction. That's your reward.
>
> (OAL 047)

In training and development for volunteering, older people can develop their personal skills to more effectively perform their (unpaid) work. The participants describe these professional development opportunities as being extremely helpful, not only in performing their job but also in acquiring new skills and a broader understanding of life's demands:

> Like refresher courses, yes. Or if something new comes up like how to treat a person if they're blind or what to do when they're deaf and they can't hear and how to talk to them and make yourself clear to them. Those sort of things, they're really very, very good. I've learnt all those through becoming a volunteer.
>
> (OAL 044)

Although learning as a volunteer can offer older adults an opportunity to be trained and have personal skills further developed (Lamdin and Fugate 1997), that is not the only beneficial learning experience reported in these settings. Learning as a volunteer also relates to a feeling of enhanced personal growth. Voluntary work can provide older adults with the knowledge and experience of searching for new information, and incorporate a strong sense of empowerment (Cusack 2000). Older adults report that even if they don't initially know about something, through voluntary work they are often able to acquire valuable new knowledge. One enthusiastic woman makes the following observation:

> I enjoy very much being a volunteer up there and I took on the job as co-ordinator, running the bureau for a while, and that was an eye-opener, looking after 30 volunteers and planning the whole thing. It gives, particularly women on their own, it gives you an enormous amount of influence in dealing with problems in your own personal life. You know what your rights are, you know where to go for help. [. . .] So I've found that it's given me an enormous amount of strength and confidence in dealing with my own life.
>
> (OAL 039)

Most importantly, the learning derived from voluntary work is connected to a sense of pleasure from helping other people in the community, coupled with the joy of being with others:

> It just gives you so much satisfaction when you're able to help somebody and you see the look on their face.
>
> (OAL 043)

Hence, volunteering is an important vehicle for on-going learning and confirming seniors' worth in their own eyes and those of the wider society (Lamdin and Fugate 1997; Phillipson 1998).

However, the contribution older adults offer to society is not always appreciated and they sometimes report a feeling that their voluntary work is not valued. This conveys a message that voluntary work is not 'proper' work.

> . . . you have to learn sometimes not to be appreciated. People don't see you as quite so valid in your role if they're not paying you or if you're not being paid and other people don't. . . . Society doesn't see you as being so important.
>
> (OAL 039)

Learning from different cultures describes informal learning where the exchange of ideas and contact with people from other cultures and backgrounds enhanced learning. Learning from people of different cultures is mentioned in home stay situations, in working in social agencies, and in travelling experiences, providing interesting insights into other people's cultures and ways of life.

> For 20 years we used to have homestays here, overseas students learning English language as a second language, so we had people from all over different countries and everything, different religions and we used to talk about all those sorts of things and we had a Muslim here once. He was here for quite a while and it was Ramadan while he was here so of course we got talking about Ramadan.
>
> (OAL 040)

Informal learning is quite often described in relation to media programmes and older adults' reading articles from magazines and newspapers. By listening to radio or watching/reading the news, many participants describe a sense of keeping updated on what is happening in the immediate community as well as extended world affairs.

Informal learning can also occur when exchanging ideas with others. Participants describe how a learning situation can be found in simply discussing opinions and exchanging views on current affairs. These situations may arise in a work environment, with friends or in family gatherings.

Friends can also offer a special shared experience for learning, where two or more older adults may exchange views and help one another in finding out how to engage in instrumental behaviour (e.g. how to operate a computer), or simply the joy of learning something new (e.g. insights gained from watching a TV documentary together).

> Yes, well I suppose we've helped each other and learned things about the computer because we both started only a few years ago and so I suppose that was, we haven't actually been in a class together but I have helped Janet with a course she was taking and then we've sort of both helped each other.
>
> (OAL 039)

Some older adults report they have attended classes and shared formal learning experiences with partners or children. Contrastingly, there is also a sense that informal learning is constantly present in family contexts. Learning among family members seems to occur through conversations and discussions on daily issues and/or exchanging of each other's experiences. An informal environment provides opportunities for exchange of inter-generational learning. Older adults can offer their expertise to children and grandchildren, at the same time that they report how much they also learn from the younger generations. At times the discussions within family might be about a current affair, with different generations presenting their views on the same subject, thus learning from each other; sometimes the older adult may report having learned about a child's job, or simply how motherhood has changed historically:

> . . . my little grandson got fascinated by tuataras and I bought him a little model and he asked questions and we had to go and find a book and we had to go and look for tuataras in the museum and try to see the one at the zoo. So I also went to hear my son lecture here on his topic which is not my topic, because he's a scientist, but that was interesting. And I also actually heard my nephew lecture. Now his field is classical studies, which is my field and that was interesting. But particularly, I've also learnt a lot about having a baby in this day and age with my daughter, and that has been very interesting.
>
> (OAL 045)

Further, inter-generational learning can also occur outside the family contexts through contact with other children or younger adults who do not necessarily belong to their families. The following volunteer in a school identifies what it means to her and others:

> Well, I think as a parent and a grandparent you're constantly learning. I really enjoy working, even though it's with older children, I used to love it when worked with little children doing music and movement because you can see them learning things, you know you can actually watch it, and you're more back from it than you were with your own children when you're all muddled up emotionally, and tired and everything, so I think that we women that go into schools and have this contact with these children once a week, we're so lucky [. . .] we're learning from them and they're learning from us. It's not just a one-way thing. You're learning all the time, aren't you?
>
> (OAL 039)

Informal learning also includes self-directed learning (SDL). This is found when a person is following a particular interest on her/his own volition, often for individualistic reasons. This is commonly found when participants mention learning from reading a book, triggering a greater interest to be followed. Alternatively,

SDL can occur through using tools such as the internet to further explore and learn about specific themes and health issues (Timmermann 1998).

Group membership and learning trajectories

The overriding impression gained from the participants in this study is that the activity theory of retirement (the notion that older adults pursue an active rather than a passive existence) is very much alive for third age learners (Laslett 1989), especially those from a largely middle-class cohort, such as those seniors involved in this study. For many, there are simply not sufficient hours in the day or days in the week to do justice to a very wide range of interests and activities.

In terms of motivation for learning, the classic study of 611 adults undertaken by Morstain and Smart (1974) identified six major clusters of purposes for participation in learning: social relationships; external expectations; social welfare; professional advancement; escape/stimulation; cognitive interest. As we might expect, apart from professional advancement and external expectations, all the other four factors are strong in inducing engagement of older learners.

The need for firm social relationships does not fade in older adulthood. While ostensibly the participants join groups for a variety of other motives, the social aspect is nearly always close by:

> . . . and one really nice thing about this particular U3A is that it encourages people to, these older people as we are, it encourages us to look after each other. You know, because we all keep in touch with each other and if somebody doesn't turn up for a meeting, then we'll find out what's happened, find out if they're ill, you know, that sort of thing, so it's actually social as well as learning.
>
> (OAL 029)

The concern for others, especially prevalent amid the women, is identified by joining action-oriented social service type groups. One woman expressed her involvement as follows:

> And I'm in Age Concern, I'm a visitor. I visit an elderly lady, or elderly people, a couple of them have died and I'm still going to see another, because they're a bit lonely on their own, so I do that.
>
> (OAL 039)

The extent of activity undertaken for stimulation is immense – while it is less likely to be a form of escape from drudgery of work (as for younger adults engaged in full-time paid work), it is usually undertaken as a point of balance in one's life. The cognitive development of older adults should not be under-estimated, as the vast majority of respondents identified joining a group (be it U3A, Probus, Grey Power[2]) as an important source of intellectual satisfaction (Illeris 2002). One enthusiastic man commented in response to a question on group membership and its benefits:

> Yes, I've been fairly heavily involved. I'm actually chairman of the local U3A at the moment, but I've run courses each year since I started. I've run a history course which goes over three sessions which ended last week, actually on the history of Scotland, so I do all the research. And in other groups, some of the groups meet monthly and members take turns at presenting papers. I did one earlier this year – art appreciation of Rita Angus. I'm doing one in November for the Comparative Religions group on the Sikh religion, so to do these things I do research putting it together.
>
> (OAL 002)

The benefits of group membership include the enhancement of the full range of human capacities – cognitive development; social networking; expressing social concern for others; building or sustaining psycho-motor skills. Learning occurs across several domains and contributes to a higher quality of life.

Two of the themes in the literature concerning older adults' learning relate to whether existing patterns are maintained or disturbed (continuity versus discontinuity) and whether learning becomes less instrumental and more expressive (Glendenning 2000). The data from this study suggest that these polarities are largely redundant and the patterns do not necessarily adhere to gender differentiation (men undertaking more instrumental activities and women, expressive).

Strategic decision-making on group membership appears to be the norm. As people get into a more fragile physical state they often self-select out of some events in favour of others:

> I used to belong to a few clubs but I've given them up mainly now. You learn certain things and you've had enough. You need a change.
>
> (OAL 023)

As suggested, there seems little evidence to support strong inclinations of men to certain (instrumental) activities, and women to other more expressive forms. Most learning events are not gender specific, for example: book clubs; Seniornet;[3] Grey Power; and Probus, where social mixing is more a priority and especially valuable to those without partners in late adulthood. One woman remarked on the good support she received after the death of her husband from the Returned Soldiers Association (RSA):

> And if you're in any need at all the RSA have got, you just phone up the secretary if there's something that you need in some way, you need your grass mown or you need a lift to the hospital; they do all that.
>
> (OAL 001)

Summary

This chapter has been constructed around the emergent themes of learning and identity for older adults. Quite clearly, a significant proportion of seniors are keen enthusiasts of lifelong learning in their lives, taking on multiple roles in groups and engaging in diverse activities. Some of them perceive themselves as inveterate learners, involved in as many activities as busy lives will permit. Most of the learning for older adults in this study derives from non-formal contexts and in informal arrangements such as the family in the role of grandparent.

This chapter has emphasised the importance of group membership to older adults and the considerable benefits which accrue to them in terms of learning opportunities. While ageing does prevent some respondents from more active pursuits, the rule rather than the exception is for seniors to maximise life's chances not only for personal growth but also for the benefit of the wider community. These findings reflect the reality of primarily white middle-class respondents and more research is required to map the behaviours and aspirations of minority groups within older adulthood (e.g. older Maori in Aotearoa New Zealand).

Learning fulfils several goals in accord with Illeris's (2002) observation of the intermeshing of cognitive, emotional and social dimensions of learning. The vast majority of respondents in this study were defying stereotypical views of retirement practices (Biggs 1993; Bury 1995) by continuing to learn in a vast array of settings.

Notes

1   A service club consisting of retired professional businesspeople.
2   A political organisation who advocate for seniors' rights.
3   An international network of seniors who have accomplished internet capabilities.

References

Arber, S. and Ginn, J. (eds) (1995) *Connecting Gender and Ageing: A Sociological Approach*, Buckingham: Open University Press.

Biggs, S. (1993) *Understanding Ageing: Images, Attitudes and Professional Practice*, Buckingham: Open University Press.

Bury, M. (1995) 'Ageing, gender and sociological theory', in S. Arber and G. Ginn (eds) *Connecting Gender and Ageing*, Buckingham: Open University Press.

Cusack, S. (2000) 'Critical educational gerontology and the imperative to empower', in F. Glendenning (ed.) *Teaching and Learning in Later Life: Theoretical Implications*, Aldershot: Ashgate Publishers, Chapter 6, pp. 61–76.

Findsen, B. (2001) 'Older adults' access to higher education in New Zealand', *Journal of Access and Credit Studies*, 3(2): 118–129.

Findsen, B. (2005) *Learning Later*, Malabar, FL: Krieger Publishing Co.

Findsen, B. and Carvalho, L. (2004) Preliminary report: 'An investigation of older adults' learning patterns in Auckland', School of Education: Auckland University of Technology.

Glendenning, F. (ed.) (2000) *Teaching and Learning in Later Life: Theoretical Implications*, Aldershot: Ashgate.

Illeris, K. (2002) *The Three Dimensions of Learning*, Leicester: NIACE.

Jarvis, P. (1985) *Sociological Perspectives on Lifelong Education and Lifelong Learning*, Athens: Department of Adult Education, University of Georgia.

Lamdin, L. and Fugate, M. (1997) *Elderlearning: New Frontier in an Aging Society*, Phoenix, AZ: American Council on Education and the Oryx Press.

Laslett, P. (1989) *A Fresh Map of Life: The Emergence of the Third Age*, London: Weidenfeld and Nicholson.

Merriam, S.B. (1998) *Qualitative Research and Case Study Applications in Education*, San Francisco, CA: Jossey-Bass.

Merriam, S.B. and Caffarella, R. (1999) *Learning in Adulthood: A Comprehensive Guide*, 2nd edition, San Francisco, CA: Jossey-Bass.

Morstain, B. and Smart, J. (1974) 'Reasons for participation in adult education courses: a multivariate analysis of group differences', *Adult Education*, 24(2): 83–98.

Phillipson, C. (1998) *Reconstructing Old Age: New Agendas in Social Theory and Practice*, London: Sage.

Taylor, S.J. and Bogdan, R. (1998) *Introduction to Qualitative Research Methods*, 3rd edition, New York: Wiley.

Timmermann, S. (1998) 'The role of information technology in older adult learning', in J. C. Fisher and M. A. Wolf (eds) 'Using learning to meet the challenges of older adulthood', *New Directions for Adult and Continuing Education*, 77, Spring: 61–72.

Chapter 6

Talking about my learning generation

The role of historical time and generational time over the life course

John Field and Irene Malcolm

It is well known to the point of cliché that people's attitudes and behaviour vary by age. Given the age-based nature of much education and training provision, then, it is hardly surprising that age has particular importance as a factor in adult learning. Nevertheless, explaining these patterns and understanding their meaning remains a challenge, and requires that we distinguish between the biological and sociological aspects of ageing.

This chapter explores aspects of learning in the everyday lives of individual British adults, of diverse ages. It offers illustrations of the ways in which generation and history are embedded in people's orientations towards learning. The work is drawn from the ESRC *Learning Lives*[1] project, which is centrally concerned with learning, agency, identity and structure in the lifespan; our own fieldwork concentrates on these in the workplace, in working learning lives. Here, we first consider the ways in which age interacts with learning, and then, drawing on the work of Ari Antikainen and his colleagues in Finland, we examine the role of generation as a particularly neglected facet of age. We also consider the ways in which working learning lives have changed and are still changing as a result of structural changes in society.

Age and adult learning

Survey findings consistently show that participation in learning declines steadily by age (Blomqvist et al. 2001; Sargant and Aldridge 2002; O'Donnell and Chapman 2006). Indeed, survey data suggest that age is a more powerful variable than gender or ethnicity, and is as important as class and prior education. Age is also an important variable in the distribution of skills and competencies across the adult population, with survey data showing a negative association between age and cognitive skills (Statistics Canada 2005: 43–45).

Until recently, though, age was a relatively neglected aspect of adult learning research. In so far as it attracted attention, the focus of much research was on learning among older adults, but even this was limited in scope. A search of papers for the Standing Conference on University Teaching and Research in the Education of Adults, for instance, shows that only three papers during the 1980s dealt with the education or training of older adults, and only five during the 1990s (Education-line no date). Recently, interest has risen, and 12 papers on this topic were given to SCUTREA conferences between 2000 and 2006.

Researchers are, then, increasingly engaging with age inequalities in educational participation. Broadly speaking, this work represents the confluence of two separate but related developments. The first is the increasing attention paid to the social and economic policy implications of aging, including implications for the provision of learning among older adults (Tuckett and McAulay 2005). The second is the development of social models of aging that investigate both the ways in which age and old age are socially constructed, and the ways in which older people seek to shape their lives (Phillipson 1998). Contextually, these developments are mirrored in the everyday experience of adult education researchers, who – at least in the UK – have a similar age profile to that of the wider educational research community (ESRC 2006), and therefore have a direct vested interest in the treatment of older adults.

Whether considered from a social policy perspective or from a more theoretical standpoint, the association of low learning participation with rising age is highly visible. A growing body of work, aimed at both scholarly and practitioner audiences, explores variations in learning with respect to age (Withnall 2002; Findsen 2005). Yet there are also important limitations to this research, at least in the British context.

First, despite the importance of the relations between age and learning across the life course, much age-related research has focused on older adults, and specifically on those experiencing or actually in retirement. This may be entirely understandable, given their relative neglect in educational studies as compared with the degree of attention paid to young people, and doubly comprehensible in the light of the highly visible inequalities that are manifest in the survey data (Withnall 2002). Literature on youth transitions deals with some aspects of the life course, but in general this work concentrates on the shift from school and adolescence, usually defined in a rather formal manner. It therefore tends to neglect age-related aspects of other developments in lifelong learning. For example, the recent expansion of compulsory training has disproportionately affected the young (particularly the under-25s), as has the growth of full-time higher education, much of which appears to represent a process of 'drift' rather than active choice (Merrill et al. 2003). Yet if age is rarely a category of analysis when looking at younger adults, it is neglected altogether when we come to those groups who fall between youth transition studies and studies of learning in the third age. We need to know more about the place of different kinds of learning more generally in the various phases of people's lives – certainly among older adults, but also among younger people, as well as among the middle-aged.

Second, relatively little current research treats age as a problematic concept. We may accept that patterns of participation vary by age, but are these variations a product of chronological age, of life stage, or of generation – or indeed of all three? Just how do time and place intersect with learning biographies? And is a sense of the learning self affected by one's sense of one's own age and life stage, as many popular sayings suggest? These issues need to be clarified if we are to move beyond mapping patterns of inequality between age groups, in order to understand precisely how age and learning interact.

Generations and adult learning

The concept of generation offers one way of investigating relationships between age, values and behaviour. Earlier social studies of generations frequently started with the influential work of Karl Mannheim, who drew a clear distinction between generations as heirarchical kinship ties, and generations as horizontal ties of solidarity; interested as he was in generations and political change, Mannheim's analysis encouraged later researchers to consider values and attitudes as well as the 'objective' shared experience of a particular historical moment (Mannheim 1952). A recent revival of interest in Mannheim's work has served to widen the framework for analysis, with considerable attention being given to the ways particular generations come to be formed. Fruitful approaches supplement Mannheim's legacy (Pilcher 1995) with concepts drawn from Pierre Bourdieu, whose work seeks to explain the ways in which privilege is transmitted across generations (Bourdieu 1993).

Essentially, Bourdieu's framework suggests that inter-generational conflicts arise from struggles over the deployment of symbolic capital as a resource, which people of different age groups will use in order to maintain and improve their status and gain positional advantages. This theoretical approach lends itself well to the study of generations. For example, some recent studies characterise the 1960s generation as an active force which owes its relative position in part to the economic security that it enjoyed, as well as the high levels of social capital and social competency that were created through participation in mass protest movements; they contrast this with the insecurity and low social capital of young people in the later 1970s and early 1980s. These studies suggest that, by contrast, people in 'Generation X' – or, in the UK, 'Thatcher's Children' – seemed to behave as a 'passive' generation. The baby boomers had closed off many career opportunities from those who followed, and their members in the dominant media (and everyday life) also tended to disparage their cultural tastes and values (Edmunds and Turner 2005; Phillips and Western 2005).

Generations are complicated. They do not have clear borders, and their membership is indeterminate. Moreover, different members of a generation will have different experiences, and will construct their sense of generational identities in different ways; most obviously, experiences and perspectives will vary according to social class, ethnicity, gender and geographical location. Generation is observably a useful category of analysis, and one which can be seen as lived and collectively constructed in specific ways that allow us to examine the intersection between history and biography (Hammerström 2004). It therefore seems to be a particularly appropriate category of analysis for a project like *Learning Lives*, which uses life history methods to investigate identity, agency and learning in people's lives.

The question, then, is how generations and historical time relate to learning and knowledge creation. Earlier attempts to analyse these issues, for example through stage theories of the life course, tended to be ahistorical (Tennant 2005). An attention to generational time and historical time may be helpful in understanding critical differences in respect of:

- *Identity* – the word itself is part of the everyday common language for some generations and not others.
- *Agency* – the language of agency and choice may change over generations.
- *Learning* – folk wisdom on learning is constructed through time, experiences of schooling vary between generations and opportunities are not equally distributed across all age groups or generations.

Alongside such generational specificities, people experience the impact of longer-term structural changes, but in varying ways and with access to varying resources.

Structural economic change is particularly relevant to the ways in which working lives have been transformed in the area where we are conducting our fieldwork. Our interviewees live mostly in the West of Scotland, a region whose economic structure has undergone dramatic, long-term transition from reliance on heavy manufacturing. During the last two decades, the region has experienced significant growth in service sector employment and, thanks to two decades of concerted civic bossterism, Glasgow, in particular, is well-known for industries based on 'aesthetic' labour (Nickson et al. 2004). However, the region has also seen considerable expansion in employment of 'emotional' labour, for example, in call centres (Thompson and Callaghan 2002). This shift has been accompanied by a degree of feminisation of waged labour, leaving in its wake a number of communities where levels of male unemployment and ill health are high.[2] From the perspective of the very long term, of course, change appears less dramatic: all the characteristics of bourgeois capitalism, waged labour included, remain firmly in place.

Whilst biographical methods have become well established in the field of lifelong learning research, relatively few British life history studies have dealt with generations. In a Finnish study, Ari Antikainen and his collaborators (Antikainen et al. 1996) argue that generational analysis has a particular value at times of rapid social change, when people from different age groups will shape their actions differently. Generation is defined as 'a group of people born during the same time period and who are united by similar life experiences and a temporarily coherent cultural background' (ibid.: 34).

Dividing their participants into cohorts on a largely statistical basis, Antikainen's team identified four educational generations (ibid.: 35):

1   Cohort with little education (born up to 1935).
2   Cohort of educational growth and inequality (1936–45).
3   Cohort of educational growth and welfare (1946–65).
4   Young people (born from 1966 onwards).

Allowing for a wide range of variations within each group, each of the four cohorts apparently shared a similar experiential base of schooling, and they tended to share particular ideas of education and its aims (education as an ideal, a means to an end, a commodity, or a taken-for-granted given). They view their educational futures in different ways, and they give different meanings to education (ibid.: 36–37, 51).

This may seem rather a schematic way of approaching the problem of generations, based as it is largely on people's experiences of formal schooling. Although Antikainen's team very much acknowledge the importance of other types of learning in principle, in practice they appear to play a secondary role in this four-part classification. When considering the group with scant formal education, for instance, the important place of informal learning is presented largely as an illustration of the limited formal education available (ibid.: 38). Gender dimensions are largely ignored, despite some evidence of their impact in the empirical data that are presented. We also note that the fourth category – young people – is not analysed any further, as though its members' short lives simply contained insufficient experience to provide data for biographical research. While we acknowledge the path-breaking influence of the Finnish group, then, we have sought to identify important examples of informal learning which form part of older and younger (post-1966) interviewees' generational experiences; and we have tried to be sensitive to the gender dimensions of the data. Nevertheless, *Living in a Learning Society* (Antikainen et al. 1996) remains a seminal text, opening up the shared experiences of generations to systematic study.

Working learning lives: two Scottish cases

In developing our own approach to biographical research, we are combining different methods to explore the place of learning in people's lives. The starting point is a series of interviews which aim to allow interviewees openly to tell the story of their lives. This section of the chapter takes the stories of two participants, and examines the interplay of generation with other factors in the interviewees' construction of learning identities. Their birthdates are separated by some 40 years, and their educational experiences as well as their socio-economic backgrounds are very different, although they do share a number of common experiences. We have selected them mainly to illuminate generational dimensions.

Jeannie Taylor is a Glaswegian in her mid-thirties, with a degree in French, who works as a call centre manager. Her job is typical of the West of Scotland's 'new economy'. Her family background, however, binds her to older ways of life. Her father, a primary schoolteacher, was born to a family who came from the

Highlands; her mother, who worked for a book publisher, was descended from Irish Catholic immigrants. This ethnic background, it should be said, is as 'traditional' in Glasgow as call centres are 'new'.[3]

Andy O'Donnell is in his mid-seventies, trained as a bricklayer, and lives in a small town. His father was on active service during the Second World War, and Andy's schooling was brief, followed immediately by a craft apprenticeship and then national service in the Army, in Egypt. Back in civilian life, Andy followed work around, moving from contract to contract. Active in the Labour Party since the 1960s, he has a long record of public service. At first sight, Andy appears the archetypal traditional proletarian, but his life story is certainly not one of static relationships and limited mobility.

Born in 1970, Jeannie went to school at a time when higher education entry was becoming the normal track for children of middle-class parents (particularly those from the service middle-class, but also those from the lower middle-class). By the time she had entered secondary education, this was well on the way to becoming the norm for middle-class girls, as it already was for boys. Her story is of a school experience that, at the time, was taken for granted:

> All the way through to primary and to secondary again fairly uneventful, very studious and very well behaved. . . . Did six years at [secondary] school and my sixth year I treated kind of a little bit of a holiday.

She attended university in her home city, spending a year in France but otherwise living with her family.

Jeannie's story seems that of an average normal (middle-class female) educational biography. In the Finnish schema, she might appear a comfortable member of the third cohort, those born into a period of educational growth and welfare. Yet her schooling and education took place later, between the mid-1970s and mid-1990s, at a time when welfarist approaches were being seriously challenged.

Andy's initial education followed a trajectory that seemed equally typical for many in his generation. He left school at 14, in the year that the Second World War came to an end. He had enjoyed some subjects (history, geography and English); arithmetic was a challenge and he was frankly baffled by algebra. At the end of his schooldays, Andy had found himself a job as a coalminer, but his father intervened:

> I got a job in the pit and he widnae, and I come in and he said, when I left the school, and he says 'Have you went and seen aboot a job?,' I says, 'Ay, I'm starting on Monday,' he said, 'Where?,' I said, 'At [name] Pit,' he said 'No yer no, yer getting a trade,' he says . . .

Andy also learned from his father, an unskilled labourer:

> My father always had a book in his hand, read everything . . . he'd bloody encyclopaedias and he used to say, 'Have a read at that, read that book' or

'Read this book', I mean I remember him, I think it must have been one o' the first books on the Holocaust, he said, 'Read that and then you'll find oot what history's aboot.'

At 21, Andy was drafted into the Army. He reflected that:

> All the education I got, I suppose, I think I got more education after I left the school than I ever did when I was at the school even though I wisnae a bad student but I wisnae the best by a long shot, but I picked up, I was, I learned a lot after I left the school and when I was in the Army, I was a Corporal in the Army for National Service and I was quite good.

Andy's educational scepticism extended to the apprenticeship: 'it's like the slavery, in't it, you were a bound apprentice and when your time's oot you get a certificate to say that you're a fully qualified bricklayer'. The certificate did not make a man an expert; rather, that was down to skill and experience.

Andy seems the typical skilled manual worker of his generation. Schooling coincided with war and paternal absenteeism, ending at 14, to be followed by a craft apprenticeship, with a decisive intervention determining that he would not follow the less-than-respectable and possibly insecure trade of coalminer. Andy experienced school as generally enjoyable, but the decision to leave was automatic. His father's influence seems to have fostered an autodidacticism in Andy, but in his story he stresses how real learning took place on construction sites, in the Army and through civic involvement: it is 'real life' rather than school that teaches you all the important lessons. He appears almost a stereotypical male in the group defined in the Finnish study as the generation of limited educational opportunity.

Similar generational experiences are traceable in the working lives of other interviewees. Jeannie might conventionally be seen as being in the early stage of middle-age, but she is not in a standardised career. The transition from full-time education into work was itself a protracted one:

> Once I graduated I just kind of bummed about for two years. I couldn't really find anything that I wanted to do. I had a job in a shop at that point and then eventually round about 25 I started working for telephone banking.

After five years in telephone banking, Jeannie moved to the call centre at which she was working at the time of our interviews, starting as a call agent, then as a team leader, then in the training department, back into a supervisor's role. Her current post involves coaching call agents:

> When you call a call centre and there's usually a wee announcement that'll say 'For quality and training purposes your call may be monitored', that's what I do, I record the calls and I listen to them and I give feedback based on the recorded calls.

Jeannie seems to present her job as being the result of happy accident:

> I know you don't think anything of the announcement at all but it suits me down to the ground cause I'm really nosey and I love to hear everything that's going on.

Jeannie emphasises the professionalism of the role, the way in which the call centre tries to meet the needs of its corporate clients through high standards of performance:

> . . . sometimes it's the same as Big Brother and the Phone Police and other times it's seen as really what it is, it's a really valuable asset because we're giving real kind of feedback.

Job fulfilment, for Jeannie, is derived from personal curiosity ('I'm really nosey'), mastery of difficult interpersonal exchanges (dealing with 'a screamer'), and passing her skills on to junior staff.

Andy's job and career seem rather more routine, with a working life spent in the trade to which he had been apprenticed. After leaving the Army, he returned to the firm where he had served his time, 'but then I wisnae going tae make enough money with them so I started going aboot plying my trade elsewhere'. In some firms he was appointed foreman, but preferred to lay bricks, at least while he was younger:

> I could make mair money laying brick than I could walking aboot and looking at drawings . . .

He also took on sub-contracting (or 'grip-work'). Andy repeatedly stresses the physical demands of the job: 'Miners couldnae live at the bricklaying, they couldnae. . . . The bricklaying's one of the hardest jobs in the world.' Mastery was presented in terms of adulthood and gender. Andy's judgement when a younger apprentice was being kept away from harder jobs, such as cornering, was that, 'A wee lassie could dae that after a couple of year, ken [laugh].' Out of a sense of commitment to the apprenticeship, Andy intervened to ensure that the youth was able to practise cornering. For Andy, satisfaction from the job was derived from the respect of the team, doing the 'right' thing and by the embodied skills and strength that he could exercise. Being a foreman, walking around and translating designs into walls, was something you did when you could no longer do the real job.

Generational experiences seem to combine with socio-economic change in shaping people's orientations towards learning. We must, of course, beware of stereotypes in trying to understand Andy's and Jeannie's lives. Andy is not a classical Fordist manual worker, but is rather highly mobile and flexible, and his story is full of examples of agency. Yet his view of skill as something learned from experience, over time, in a disciplined manner, combined with the physical strength and masculinity of the trade, is very much generational. It is bound up with a sense of independence, of leaving school, serving one's time and then earning one's living without depending on others: by the labour of one's back, the use of one's hands.

This habitus is in decline (Savage 2000). Andy's generation may not be the last of its kind, but in post-industrial societies it is being eclipsed. Jeannie, in many respects, may be described as belonging to a pathfinder generation, characterised by prolonged adolescence, a blurring of boundaries between dependence and independence, attention to the development of emotional skills, and mobility.

Finally, the interviews provide important evidence of social and civic networks – of the ways in which interviewees build and use their social capital. Jeannie and Andy share a common background of support for the Labour Party, although their trajectories differ. Andy's involvement in the Labour Party dates back to his thirties, when he first joined, became a councillor, and eventually became Deputy Leader of the Labour Group. For Andy, Labour Party membership appears an expression of comradeship, as well as representing a degree of continuity with his father's beliefs, and dovetailing with his trade union activities, expressing a sense of social justice. His active involvement ceased after the second invasion of Iraq. Initially, Andy decided to renew his membership: 'I couldnae, no be a member, I had been a member for about 45 year.' By the time of the third interview, he had left: 'I didnae put in a resignation or anything, I just didnae go back, because o' the war, that was the main thing, I didnae go back.'

For Jeannie, politics was a consequence of family. She joined the Labour Party while an undergraduate, describing her allegiance as 'the kind of nice, middle ground Socialism that you always look out for each other'. Her parents both campaigned for the Labour Party and she stresses that her family was extended and close:

> Tremendously social family really, really my aunt and my uncle were both Councillors. . . . There's always been even from a young age we were always out on demonstrations . . . so there was all this 'Maggie Maggie Maggie Out Out Out' demonstrations that we would go on and May Day was an event we would go and . . . cause there's always been that element of, this is just what you do, this is how you're brought up.

Jeannie seems to be telling a quite unreflective story, where her politics are 'just what you do'. This is repeated when describing student politics:

> I'd started uni in '88, so it was all the same thing, the education, what I always remember was 'Sit down, join the fight, education is a right' and you would go and you would sit in the middle of the road during the demonstration and again it was just that it was there and you did it because that's the way you were brought up.

Now, though, Jeannie felt that the parties were 'all kinda much of a muchness'. At this stage of her life, 'I think it's more issues rather than parties'. After university, she said, 'it falls away; you just don't kind of go back to it'.

Once more, the traces of generational differences seem clear. Andy's party loyalty is certainly not unreflexive, and the political trajectory in his story evidences agency. He learned his political and leadership skills just as he had learned everything else: 'Just learnt it, aye, ye learned by yer ain mistakes, the same as ye dae with most things.' In his view, local politics was 'common sense'. Jeannie's political allegiances, by contrast, were much more conditional and, at an organisational level, more transient. Her account appears to be much more passive, telling the story of someone who is only involved because it was how she was brought up, and who left politics behind when she ended full-time education. Whereas Andy's generation was one that got involved in politics as a long-term project, it was Jeannie's parents who were long-term party activists; her own generation was more inclined towards issue-based politics. Her learning was more about how to move on and take her allegiances and capabilities from one hot issue to another.

Conclusions

These two life stories exemplify generational influences on people's sense of self and of agency, and on their orientations towards learning. We have taken a broader canvas than Antikainen's group against which to examine these issues, taking into account significant informal learning that arises in everyday life, situated in a wider history. We give greater emphasis to experiential learning which allowed Andy, for example, from the generation of limited educational opportunity, to develop his role as a local political leader and JP (Justice of the Peace). In Jeannie's case, new learning about call centre emotional labour is ongoing in her training of others.

At this stage in our research, we see the schema that Antikainen's team adopted (1996: 51) as offering an interesting basis for further analysis of the impact of generational time on learning, identity and agency in the life course. It is hoped that the methodologies employed in *Learning Lives*, as well as our inclusion of experiential learning and attention to gender dimensions, will allow us to develop a more detailed, and possibly more complex, understanding of the impact of generation as it interacts with other factors such as gender, class, ethnicity and experiences of macro-level changes to affect people's agentic, working learning lives.

Notes

1 *Learning Lives: Learning, Identity and Agency in the Life-Course* is funded by the Economic and Social Research Council, Award Reference RES139250111, and is part of the ESRC's *Teaching and Learning Research Programme*. *Learning Lives* is a collaborative project involving the University of Exeter (Gert Biesta, Flora Macleod,

Michael Tedder, Paul Lambe), the University of Brighton (Ivor Goodson, Norma Adair), the University of Leeds (Phil Hodkinson, Heather Hodkinson, Geoff Ford, Ruth Hawthorne) and the University of Stirling (John Field, Heather Lynch and Irene Malcolm). For further information, see www.learninglives.org.

2 This is a broad and complex group. For a graphic portrait, see Turner (2000).

3 The quote marks are meant to remind us that not only are 'traditions' always invested, but so is 'newness'.

References

Antikainen, A., Houtsonen, J., Kauppila, J. and Huotelin, H. (1996) *Living in a Learning Society: Life Histories, Identities and Education*, London: Falmer Press.

Blomqvist, I., Ruuskanen, T., Niemi, H. and Nyyssönen, E. (2001) *Participation in Adult Education and Training in Finland*, Helsinki: Statistics Finland.

Bourdieu, P. (1993) *Sociology in Question*, London: Sage.

Economic and Social Research Council (2006) *Demographic Review of the UK Social Sciences*, Swindon: ESRC.

Edmunds, J. and Turner, B.S. (2005) 'Global generations: social change in the twentieth century', *British Journal of Sociology*, 56: 559–577.

Education-line (no date) Online at http://brs.leeds.ac.uk/~beiwww/beid.html.

Findsen, B. (2005) *Learning Later*, Malabar: Krieger.

Hammerström, G. (2004) 'The constructs of generation and cohort in sociological studies of aging: theoretical conceptualisations and some empirical implications', in B.-M. Öberg, A. L. Närvänen, E. Näsman and E. Olsson (eds) *Changing Worlds and the Changing Subject: Dimensions in the Study of Later Life*, Aldershot: Ashgate.

Mannheim, K. (1952) *Essays on the Sociology of Knowledge*, London: Routledge and Kegan Paul.

Merrill, B., Crossan, B., Field, J. and Gallacher, J. (2003) 'Understanding participation in learning for non-traditional adult learners: learning careers and the construction of learning identities', *British Journal of Sociology of Education*, 24: 55–67.

Nickson, D., Warhurst, C. and Dutton, E. (2004) *Aesthetic Labour and the Policy-making Agenda: Time for a Reappraisal of Skills?*, Oxford/Coventry: SKOPE, Research Paper 48.

O'Donnell, K. and Chapman, C. (2006) *Adult Education Participation in 2004/05*, Washington, DC: National Center for Education Statistics.

Phillips, T. and Western, M. (2005) 'Social change and social identity: postmodernity, reflexive modernisation and the transformation of social identities in Australia', in F. Devine, M. Savage, J. Scott and R. Crompton (eds) *Rethinking Class: Culture, Identities and Lifestyle*, London: Palgrave Macmillan.

Phillipson, C. (1998) *Reconstructing Old Age*, London: Sage.

Pilcher, J. (1995) 'Mannheim's sociology of generations: an undervalued legacy', *British Journal of Sociology*, 45: 481–494.

Sargant, N. and Aldridge, F. (2002) *Adult Learning and Social Division: A Persistent Pattern*, Volume 1, Leicester: National Institute of Adult Continuing Education.

Savage, M. (2000) *Class Analysis and Social Transformation*, Buckingham: Open University Press.

Statistics Canada (2005) *Learning a Living: First Results of the Adult Literacy and Life Skills Survey*, Ottawa/Paris: Statistics Canada/Organisation for Economic Co-operation and Development.

Tennant, M. (2005) *Psychology and Adult Learning*, London: Routledge.

Thompson, P. and Callaghan, G. (2002) 'We recruit attitude: the selection and shaping of call centre labour', *Journal of Management Studies*, 39: 233–254.

Tuckett, A. and McAulay, A. (eds) (2005) *Demography and Older Learners: Approaches to a New Policy Challenge*, Leicester: National Institute of Adult Continuing Education.

Turner, R. (2000) *Coal Was Our Life*, Sheffield: Sheffield Academic Press.

Withnall, A. (2002) 'Thirty years of educational gerontology: achievements and challenges', *Education and Ageing*, 17: 87–102.

Chapter 7

Researching literacy for learning in the vocational curriculum

James Carmichael, Richard Edwards, Kate Miller and June Smith

Introduction

The *Literacies for Learning in Further Education* (LfLFE) project was a collaboration between two universities – Stirling and Lancaster – and four further education (FE) colleges – Anniesland, Perth, Lancaster and Morecambe, and Preston in the UK. It was funded for three years from January 2004. The project drew on work already done on literacy practices engaged in by people in schools, higher education and the community and sought to extend the insights gained from these studies into further education. It aimed to explore the literacy practices of students and those practices expected in different parts of the curriculum and to develop pedagogic interventions to support students' learning more effectively. This project involved examining literacy across the many domains of people's experiences, the ways in which these practices are mobilised and realised within different domains and their capacity to be mobilised and recontextualised elsewhere to support learning.

The project sought to examine the literacy requirements of four curriculum areas in each of the four FE colleges. It also sought to explore the literacy practices in which students engage outwith their college-based learning. We were investigating the interface between the literacy requirements which students face on their courses and the resources that they bring with them to their studies. This interface was described as 'border literacies', which, if they exist, enable people to negotiate more successfully between vernacular and formal literacies. We were exploring the extent to which such border literacies can positively affect learning outcomes and can serve as generic resources for learning throughout the life course. These border literacies are potentially the altered literacy practices that students are already familiar with which become relevant in college contexts.

One of the premises for the project was that the literacy practices of colleges are not always fashioned around the resources people bring to student life and that students may have more resources to draw upon than people working in colleges might be aware of. The intention was to achieve a critical understanding of the movement and flows of literacy practices in people's lives: how literacy practices are ordered and re-ordered, networked or overlapped across domains, across social roles in students' lives and what objects might mediate such mobilisations. Ivanic et al. (2004: 10) warn that the processes of mobilising these border literacies are 'not simple "border-crossings", but are complex reorientations which are likely to entail effort, awareness-raising, creativity and identity work on the part of the learner'.

A project such as this raised many theoretical, methodological and practical challenges, not least in ensuring validity across four curriculum areas, in four sites, drawing upon the collaboration of 16 practitioner researchers. This chapter examines some of the challenges and findings from the initial phases of the project. The chapter explores some of the findings regarding students' literacy practices in their everyday lives and those required of them in their college studies, and focuses on different aspects of partnership within the project, in particular the attempts to enable students and lecturers to be active researchers rather than simply respondents. First, however, we outline the theoretical and methodological terrain of this project.

Theoretical and methodological terrain

The policy agendas of widening participation and social inclusion often position literacy as a key issue to be addressed. Literacy is identified as a significant factor affecting retention, progression and achievement in further education courses in the UK. Much of that agenda focuses on basic skills and works with an individualised deficit model of literacy (DfES 2003). New Literacy Studies (NLS) provides a social view of literacy which locates literacy practices (different forms of reading, writing and representation) in the context of those social relations within which they are developed and expressed (Barton and Hamilton 1998; Barton et al. 2000; Gee 2003). NLS offers a view of literacy as multiple, emergent and socially situated in particular contexts. This work has demonstrated the rich variety of literacy practices in which people engage as part of their daily lives, but also that these are not always mobilised as resources within more formal education provision.

One initial premise of the project was, then, that 'vernacular' literacy practices exist (Barton et al. 2000) and students engage in them. These practices are seen as the sorts of resources for learning that may not be tapped into in all their richness. Research within the NLS umbrella recognises the importance of making the 'vernacular practices' of everyday life visible. Ivanic et al. (2004) argue that text-related practices increasingly involve an element of multi-modality and have been influenced by digital and new technologies. They argue that the use of new technology has facilitated a shift in the semiotic landscape towards the iconic and visual as well as the written word. They question whether educational provision has changed to accommodate these wider cultural shifts.

Furthermore, NLS questions the view that literacy is a skill that can be transferred unproblematically from one domain to another. Barton and Hamilton (1998) describe a domain as a structured and patterned context in which literacy is learned. The notion of transfer has been further problematised by Tuomi-Grohn and Engeström (2003), who argue that both cognitive and situated explanations of transfer are not sufficiently robust, especially when discussing transfer across domains.

Given the focus on the situated nature of literacy practice, it is unsurprising that ethnography is a preferred methodology for NLS studies. Ethnography is very close to the ways in which people make sense of the social context they find themselves in and has its roots in anthropology (Street 2001). The approach is that of illumination and de-cloaking existing practices to provide 'thick description' (Geertz 1993). Our aim therefore was to provide depth of description. The data-gathering process involved the practitioner researchers (of whom there were 16) and university-based researchers (of whom there were four). Where possible, the students themselves became involved in the process as co-researchers, not simply respondents. However, it was recognised that for many of the students, the use of the term 'co-researcher' to represent their involvement was more aspirational than evident from practice.

Smith (2004) found in her study of FE students' literacy practices that, when asked directly about their home-based literacies, students tended to say either that they did nothing or that they did very little. To overcome this direct approach, the LfLFE team used a series of 'conversations' with each student. Nevertheless, despite being informal and unstructured, the conversations were focused. Initially, there was an informal discussion about each student's life history, in which they were encouraged to talk about their family, education to date and reasons for joining the course. The second conversation was based around a 12-hour clock face. Each student was asked to choose a non-college day and write down what they did that day. When it was completed, they were engaged in a taped conversation around the literacy practices that were embedded in the social practices they had identified. In this way students came to a closer understanding of our use of the term 'literacy practices' and they began to move away from a paper-based view of text. After this conversation, they were given a disposable camera and asked to take photographs of their home- or work-based literacies. In this third conversation, the students were encouraged to think about any potential or existing links between home- and college-based practices. In addition to these individual interviews, two focus group events took place. The first focused on one literacy event within a class observation. The second was an icon-mapping exercise where students were asked to select a number of icons that represented literacy practices that were important to them. Once these were selected, the students were asked to place them on a Venn diagram of three overlapping circles, each named as either College, Home or Work. The overlapping spaces represent those areas where a literacy practice might take place in more than one of these spaces. From this, we were able to talk about the practices that they felt shared some borders.

Student literacy practices

> I just can't believe how much they do at home. Before becoming involved in this project, I thought most of them [students] maybe skimmed through a magazine occasionally or texted their friends, but no more than that.
>
> (Mike, a practitioner researcher on the LfLFE project)

Mike, and his fellow practitioner researchers within the Scottish end of the project, have all remarked on this aspect of their involvement. FE students, particularly those under 19, are regularly portrayed as a media generation who have no interest in literacy practices beyond playing computer games (Luttrell and Parker 2001). Furthermore, those practices which they are thought to be involved in are often devalued (Gee 2003). Yet the data collected have shown that, in the main, students engage in rich and varied literacy practices outwith their formal educational institutions, but these are largely not drawn upon by their experiences within their vocational areas.

Here we will focus on two students to illustrate this situation: one from multimedia – Tony; the other from childcare – Rachael. Both are studying at the same level – Higher National Certificate (HNC). These students were not selected because they are exceptional, but because they are 'telling cases'.

Tony

Tony was a mature student who had been an engineer for over 12 years. He had studied and passed the NC multi-media course the previous year. He was separated from his child's mother and saw his daughter on Saturdays. He lived with his new partner.

Tony described spending much of his leisure time at home involved in literacy practices he felt were directly connected to learning his chosen vocational area. These practices included reading textbooks and computer specialist magazines, downloading tutorials from specialist websites and joining multi-media forums where he could ask for advice and guidance on aspects of the software he was finding challenging. He 'played' with his computer most evenings. He said he did this for fun, not to pass the summative assessments within the units. He could do that without doing any extension work at home. He was motivated to learn more about his area for its own sake. Tony did not feel that what he was doing involved reading and writing. Before participating in the project, he had said he had never explicitly articulated what he did with computing. He was surprised to realise that his work was as literacy rich as it is. In our discussions, he came to understand that his attitudes towards his practices around reading had changed.

Tony described how his reading (and learning) had changed over the course of his time at college. At the beginning of the NC course, to learn a new aspect of computing, he said that, after listening to the demonstration given by the class teacher to the entire group, he used the step by step guides supplied by the class teacher, reading each step one at a time and then carrying out the step before reading the next instruction. He felt these were more significant than other hand-outs. However, now halfway through his HNC year, Tony describes a different process when he is using a tutorial at home. He quickly reads through the entire tutorial, whether it is from a book, a magazine or a website, to get a feel for the outcome. Then, with the tutorial to one side rather than at his side, he tries out the new feature of the software. He refers to the written text only if he needs some help. He feels that he now needs to visualise what the end product will be and the stages in-between are less important to him. He has the confidence and the experience to experiment and not rely on following step-by-step written instruc-tions. Another difference is that he now feels he would consult with textbooks to help his learning, whereas prior to his HNC year he felt they made no sense to him. Prior to this year, Tony felt textbooks were for academic people and not for people like him. After nearly two years of multi-media, for Tony the physical location where these activities take place may be different, but the main features of a literacy practice (Mannion 2005) remain the same: medium used, the text types, the purpose, values and expectations. He does not have significant borders to cross, although he is not himself aware of the border crossing in which he is engaged.

We would suggest there are two reasons for this. Firstly, both the class teacher and the students view the nature of knowledge and learning as a joint activity and, secondly, the use of ICT itself. Both students and the class teacher acknowledged that he (the teacher) was not an expert in all aspects of computing. Although the teacher provided demonstrations of aspects of a computing package, it was recognised that he could only provide a starting point from which the students had to move on. In the multi-media classroom students learned from each other as well as from the teacher. They brought into college tutorials they had found on the internet; they shared magazines and textbooks and they told each other of new sites or forums they found. The students were co-constructing their understanding. We would argue that the multi-media classroom is potentially more suited to learners' expectations, experiences and home-based literacy practices. For Tony, this certainly appears to be the case.

Rachael

Rachael is a quiet student who, despite being articulate, found it difficult to explain her motivations and actions. In interview, she often responded: 'I don't know'. She had passed some higher level courses while at secondary school, but had decided to leave halfway through her final year because she did not want to go to university. She lived at home with her parents.

Rachael described a variety and depth of home-based literacy practices around her passion – music. She downloads music from the internet and burns her own CDs. She follows the progress of her favourite bands in magazines and news-papers, wherever possible attending concerts at local venues. Often she uses the internet to buy tickets or music. She also accesses websites to find out more about her favourite style of music. She loves to read novels and keep in touch with friends through email and texting.

Like Tony, Rachael did college work at home. However, all the college literacy events she carries out at home are connected to the completion of assessments, not extension work connected to learning about her vocational area. She reads her handouts as reference material, selecting the parts which refer directly to her assessment. Rachael understands the purpose of her academic reading and writing as a need to pass her assessments, which would then allow her to work with children.

In the classroom, Rachael and her classmates had requested that their teacher adopt a teaching method that relied on them copying down bulleted notes from an overhead. The teacher talked the students through each point at a pace with which they could keep up. The students felt this approach helped them to memorise the details which they needed to pass the assessments. They felt confident that the teacher had already selected the elements they would be assessed on and they would then later refer to these notes when writing their summative assessments. In this classroom, the teacher is the expert who provides the students with all the information they need to pass their assessments. The teacher is seen by herself and by her students as someone who has access to knowledge which she passes on to her students directly or through guided reading. Reading is geared to focusing only on the aspects of the subject which are required by the assessment.

This view of knowledge fits within a traditional cognitive paradigm which portrays learners as 'disconnected knowledge processing agents' (James and Bloomer 2001: 2). This view has been challenged by socio-cultural theories which argue that learners construct meaning in a dynamic way from their interactions with others, their activities and their environments. Rachael may have carried out college-based tasks in the context of her own home, but the medium, text types, purposes, values and expectations of these literacy events were radically different from her home-based literacy events. Rachael's home-based literacy practices and those of her vocational classroom are so divergent that she is unable to bridge the gap between the two worlds. For Rachael, her home-based and her college-based literacy practices are kept strictly separate.

Gupta (2004) discusses two kinds of reader: transactional and reduced. The transactional reader is one who can interact with the text to create meaning and enjoy reading; the reduced reader perceives reading as painful and is reluctant to read. Before joining the multi-media course, Tony could have been described as a reduced reader at home and at college. But his approach to reading changed to that of a transactional reader when he found his passion. He developed an active meaning-making strategy which was based on context and prior knowledge. Rachael, on the other hand, described her home-based reading as transactional, but her college-based reading remained one of a reduced reader whose goal within academic reading was to select the parts of the text which were relevant to passing the assessment.

For Tony, the literacy practices around learning multi-media in and out of the classroom and his vernacular practices blended together. The culture of education and that of the everyday were resonant with each other to enable a translation from one domain to another. He believed he had an active role to play in constructing his knowledge and learning. There were no border literacies because there were no borders. In contrast, for Rachael the literacy practices around both learning and assessment were academic literacy practices, which were removed from her vernacular practices and passions. Her experience of her vocational learning in college was one where meaning and knowledge came as a set of fixed ideas to be learned by rote, rather than constructed through her literacy practices. Here, the culture of further education and that of the everyday were clearly distinct. For her, there was no evidence of border literacies because the two domains were too distinct. As argued by Ivanic et al. (2004), here there would appear to be a requirement to construct border crossings.

Participant researchers

Members of teaching staff in the four colleges were recruited as participant researchers within the LfLFE project. The research began with the perspective that a collaborative, team-driven approach was desirable, as 'asking how participants understand, value and construct ideologies around what is being done, clearly points to the collection of first-hand, "insider" accounts in which subjects talk/write/reflect about their own literacies' (Street 1995: 258). The use of participant-researchers is an appropriate and powerful method of plunging deep into the culture and environment of the research setting in ways that would be very difficult and time-consuming to achieve otherwise. So potentially the research should benefit from working with the immersed practitioner-researchers, but then also gain the insights brought to the process by the 'outsiders' from the higher education (HE) institutions involved.

All these are positive constructions but they do carry with them certain costs. Utilising participant-researchers presented us with the immediate challenge that the perspectives, values and language-codes of both the FE and the HE members of the team have to be transcended in order for effective dialogue to take place. This is never a completed process but was ongoing throughout the project. In a real sense, therefore, both FE staff and FE students ideally had to become actively, not passively, involved in the progress of the research project. By itself, this was difficult to achieve. A tenet of the ethnographic approach adopted within the project is the assumption that the researcher from one cultural situation can understand and 'read' the cultural artefacts and discourses generated within the processes under study. However, sometimes it is valid to question that assumption. Whilst the gulf between HE and FE is not so complete that communication cannot occur, there are still issues in that process. They are, so to speak, two sets of educators separated by a common language!

This can be addressed by drawing upon dialogical traditions. An important tenet of these is that forms of thought are determined by forms of practice. For new forms of thought to develop, changes in practice are sometimes required. To develop new ideas one must have possibilities to test these ideas and to interact directly with those engaged in the practices under study (Chaiklin and Lave 1993). Reconstructive analysis seeks the insider's view. However, there is a dialectical play between insider and outsider views. There is never a totally inside view, just as there is never a totally outside one. People constantly make outsider claims, third person claims, about events. We are inside a culture, when we understand how our subjects themselves distinguish between outsider positions and insider positions. Understanding someone else necessitates a movement between an outsider and an insider position. Understanding occurs not through occupying one position or the other but rather in learning the cultural movement between them. Understanding is inter-subjective, not subjective nor objective. The hope is that by creating a dialogue between the practitioners and their students with their insider knowledge and the researchers with their outsider knowledge, new insights and new practices will develop.

This requires of a research team attempts to 'bridge the gap' between the two institutional forms, a constant process of examination and reflection as the research proceeds in order to establish a common language and common procedures. Even so, there are and will be points of discontinuity. For example, to begin with, the process of setting up the research and launching it took much longer than was anticipated by the HE members of the team. Further, many of the FE staff involved started with an expectation that HE staff would provide them with an established set of procedures and operations that they would be required to carry out, without themselves having to take responsibility or be involved in making decisions that would shape the research. Teacher practitioners are concerned to get tangible results from research that means something in terms of their work. University-based researchers are aiming to do the same thing, but it might be that both parties have a different perspective as to what the work is.

What of the response to the research project from staff in the FE sector itself? In the first case, the challenge was to find FE staff willing and able to become participant-researchers. It might be thought that FE staff would welcome the notion of being involved in a very positive way with the business of developing a richer understanding of the practices and processes of learning. Whilst many were, matters are in fact not that simple. In effect, the sub-text of discussions with potential recruits was about the concerns with being required to take on additional work for which they would probably not be properly paid, and for which they would not be given adequate time.

Aside from this worry, some were intimidated by the view that it would involve them in 'academic' activities. There were some indications from staff that their perceptions of the kinds of skills and literacy practices possessed by HE researchers was that they were appropriate and necessary for the purposes of carrying out research. By contrast, their own skills and literacy practices were inadequate to the task. Many of the practitioner-researchers thought it would be the role of HE staff to check their procedures and activities to make sure that they were 'getting it right'. The practitioner-researchers persisted in assuming that HE staff were not only going to provide the 'right' way to carry out research, but would also 'judge their performance' and would re-direct what they did.

At the same time, this perception that HE staff were trained and able to do research in ways that FE practitioners were not, was also coupled with a view that HE practitioners would ask of the FE staff things that were unreasonable or in important ways 'artificial'. That is to say, there was a perception among FE staff that the ways of the theoretical and academic world have nothing to do with the world of the actual and the practical.

However, it was also the case that many FE staff were keen to participate but often found that their enthusiasm was not matched by other staff in their department or by their department head. Indeed, it quickly emerged during the opening phases of organising the research that the 'culture' of the department was at least as, if not more, important to the research, and for that matter to the day-to-day practice of the staff concerned, than the culture of the whole college as an institution. FE staff working as practitioner-researchers on the research project functioned within the normal operations of the department and sometimes priorities clashed.

As a result FE staff, engaging upon research projects, are stepping out of the institutional norms. Even in institutions that are supportive at a management level, the perception of colleagues is really more significant on a daily basis. For colleges and for departments, research can seem no more than something of a diversion and an indulgence that is tolerated as long as it does not interfere with the 'real work'. It does not do to overstate this element of the experience of the project. It is not outright opposition to the research, but an attitude that can and does exist, in some instances, alongside a supportive rhetoric and is therefore a subtle pressure rather than an obvious hostility. Nonetheless, it is an attitude that arises out of the cultural norms and is therefore quietly powerful.

In the attempt to construct a working relationship between HE and FE, therefore, the challenge of the different cultures is one that is, in some respects, quite obvious and direct, but it can also be quite subtle and difficult to identify. FE and HE staff live and move within institutional cultures that have much in common, but these very similarities can and do conceal significant differences, which in fact are exposed and made concrete within a research project that thrusts the two sets of institutions into direct contact.

Conclusions

Practitioner-research as a method of pursuing ethnographic research is challenging and difficult. In some respects the process is itself the point of the research. Being engaged in such work challenges the world-view of each member of the research team. It challenges practitioner-researchers to re-examine the nature of their practice. It also focuses upon the assumptions, the implicit value judgements, that often affect and direct the ways in which practice operates. For all these reasons, this kind of research is of great value to those who participate in it, at whatever level.

Still it is valid to ask if the advantages outweigh the disadvantages, particularly when trying to research the sensitive terrain of literacy. Research work carried out this way is slow, as each step of the process is hedged with difficulties. Negotiations around arriving at working practices, shared understanding of language, and on the very manner in which the research is conducted, are not resolved quickly and indeed carry on throughout the project. That in itself, of course, is not a negative, as the process of negotiation and communication carries its own value for the members of the team and for the research work, but it does take valuable time. It also carries certain costs for those who are participants, as they find that their own practice is challenged in various ways, and as they meet certain institutional barriers and problems, experiences can be painful. In some respects it might be said that a research project could be carried out a great deal more efficiently and effectively simply by taking on professional researchers and setting them loose to get on with it. But it would be an importantly *different* exercise.

The power of participant research lies in the partnership of researchers and practitioners in that both have to question their own practice by the very nature of the process. Yes, there are costs. However, it is important that these costs are borne and that the value of participation is recognised at both an institutional and a departmental level in institutions, but also at the level of policy making. Such recognition has to go along with an awareness of the fact that participant research takes time. It may provide valuable insights into the literacies for learning in which people engage, but it is itself a sensitive terrain.

References

Barton, D. and Hamilton, M. (1998) *Local Literacies: Reading and Writing in One Community*, London: Routledge.

Barton, D., Hamilton, M. and Ivanic, R (eds) (2000) *Situated Literacies: Reading and Writing in Context*, London: Routledge.

Becher, T. (1989) *Academic Tribes*, Buckingham: Open University Press.

Chaiklin, S. and Lave, J. (eds) (1993) *Understanding Practice Perspectives on Activity and Context*, Cambridge: Cambridge University Press.

DfES (2003) *21st Century Skills: Realising Our Potential*, London: Crown Copyright.

Gee, G.P. (2003) *What Video Games Have To Teach Us About Learning and Literacy*, New York: Palgrave Macmillan.

Geertz, C. (1993) *The Interpretation of Cultures*, London: Fontana.

Gupta, R. (2004) 'Old habits die hard: literacy practicies of pre-service teachers', *Journal of Education for Teaching*, 30(1): 67–78.

Ivanic, R., Edwards, R., Fowler, Z. and Smith, J. (2004) *Literacy Practices as Resources for Learning: Issues of Identity, Multi-modality and Fluidity*, TLRP Annual Conference, Cardiff, November.

James, D. and Bloomer, M. (2001) *Cultures and Learning in Further Education*, British Educational Research Association Annual Conference, University of Leeds, 13–15 September.

Luttrell, W. and Parker, C. (2001) 'High school students' literacy practices and identities and the figured world of school', *Journal of Research in Reading*, 24(3): 235–247.

Mannion, G. (2005) 'Mobilising a Literacy Practice', unpublished LfLFE project.

Smith, J. (2004) 'Furthering Literacies: A Study of Literacy Practices in Further Education', unpublished MSc, University of Stirling.

Street, B. (1995) *Social Literacies: Critical Approaches to Literacy in Development, Ethnography and Education*, Harlow: Longman.

Street, B. (ed.) (2001) *Literacy and Development: Ethnographic Perspectives*, London: Routledge.

Tuomi-Grohn, T. and Engeström, Y. (eds) (2003) *Between School and Work: New Perspectives on Transfer and Boundary-crossing*, London: Elsevier Science Ltd.

Chapter 8

Exploring learning in a small rural community

Darryl Dymock

Introduction

In Australia, residents in some rural areas in particular have taken up the concept of learning communities in an attempt to address changing and challenging economic and social circumstances (CRLRA 2001; ANTA 2002; Kearns 2005). Faris (2001, in Martin and Faris 2004: 2) defined a learning community as 'a form of learning-based community development in which the concept of lifelong learning is explicitly used to mobilize the learning resources of all community sectors'.

The benefits claimed for learning communities can be broadly classified as stimulating economic development; promoting social cohesion and inclusiveness; and encouraging personal development (Yarnit 2000; Wong 2002; Longworth 2004). Black et al. (2000: 58) noted the emergence of such initiatives in rural areas of Australia as an indication of the ability of communities to chart their own futures instead of being dependent on distant governments or commodity price movements. In a review of rural research priorities, Black et al. (2000: 62) suggested that education and learning were important for rural communities in Australia for three reasons: education, broadly defined, is vital in helping farmers respond to changing markets and technologies; that lack of educational opportunities in rural areas is one reason for people moving to metropolitan areas; and that 'the knowledge and skills of their members influence the resilience of rural communities'. The last finding is in line with the OECD's conclusion (2001, in Martin and Faris 2004: 2) that the 'knowledge base' of a community is a critical factor in local development.

This knowledge base is not developed only through formal learning. The significance of informal but planned learning was first highlighted in Canada more than 30 years ago by Tough (1979) and reconfirmed in more recent studies in that country (Thomas 1999; Livingstone 2000). Livingstone (2000: 1–2) identified three basic sites of adult learning: formal schooling (the formally constituted system with some mandatory attendance), further education (all other organised educational activities, including training programmes and workshops 'offered by any social institution'), and informal learning. The latter he characterised as 'any activity involving the pursuit of understanding, knowledge or skill which occurs outside the curricula or educational institutions, or the courses or workshops offered by educational or social agencies' (ibid.: 2).

There are questions, however, as to the extent to which small rural towns, with limited government and community resources, can sufficiently utilise all the formal and informal learning in the community for development purposes. For example, Martin and Faris (2004: 1) observed that internationally people and institutions at both government and community level had difficulty in implementing institutional mechanisms that facilitate the development of learning communities. A review of ten regional learning communities in Australia (CRLRA 2001: 135) noted that there was often no 'critical mass' of training providers in such communities, and that small communities sometimes lacked enough people to form committees and share the tasks needed for collaboration in vocational education and training.

In considering such issues for rural communities, it would seem important to understand both the attitudes to learning and extent of the knowledge and skills base on which a learning community might be built. This seems particularly critical in rural areas that have limited formal educational provision, are at some distance from the facilities of larger towns and cities, and where a small population is spread across farms, villages and towns. It was in such a rural area that the research reported here took place.

The purpose of the research was to explore attitudes to learning in a relatively isolated rural area, as well as to identify the resources available, including the formal education and training institutions and local knowledge and skills. In other words, it was an attempt to determine the extent to which there was a learning culture, as described in this adaptation of a definition by Johnston and Hawke (2002: 9):

> A learning culture is the existence of a set of attitudes, values and practices within a community which support and encourage a continuing process of learning for the community and/or its members.

The trigger for the study reported here came from a local council, elected by the residents to be responsible for the administration of a rural area, usually identified in Australian local government as a 'shire'. The council was anxious to learn about the concept of a 'learning community' and whether such an initiative might contribute to the social and economic development of an area that was reasonably prosperous from primary production, but losing many of its residents in their twenties and thirties to education and employment elsewhere. The area is referred to in this chapter as Bunjeroo Shire, and the names of the towns have also been changed.

Background

The Bunjeroo Shire Council was responsible for a rural area of approximately 3,000 square kilometres (740,000 acres), located some 200 kilometres (125 miles) from the state capital, Bigcity. There were a number of small towns and villages in the shire, the largest being Maintown, with a population of almost 2,000 people. At the 2001 census (ABS 2002), the total shire population was around 4,500, almost exactly half male and female. Eighty-nine per cent were born in Australia, including 1.2 per cent Aboriginal and Torres Strait Islanders. The largest overseas-born group in the Bunjeroo Council area came from the United Kingdom (3.9 per cent).

Two per cent of the population were in the 0–14 age group, while at the other end of the spectrum, 18 per cent were aged 65 years and over. The 15–24 age bracket comprised only 9 per cent, compared with 13 per cent in the state, reflecting the Australian trend for young people to leave rural areas for education, training or employment. Local industries were very strongly in primary production, with cattle and pig-raising, crop farming and forestry prominent.

Research approach

The researchers undertook an initial 'environmental scan' to identify learning resources available to the residents. With the support of Bunjeroo Council staff, they then explored the learning 'attitudes, values and practices' (Johnston and Hawke 2002) in the community, utilising several sources of information: focus groups, interviews with a cross-section of the local population, and a questionnaire survey. Initial interviews to identify possible themes and issues were undertaken with several interested individuals identified by the council, and a pilot question-naire was tested with a cross-section of council staff. For the purposes of this chapter, the main question was: To what extent was a learning culture evident in the Bunjeroo Shire? This question was addressed through three research questions:

1 What are residents' attitudes to learning?
2 What are people currently learning and planning to learn?
3 What skills, knowledge and talents exist locally which might be drawn on?

The *focus groups*, comprising a reasonable cross-section of the community, were all residents of Maintown a seniors group in a home for the aged, a group of young people within the 18–25 age range, a group of adults aged 26–45, and a group of Bunjeroo Council staff. Each focus group ran from 1 to 1.5 hours. With the exception of the residents of the aged care home, where detailed notes were taken, all focus groups were audiotaped and transcribed.

Interviews were undertaken with 20 people in order to obtain detailed information to supplement the responses obtained through the focus groups and questionnaires. The interviewees were invited to participate by a senior officer of

Bunjeroo Shire Council and covered a wide cross-section of the community, although only four (i.e. 20 per cent) were male. Age groups ranged from 16–19 to 65 and over.

The *survey* form was mailed to the 2,100 ratepayers in the Bunjeroo Council region, of which 137 forms (7 per cent) were returned to the Council's offices. Although this response rate is low, one positive factor was that the questionnaires were returned from locations across the Bunjeroo Council region. Respondents came from a wide age range, although there was no male representation in the 20–24 age bracket. Overall, nearly three-quarters of the respondents were female, with the majority of these in the 25–44 age group.

Findings

Current learning opportunities

Using the categories identified by Livingstone (2000) and outlined above, in terms of *formal schooling*, the Bunjeroo Council communities were served by a range of learning providers spread across the region, including four kindergartens/ pre-schools, four government primary schools, and two church-operated primary schools. There was also a 'community school' in Maintown that covered primary and high school, and five other schools that offered secondary education, three only in the junior years. There was a collaborative arrangement among these latter six schools, providing opportunities for students in sport and social activities, for staff in curriculum development and training, and for resource sharing.

There was also some formal schooling for adults at a campus of the regional Technical and Further Education (TAFE) College on the Maintown Community School site, which shared administration facilities and IT infrastructure with the school. Occasionally a representative of a private training provider visited to run a short vocational course. Some of the TAFE courses were non-formal, i.e. not accredited, and therefore fell into the second of Livingstone's categories, *further education*. Other organisations with an education and training focus, but based outside the council area, also provided formal learning for people in the area, including universities and TAFE institutes, both in and beyond the state.

A mix of further education and what Livingstone called *informal learning* occurred through a number of community and voluntary organisations in the Bunjeroo region. These included an arts society, a history museum, various service clubs, and the rural fire service. Other examples included community development and tourism associations, which had been formed in half a dozen towns to raise awareness of local priorities with the council, develop ideas for community-based projects, and assist in running some sporting and community facilities. Similarly, sporting clubs offered various learning opportunities for community members, including coaching experience. There was also informal learning through the Community Library, which shared its facilities with Maintown Community School, including free internet access and word processing facilities for local residents.

Education participation rates

Formal education participation rates of residents of the Bunjeroo Council region compared favourably with those of Bigcity at the pre-school, primary, secondary school and TAFE levels (see Table 8.1). The TAFE presence in Maintown was undoubtedly a positive factor, stimulating involvement in vocational learning particularly. However, the university participation rates in the Bunjeroo Council region were substantially lower than in Bigcity: 0.7 per cent versus 4.2, reflecting the fact that residents had to move elsewhere to undertake university and some vocational studies.

Attitudes to learning

It was clear that the community contained many active learners across all ages. Most responses associated learning with the acquisition of knowledge and skills, and identified perceived benefits to be derived from engaging in learning. These included improving the quality of life, expanding the mind, and self-improvement, as described by one resident:

> [It's] about achieving goals. I think you learn throughout your life. It is a lifelong process, so you learn something, you achieve one goal, which leads to more learning and achieving of the next goal, and it helps you to find your path in life.

A number of respondents associated learning with institutions such as school, TAFE and university. Others outlined specific areas of interest which they wished to learn more about, and some respondents related learning to the methods used to acquire knowledge. Apart from at the aged care centre, most people reported learning activities related to work or career development. One farmer initially said that the term 'learning' reminded him of school, but he then paused and said: 'No, well I'm a farmer. I learn every day on the farm.'

Table 8.1 Education participation in Bunjeroo Shire, 2001

	Bunjeroo Council Area (N = 1,024) (%)	Bigcity (%)
Pre-school	1.5	1.2
Infants/primary school	13.1	9.6
Secondary school	5.2	6.1
TAFE	1.9	2.6
University or other tertiary institution	0.7	4.2

Source: ABS Census Population and Housing, 2001.

The generally broad view of learning expressed by people in the area was also reflected in the different ways they liked to learn. For hobbies and recreational learning, the most significant sources of learning were books and magazines, whilst for workplace learning, the preferred method was a class or workshop. Residents generally seemed to be satisfied with the extent of access to computers and the internet, and there was a strong uptake of information and communications technologies (ICT), at home and at work.

Learning needs

Two major themes emerged in discussions of current learning activities. First, most people's reported learning activities related to work or career development. Second, undertaking courses by distance education was a popular approach to learning since this mode of learning could be more easily incorporated into a busy lifestyle.

Survey respondents were asked if they were planning to undertake any new learning projects, described as 'when you decide to find out something new, or how to do something better than you could before', a definition adapted from the 1998 NALL survey (Livingstone 2000). Almost exactly half said they planned to undertake a new learning project, and of those, 93 per cent indicated they were definite/highly likely or moderately likely to undertake them. In other words, there was a strong commitment by half the respondents to pursuing learning in the immediate future. The responses were categorised as shown in Table 8.2, indicating that the majority of learning needs expressed by community members focused on learning related to hobbies and leisure activities.

Learning needs in work-related fields reflected the increasing demands in the workplace for individuals to hold formal qualifications and regularly update their knowledge and skill sets. These included certificate courses in various areas (e.g. hospitality, business management, office administration, farm management), together with the provision of opportunities to develop job search skills and enterprise skills (e.g. public speaking, networking skills). Other learning needs identified included computer-related learning for skills ranging from basic computer use, email and internet, to specific software programs. There also seemed to be a need for the provision of computing courses specifically for older people.

Table 8.2 Planned learning activities

Category	% of responses
Hobby & leisure	44
Work-related	32
Computer-related	19
Other	5

Another key area of need uncovered in the questionnaire related to learning more about business and enterprise skills, e.g. running a small business, marketing/ publicity, bookkeeping, networking, financial management. Small businesses are essential to the economies of rural communities and provide a livelihood for significant sections of the population, so the provision of learning opportunities in these areas was likely to deliver considerable benefit to the community overall.

On the other hand, there was considerable local expertise which could be drawn on to help meet some of these learning needs. The skills audit within the questionnaire identified a small but significant proportion of people who felt confident enough to teach in the areas of business skills, enterprise skills and ICT skills. In addition, respondents self-identified specialised skills in areas ranging from primary production and aged care, to photography, story writing and gardening. This collective pool of skill, knowledge and expertise held by members of a community is often unrecognised.

One unexpected outcome of the research was that, without prompting, a number of focus group members emphasised that Maintown was a community where support was generally always available for community initiatives and projects. There was also reference to the extensive support networks and services available for parents, particularly in Maintown.

Barriers to learning

While the study showed that people in the area generally had a positive view of learning, it also identified some barriers to learning which affected their capacity to take advantage of opportunities. The location of the Bunjeroo local government area, its relatively small population, and the scatteredness and size of its towns give the area a certain kind of vulnerability to factors that may not impact to the same extent on larger metropolitan communities. The main learning barriers identified in the study were the high cost of courses and the pressure of competing activities at work and at home. Inadequate childcare facilities and lack of access to transport, were ranked relatively lowly.

More distinctive for a rural community were the concerns about the limited range of courses available, the travelling distance to courses in (more populated) towns beyond the local government area, and the difficulty of finding out what learning opportunities were available. There was also the disincentive of lack of employment opportunities in the area even if training was undertaken. In addition, the need for two different forms of student support was identified: when students had to move away from home in order to pursue a course of study, and for students who stay in the area but were studying by distance education. Some respondents expressed particular learning preferences, such as those who said they disliked learning in classes, and older people who preferred to learn with a similar-aged group, particularly in computing.

Learning opportunities

Community members' perceptions of learning opportunities currently available in Bunjeroo Shire ranked along the continuum from very good to very poor. While a third viewed learning opportunities as good to very good, almost half perceived them as only reasonable, with a considerable number regarding them as poor.

There was a wide range of sources identified by respondents in relation to finding out about learning opportunities available to them beyond school. The TAFE office in Maintown was the most often cited, presumably because it was the most visible post-school educational contact point in the Bunjeroo Shire area. However, the role of this one-person office was understandably focused on activities that TAFE could provide, so it did not have a general educational advice function. Hence people sought such information from such diverse sources as the council office, the local school and the local newspaper, or contacted institutions direct, sometimes through the internet, or they used individual contact people.

Discussion

While the number of respondents to the survey and in the interviews and focus groups was relatively small, the multiple sources of data collection meant that a variety of people was reached, so the responses summarised in this chapter might reasonably be seen as *indicative* of the range of views of a broad cross-section of the population.

In relation to the first research question, the responses suggested that people in the Bunjeroo Council region had a positive view of learning and did not see it only in terms of formal education. They valued learning as an activity in itself and believed that it was not only about obtaining qualifications and career advancement. Indeed, it seemed that people understood and supported the link between the benefits of learning to the individual and the community to which they belonged. This finding supports Thomas's (1999: 2) conclusion from the 1998 Canadian community learning survey, that adults can and do engage in learning, and that they enjoy it, despite sometimes 'impressive challenges'. He also claimed that 'their learning is where their hearts and hopes are'.

It needs to be kept in mind that the respondents to the survey might well have been those who already had a positive view of learning, and who may well fit what Merriam and Cafarella (1999: 71) said was the typical profile of an adult learner: 'white, middle-class, employed, younger, and better educated than the non-participant'. These descriptors are, of course, referring particularly to US adults, but there appears to be considerable transfer to the Australian situation, so it may well be that the views of those with low levels of education and/or with poorly developed literacy and numeracy skills are not represented in the findings.

In terms of the second research question, regarding current and planned learning, the areas of learning fitted all three of Livingstone's (2000) three categories: formal schooling, further education and informal learning. These responses were a reminder that purpose and context are important: people learn in different ways for different purposes at different times of their lives (Merriam and Caffarella 1999). In Maintown, at least, the presence of formal educational institutions, limited though they were, appeared to have made some impact on the learning culture of the town, although it is difficult to assess the extent of that influence.

The other side of the coin is that half the population had no plans for further learning, even when 'learning' was broadly defined. However, in a mailed questionnaire, it may be that 'learning' was considered only in a formal sense, a tendency noted by Tough (1979) and Livingstone (2000) when there was no prompting. Secondly, the range of potential impediments to learning may have influenced those attitudes. Some of the barriers, such as cost, are commonly identified in the adult education literature (e.g. Merriam and Caffarella 1999), but in the words of one respondent, 'distance from everything' is a continuing concern for face-to-face formal learning in rural areas. For the more isolated villages, this was a particularly significant issue.

Issues relating to transport and childcare, respectively, drew only very minor responses in the survey. This could be because people living in rural areas are used to having to travel distances to attend various functions such as sporting activities, and also have organised their lives to accommodate childcare needs. Alternatively, it may reflect the circumstances of those who responded to the survey. In any event, the high take-up of computer technology would seem to provide potential alternative access for some people to a range of formal learning, and to many sources of informal learning.

One factor identified in the study which had the potential to discourage further learning was the lack of a clear point of information about learning opportunities, both locally and elsewhere. It seems that there were pockets of information available but no one central point discernible to residents. On a related theme, it is possible that lack of knowledge contributed to the strong perception that learning opportunities were only reasonable, or the latter opinion may indicate that another role for the 'central point' would be to co-ordinate and act on requests for learning and negotiate with potential providers. In line with the learning community model, this function may best be undertaken by a community committee, which would also help ensure that the needs of those with poor basic skills are also met.

In respect of the third research question, there appeared to be considerable local expertise, which could be drawn on to help meet some of the learning needs expressed. The findings show that it is important to remember in any discussion of learning in communities that individuals and groups are both 'consumers' and potential sources of it.

In the context of explorations of learning, the research found that there was community recognition of local support and local networks for activities that were perceived to benefit the community. This supports the CRLRA (2001: 135) observation that personal linkages are stronger in smaller centres and that the lack of resources in such communities can lead to collaboration. Such networking is, of course, a key feature of the concept of 'social capital', defined by Falk and Kilpatrick (2000: 103) as 'the product of social interactions with the potential to contribute to the social, civic or economic well-being of a community-of-common-purpose'. It is noteworthy that in the research reported here, the residents themselves recognised the relationship between learning and social capital, a link that has been discussed by authors such as Balatti et al. (2006) and Field (2005).

In considering the definition of a 'learning culture' adapted from Johnston and Hawke (2002: 9), and presented earlier in this chapter, the research findings presented above suggest that this particular population in general had a positive attitude to learning, and that learning was valued not only for its own sake but also for the contribution it made to the community. In terms of 'practices', the response was not as strong, with only about half the population indicating plans for new learning projects. On the other hand, this initial study unearthed a significant pool of local talent, which suggests that there might be considerably more local skills and knowledge to draw on. Overall, there was substantial support for learning, and there was sufficient interest and involvement in learning from a wide range of residents of the area to indicate that there was a strong learning culture, one that would support a 'continuing process of learning for the community and/or its members' (Johnston and Hawke 2002).

The one element missing seemed to be some way of bringing all the learning together to work towards a common purpose, and the council appears to be a key player in that process. In an international comparative study, Martin and Faris (2004) identified leadership by local government as a key factor in the development of a learning community culture. Although not a traditional role for councils in Australia, the increasing concern for the quality of rural life that Black et al. (2000) noted has seen local government in rural areas in particular broaden their vision of the part they can play in helping sustain their communities (ANTA 2002; Kearns 2005). The study reported here serves only to emphasise what an important role that can be in the development of a learning culture.

Conclusion

The significance of learning for the social and economic development of smaller communities is only gradually being recognised. Rural areas, with their sparser populations and distances from major educational facilities, face particular problems in providing access to a wide range of learning opportunities. The research presented here, limited though it is, suggests that small rural communities have the resources and the resilience to develop into learning communities, i.e. the 'sub-stratum' of a learning culture is highly likely to be there. In particular, the findings indicate there should be considerable understanding of learning as both formal and informal, a significant local pool of knowledge and skill and a reasonable willingness to share them within the community, familiarity with information and communications technology, well-developed and recognised local networking and co-operation (social capital), and a recognition of the individual and community benefits of learning. It could also be that the small size of some rural communities may be a positive feature if the opinion leaders and network members are both learning role models and public proponents of learning. And local government has a role as both a driver and facilitator of a learning culture.

Thomas (1999: 2) concluded from the 1998 Canadian survey of informal learning that 'learning frequently begets learning, and its associated vitality, in its immediate human neighbourhood'. For rural communities, the distances may be vast, but the human neighbourhood may be quite small. It seems that learning and its 'associated vitality' have the potential to help sustain such communities and make them attractive places to live, work, recreate and re-create.

References

Australian Bureau of Statistics (ABS) (2002) *2001 Census Basic Community Profile and Snapshot: Bunjeroo* (DC) (LGA 45210), at: http://www.abs.gov.au/Ausstats/ABS%40 Census.nsf/4079a1bbd2a04b80ca256b9d00208f92/e9f90afb33fdf0bdca256bc00014566 e!OpenDocument.

Australian National Training Authority (ANTA) (2002) *Learning Communities Audit Reports*, Brisbane: ANTA.

Balatti, J., Black, S. and Falk, I. (2006) *Reframing Adult Literacy and Numeracy Outcomes: A Social Capital Perspective*, Adelaide: NCVER.

Black, A., Duff, J., Saggers, S. and Baines, P. (2000) *Rural Communities and Rural Social Issues: Priorities for Research*, Canberra: Rural Industries Research and Development Corporation.

Centre for Research and Learning in Regional Australia (CRLRA) (2001) *Building Dynamic Learning Communities: Ten Regional Case Studies*, Hobart: CRLRA, University of Tasmania.

Falk, I. and Kilpatrick, S. (2000) 'What is social capital? A study of interaction in a rural community', *Sociologia Ruralis*, 40(1): 87–110.

Faris, R. (2001) 'Learning communities: villages, neighbourhoods, towns, cities and regions preparing for a knowledge-based society', paper presented at the Centre for Curriculum Transfer and Technology, Victoria, British Columbia, at: http://members. shaw.ca/rfaris/docs/LCdigest.pdf.

Field, J. (2005) *Social Capital and Lifelong Learning*, Bristol: Policy Press.

Johnston, R. and Hawke, G. (2002) *Case Studies of Organizations with Established Learning Cultures*, Adelaide: National Centre for Vocational Education Research.

Kearns, P. (2005) 'A tale of two towns: learning community initiatives in Bega Valley and Thuringowa', *Australian Journal of Adult Learning*, 45(3): 371–384.

Livingstone, D. (2000) *Exploring the Icebergs of Adult Learning: Findings of the First Canadian Survey of Informal Learning Practices*, at: http://www.oise.utoronto.ca/ depts/sese/csew/nall/res/cjsaem.pdf.

Longworth, N. (2004) *Lifelong Learning in Action: Transforming Education in the 21st Century*, London and New York: RoutledgeFalmer.

Martin, J. and Faris, R. (2004) 'The likelihood of learning communities: a Canadian Australian perspective', paper presented at the ACANZ Conference, Macquarie University, 23–26 September, at: http://members.shaw.ca/rfaris/docs/The%20Like lihood%20of%20Learning%20Communities%20160904.pdf.

Merriam, S. and Caffarella, R. (1999) *Learning in Adulthood*, San Francisco, CA: Jossey-Bass.

OECD (2001) *Cities and Regions in the New Learning Economy*, Paris: OECD.

Thomas, A. (1999) 'Wrestling with the iceberg', address to 3rd annual NALL Conference, 'Wrestling with the iceberg of informal learning', Toronto, 19 February, at: http://www.oise.utoronto.ca/depts/sese/csew/nall/res/02thomas.htm.

Tough, A. (1979) *The Adults' Learning Projects*, Toronto: Ontario Institute for Studies in Education.

Wong, S. (2002) 'Learning cities: a European perspective', *Adult Learning Australia*, 2: 14–16.

Yarnit, M. (2000) *Towns, Cities and Regions in the Learning Age: A Survey of Learning Communities*, London: LGA Publications.

Chapter 9

Fire wall

Words and action in vocational training

Anna-Lena Göransson

This chapter presents the main results of my doctoral thesis (Göransson 2004). It describes how a group of firefighters, who consistently maintain that they are 'practitioners and not theorists' relate to various forms of language-based knowledge and language-based 'knowledging' in their vocational training which is based on problem-based learning. The study was carried out at a training college of the Swedish Rescue Services Agency (SRSA). The SRSA is a government authority working within the field of emergency and rescue services and other societal safety issues. The SRSA has four colleges where firefighters are trained. Data was gathered during ten weeks on scene and consists of classroom and training field observations, 14 qualitative interviews with six students and several informal discussions with learning firefighters. I also studied the curricular directives from the SRSA and compared them to what the students told me and their actions in the educational setting.

According to Vygotsky (1962), linguistic interaction is the fundamental condition for learning. The Swedish linguist, Larsson (1995: 105), says that language constitutes us and our knowledge and that it is in 'languaging' that knowledge is created. But both as a researcher and as an editor I have come to understand that human beings can build bridges between them with words but also raise fire walls. Our social contexts are of crucial significance to what and how we communicate, read, write and learn. That is why language that we use can create problems. When presenting his library findings, after two weeks of self-study, one of the firefighters in my study clearly articulates the gap between his own everyday language and the *logical-scientific paradigm* (Bruner 1986) of the textbook in this way:

> Fire. A rapid often uncontrolled oxidation process, the result of which is the development of heat and light of varying intensity, *I've written there. And of course*, the principal qualities of a fire *I've mentioned a little as well*. A flammable liquid vaporises and the pyrolitic gaseous fuel, created during vaporisation, consists of various . . . reacts with oxygen and forms products of combustion, such as carbon monoxide, carbon dioxide *and water and a little of that stuff. That's what I've mentioned . . . I've written a short story of how fire spreads, or of a fire's progress then . . .*
>
> (Firefighter 3)

It is obvious that he has not appropriated the chemist's language. Thinking 'didactics', considering the relation between actors, content and methods in a situated learning space, one can of course ask oneself whether the chemist's definition of fire is a functional definition for a firefighter, and also what the firefighter should or could do with that definition in his or her working practice. But whatever the answers to those questions are, we cannot get around the fact that in vocational training students and teachers are also faced with more and more 'theory' in the form of written text-based, often abstract information which they are supposed to read, critically study, question and reconstruct into new knowledge of their own. In other words, theory and practice must meet. Considering the significance of 'languaging' for learning, I therefore find it urgent to examine how students who call themselves 'practitioners and not theorists' and who primarily want to learn by physical practice, relate to various forms of verbal-based learning; and try to understand what this 'knowledging' implies for them. That is, I seek to understand and describe learning in terms of socialisation, interaction and communication and, for example, try to find out where, when and why communication works and where, when and why verbal learning difficulties occur.

Method and theory use

With the focus on the students as learning language users, I searched for an understanding of what was going on in the educational setting from a socio-cultural perspective to learning (Säljö 2000) and within the parameters of a didactic perspective (Uljens 1997) from external contexts to the actions of the students and teachers in the educational setting. I noted and analysed communication in the educational setting with support from those aspects compiled by Hymes (1986) to describe what he calls *situation context* and to understand text[1] in context: **S**etting/scene, **P**articipant, **E**nds, **A**ct sequence, **K**ey, **I**nstrumentalities, **N**orms, **G**enre. This means I noted the communication in the educational setting by focusing on where, who was communicating what with whom, with what aim and object, and in what way. I wanted to know how and about what, when and where, and in what way students and teachers talked, read, wrote and listened to each other, and how all this influenced learning in relation to the course objective.

Inspired by McCormick (1994), I consider the learning process as a meeting between the *educational text* and the student. By educational text, I mean that which the student encounters in the educational setting in the form of teachers' actions, teaching methods and textbooks, together with underlying factors, such as curricular directives and educational ideologies. McCormick's view is that reading and comprehension always occur within a collective, in a social and cultural space, and that the reading is steered in different directions due to the varying features of the text, who is reading and in what context the reading is taking place. McCormick says that readers create their own texts in relation to the author's text, aided by the *repertoires* and *strategies* they have at their disposal while reading and their underlying ideology. She describes the *general repertoire* as: 'A set of culturally conditioned experiences, beliefs, knowledge and expectations, about such matters as politics, lifestyle, love, education, integrity and so forth' (McCormick 1994: 79). In *matching*, the repertoires of the text and the reader are in agreement and so the reader feels at home while reading the text. *Mismatching* occurs if the repertoires of the reader and the text are not in agreement. A *tension* between repertoires occurs when the reader is sufficiently familiar with the text's repertoire but disagrees with it or opposes it for various reasons. Where McCormick works with *literary ideology*, I focus on 'culturally conditioned experiences, beliefs, knowledge and expectations' about *language and language use, knowledge and learning* and also about *the municipal fire services*, which influence the behaviour of the different actors in the situated meeting between the students and the institutional educational text (see Figure 9.1).

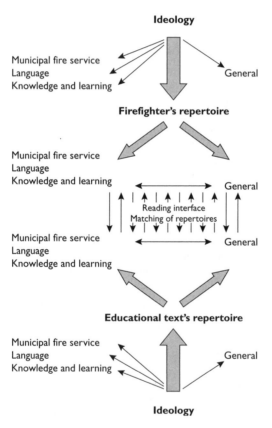

Figure 9.1 The learning process as a meeting between student and educational text (after McCormick 1994: 73).

Results

I understood from the firefighters that they work in a hierarchical, greedy organisation (Coser 1974), in which the brigade and the watch are of major significance to the individual firefighter's socialisation into the profession and his vocational role. The acclimatisation period reminds me of an apprenticeship whereby the newcomers gradually become full members of the group. Practical work-knowledge is developed by doing, while simultaneously learning to use the group language. And in that way one also becomes party to the attitudes and values that go with the language. The newly arrived firefighters learn, *inter alia*, to know their place, to listen and to be respectful towards older colleagues.

The bonds between the individual firefighters and the job are strong. A firefighter's identity is based on his professional role, of which he is very proud. Firefighters find meaning in their work and feel a strong affinity with their watch, which they often describe as being like a family working together to achieve a common goal. There are many common personality traits amongst brigade members, for example the desire for challenges at work, physical strength, a competitive spirit, an interest in practical work and the desire to work in groups. Clothing reinforces the professional identity. Firefighters have station uniforms when they are in the firestation and overalls for emergency response call-outs. This clothing also applied during training, which meant that the professional identity was also maintained in the educational setting.

The firefighters expressed a common point of view about how and what they wanted to learn: they wanted to learn from professionals who knew what it meant to be a firefighter in practice and who could provide them with insight, experience and what they called 'real' knowledge. They also stated that they wanted to know *why* they should act in a certain way. They recreate and reconstruct their work culture in practical actions and in informal discussions and stories of past incidents. The firefighters' creation of meaning is multi-modal. They articulate facts, skills, understanding and familiarity in words and body language. They 'read' emergency situations with all their senses. They search for people in smoke-filled rooms where it is not possible to see with one's eyes, but where it is possible with one's arms and legs. They watch and listen to how casualties behave, what their colleagues are doing and based on their actions act themselves. They willingly exchange examples, tips and advice with each other verbally. But they haven't documented much of their knowledge in writing:

ALG: You mean firefighters remember situations as pictures?

Firefighter 5: Yes, I think so. That's the way you learn. I mean, to be a firefighter, that means lifelong learning, so to speak . . . and then you get used to taking things in that way. You remember what it looked like, what happened there. It is very important to have that ability.

I understood that these students did not look upon themselves as readers. They do talk a lot. But it is a fact that they seldom read or write at work:

Firefighter 5:   Well, we read nothing except the daily papers.
ALG: And at work you do not have to read at all? It is not even necessary for you to be able to read?
Firefighter 5:   No, but it is . . .
ALG: Traffic signs, of course . . .
Firefighter 5:   Yes, but it's not really like that. If you know everything a firefighter knows, then you can also read, I believe.
ALG: Yes, of course. I did not mean it that way. But how much text do you have to read in your daily work, except for the traffic signs?
Firefighter 5:   No, traffic signs and the map. That's it.

In spite of all of this, reading and writing were considered to be natural activities in connection with learning:

Firefighter 6:   Is it a natural thing to read? You mean textbooks? When you participate in a course, it is. Of course, it is.
ALG: So there is no resistance to books?
Firefighter 6:   No, there is no resistance to books!

Intentions and strategies of the educator

The curricular directives are detailed and very directive concerning both content and method. There is almost no pedagogic freedom for the teachers who are to carry out the intentions of the central administration of the SRSA. From several documents and curricula directives one could understand that the SRSA wants to change both attitudes and the practical actions of the municipal fire services through its education and training. SRSA points out a necessary change of focus from operational fire and rescue actions towards risk prevention and fire preventive measures. As a result, education and training contain more and more text-based knowledge, which means more reading, writing and formal 'languaging'. In the documents 'modern pedagogy' (meaning problem-based learning) is a keyword. What is called 'traditional teaching' (meaning lecturing) is 'out' and teachers are instructed to remain in the background and not to steer the students' knowledging. There are high verbal demands on the students, who are told to search for knowledge, to take responsibility for their own studies and to work in small groups with so-called situations in accordance with the seven steps of the problem-based learning method:

1   Explain unclear terminology in the situation.
2   Establish the problem.
3   Analyse the problem through brainstorming. List support words and keywords on post-its.
4   Group and categorise.
5   Formulate learning objectives.

6   Private study – individually or in groups. Searching for information.
7   Discussion.

Reading interface

I found a great discrepancy between the activities, participation and involvement in the different learning scenes. When the setting changed the students changed and so did the communication and the atmosphere. But there was a marked change over time. At the beginning of the course all the interviewed firefighters explained that they were prepared to read and write as the course demanded. But having expressed joint ownership and a will to participate in the knowledging with their own contributions, they backed out and at the end of the course rejected large sections of the educational text as something that belonged to others:

> Maybe you've been out on the training ground and trained and worked like hell and extinguished fires and been all in a sweat and come home and had a shower. . . . Then you don't want to sit down and read a book, do you? But that's what they want us to do here.
>
> (Firefighter 1)

The clearest example of mismatching was problem-based learning, which the students understood to be working-group meetings, and reading and writing. Without any more explanation, than that this is modern pedagogy, the firefighters were taught by teachers who did not act in a way that they were used to from school. They were also taught by some teachers who were not experienced firefighters. This made the firefighters distrust the teachers' knowledge and their pedagogical skills:

FF: If the teachers don't have genuine skills from the field, you don't respect them.
ALG: That is how you feel?
FF: Well of course you respect them, they are good people. But they must be skilled firefighters. This is a school, an institution. It doesn't matter how many years you've worked here, or how many times you've put the training container on fire, you can never get real contact with us who work full time in a fire brigade.

The firefighters can hardly be said to have lived up to the role of active, knowledge-seeking, responsible PBL-students. They displayed no desire for deeper theoretical study; instead, they limited themselves as much as possible and searched only for functional knowledge that they could use in practical situations. The firefighters were not familiar with and had not previously encountered the method; and several of them were 'rusty' when it came to reading and writing. Confusion, despair and irritation were all mixed together when the students had to formulate study questions in writing, search for information and report on the knowledge in compendium form. A lot of knowledging became instrumental and would come to consist of strategic and ritual actions. The strategies they chose were to divide the work up between them and operate as messengers of written text, which they reduced to compilations in bullet-point form. The study questions that they formulated did not stimulate critical and analytical knowledge searching. And at the end of the course they were so frustrated that they did almost nothing:

Firefighter 6:   We just got frustrated when we didn't get any further. . . . And that last assignment you know . . . we did Chemicals . . .
ALG: Yes?
FF: I only worked for one hour and S did nothing at all.
ALG: No he did not.
FF: But still it passed. . . . Then you might ask yourself what did we get out of it?

Much of the open classroom discourse was experienced as meaningless, as were the written reports. The firefighters felt that 'theory' took up too much time in relation to the practical exercises, and they saw much of the library and classroom work as a waste of time.

The firefighters' classroom was monologic. It was mainly the more experienced firefighters that did the talking. It was them the teachers turned to, they controlled the discussion, and it was to them people listened and in accordance with what they were saying, corrected themselves. Several less experienced firefighters digested parts of the educational text in silence, for example, because they felt inferior to the more experienced ones and felt that they had nothing to add to the lesson. On the other hand, outside the classroom and during the whole learning period there was an uninterrupted informal learning dialogue going on between the students with a great amount of exchange of information and experience. Quite often these discussions took the form of lively stories about various incidents the firefighters had been involved in. Sometimes this also happened in the classroom and then one could see marked enthusiasm among the students:

Firefighter 6:   You noticed that in the classroom, didn't you? When someone with experience tells us something. Then you wake up and listen. Then you learn. And vice versa, when someone without practical experience talks about something . . .
ALG: Yes, then you just switch off.

The training ground and the practical exercises were appreciated. From the start in the garage, when preparing for an exercise in the training ground, the atmosphere was highly positive. The firefighters moved faster, talked more and there was tension in the air. The more fire, the more involvement:

When we practise we learn something instead of getting stuck in the PBL-method. Firefighters are practitioners and not theorists, I think.

(Firefighter 6)

On the training ground there was absorbing dialogue. After common emergency excercises the different groups often stood in a circle and had a lively discussion with their instructors about what they had done, how it went, and how one possibly ought to have acted. Thanks to these dialogues and the practical training, several of the less experienced firefighters said at the end of the course that they could now see and do more in different work situations and they felt more secure in their actions. They had learnt a lot during the exercises and informal discussions with their class mates, which allowed them to operate in their zones of proximal development.

Working didactics

Matching and tension also arose indoors when the firefighters encountered teachers that based their teaching on the firefighters' work situations and shared their experiences. One teacher who had a much appreciated lesson told me that he once had seen a picture in a magazine with three firefighters entering a burning building. What do these guys have to know in this situation?, he asked himself. He used the picture as a point of departure for his lesson. As an experienced fire-fighter and fire service officer he also knew the answer to this question from practice. This made the students trust him and they were also eager to learn what he had to in the classroom. A very ambitious fire protection engineer who taught almost the same lesson did not succeed at all. The students did not accept him, as they thought he had collected his knowledge from books and not from reality.

ALG: You have said that a lot of times now.
Firefighter 5: What?
ALG: That you want experienced firefighters as teachers.
FF: Yes. We do talk about that. That's the problem here. There is no firm link with reality. I mean if you have a class of students who are going to be dentists and learn how to drill a hole in a tooth, then you don't ask a helicopter pilot to teach them that, do you!?

But also some 'helicopter pilots' did succeed in stimulating learning and created constructive tension in the learning space. A female teacher teaching First Responder Medical Aid once let the students create their own 'situations' from their own experiences of traffic accidents. She supplied 'blood', bandages and other things they needed to make true pictures of the situations, which were then described by the different groups and discussed in front of the class. The students were acting, telling and talking and they stimulated each other by giving good examples. They were allowed to use their own working day language and everyone was very active during the lesson.

My favourite example is a lesson which had all the prerequisites needed to become a failure: it took place at the end of the course when most of the students had given up and changed into rather sad or displeased pupils. It also took place in a late afternoon just before the students were to go home for the weekend. The subject was leadership, which was not a field of practice for these students. It was led by two military officers who did not know much about the municipal fire service. But with conscious teacher support they created a stimulating learning environment with involved students who did more talking and writing than in any other lesson during the course.

These teachers were clear and well structured. They started by introducing themselves and presented the objectives for the lesson in a clear and well-structured way. They then took the working situation of the firefighters as the point of departure for the lesson and asked the students to think of and articulate the new demands that were put on them from society and which they were to meet with more education and knowledge. This made the firefighters articulate the diffuse demands of a changing society, which are so often referred to in the abstract documents of the SRSA, in concrete language and from their perspective. Every firefighter thought for himself, discussed with his group members, took notes and made himself ready to present the results.

When discussing the results, the teachers showed a great interest in what the firefighters said and *used* it when they continued the lesson. It resulted in a new task for the students, who now had to write down which demands one can put upon a firefighter who is supposed to talk to an audience about fire prevention measurements (which was one of the demands that the students had identified). A secretary had to take notes and write down all the demands, as the teachers said they were going to give them to the educator. Thus they made writing authentic and meaningful.

The officers looked at the students steadily, seeming secure and self-confident. They had appropriate tools at hand to create a dialogic classroom. They asked many authentic questions and demanded answers. They immediately saw the most silent student in the class and asked him if he had felt that the others listened to him. He said yes, they had voted on a question in his group and thereby he felt that his voice was heard. Thanks to the teachers, it was also heard in the classroom. The officers did not avoid silence, but made thinking possible and gave everyone the opportunity to think before talking. Apart from all this, they broke the lesson a couple of times so that the firefighters, who so easily tired of sitting still, could go out and have some fresh air. (Five minutes. No less. No more!)

This lesson functioned as a breeding ground for dialogue, reflection and critical thinking by giving the firefighters the possibility to diversify languaging. And the firefighters answered by acting in accordance with this, and used their language tools with both involvement and skill. Mini-lecturing, thinking, well-prepared serious discussions, writing, small talk and laughter were combined in a good tempo. Finally, the officers came back to the objectives and asked the students for comments, first in the group, then in the class.

During all these examples of good lessons, I noted how the atmosphere changed in the classroom and how the students became active and involved in accordance with the teachers' actions and the possibilities they created.

A conscious pedagogy indeed makes a difference

Different practices with different patterns of acting and different tools for handling reality meet in an educational setting, which in itself is a situated practice with its own rules for interaction (Säljö 2000: 128). The students in my study form a collective of more or less experienced firefighters. This means that the workplace context's written and unwritten rules follow them into the learning space and influence learning. In addition to this, the individual firefighter acts in accordance with his own knowledge and experience of what he consciously or unconsciously believes that the surroundings require, will permit or make possible in a certain activity. When the demands were neither explicit nor followed up, the students appeared to be lazy and also very critical of what was going on. It is obvious that a non-steering teacher can create confusion amongst students who are used to authority, if he or she does not succeed in explaining his or her actions so that they can be experienced as meaningful.

The firefighters acted as practitioners, with a way of thinking and acting that was partly explained by Schön (1987), who has argued that professional knowledge is part of a collective knowledge system in which ambitions, language, value systems and much more are shared. According to him, skilled practitioners do not apply general theories or general rules in their actions. Instead, they have access to a repertoire of examples, pictures, interpretations and actions, which they have adopted from their working community or have access to via their own experience.

To appropriate new physical and intellectual tools changes our way of thinking and acting. It changes our view of the world. Therefore, learning can be both difficult and painful. It may lead to rejection. The study shows that strong bonds between individuals and the collective can mean that a group collectively rejects or accepts certain knowledge or ways of learning, which can lead to deadlocks in the educational setting. The handling of the learning methods is therefore of vital importance for what occurs in the learning space.

The PBL-method involves reflection in and on action and activities that involve practising problem formulation, searching for knowledge, arguing in favour of one's viewpoints, and evaluation of the learning process. Here the PBL-method was contra-productive. Many students told me that the PBL-method was 'not their cup of tea', although they actually worked in a problem-based fashion in the field, without the seven-step instruction, without reading and writing, and without knowing it. But in the classroom, knowledge was silenced when the students were adapting to each other and to the prevailing power structures. The firefighters in my study also silenced the knowledge of the fire protection engineers and the educationalists by rejecting it.

The realisation of the intentions of the educational text had required a lot of work and support from the teachers. But the teachers had been instructed to remain in the background and not to steer the students' knowledging. It is obvious that students change their action patterns together with the person leading the lesson, regardless of whether the teachers act as active mediators or unobstrusive tutors. In addition, the group has a huge influence on the individual's creation of meaning. This means that the teacher not only needs to find and operate in the individual's zone of proximal development, but also needs to find and operate in every student group's collective development zone. To listen to and challenge the person learning is important, both on an individual and collective level.

A socio-cultural perspective allows us to combine physical and mental actions and see the teacher's most important task as facilitating creative understanding by creating a good breeding ground for both verbal and non-verbal interplay in educational settings. Madsén (1999) emphasises the importance of learning support and working scaffolding, not as techniques to break down and simplify tasks, but rather as a subtle interplay that builds on mutual understanding between the various actors in the educational setting. A constructive meeting between educational text and a work culture requires, I believe, that the students display openness towards those who want to convey knowledge; but also that the educational institution in question is sensitive to and makes use of the students' action patterns, attitudes, outlooks and language.

Within the work experience of firefighters, and other professions, there is important learning potential that can be realised through common articulation. Work-related narratives can function as a bridge between unique incidents and generalised knowledge, between everyday language and abstraction. It can allow practice and theory to meet and pave the way for a developed languaging in which the student can raise his or her own experience to a common general level with the help of an analytic teacher. And the firefighters ought, I believe, to be allowed to communicate with teachers, fire protection engineers and researchers on the same terms, in order to understand and make clear the relationship between their own practice and that of the engineers and researchers; and perhaps see possibilities for using the knowledge of those professions in their own practice or in reflection about it. Experience-based examples and scientific theories can both play an important role, providing that mediation is occurring and working. But personal reflection, as distinct from small talk between colleagues, must be learnt and practised.

The advantage of verbal articulation is that an opportunity is provided to question, critically examine and discuss one's own knowledge and one's own action patterns. By verbalising, systematising and generalising around one's own knowledge and placing it in relation to the knowledge of others, both firefighters and teachers can attain an increased awareness about how they do things, what they do, and why one way of acting can be better or worse than another in a given situation. The professions can then better defend what they do, and more convincingly, than by saying, 'this is how we've always done it' or 'this is said to be modern pedagogy'.

The firefighters looked for tried and tested 'recipes' to follow. But at the same time they maintained that every work situation is unique and that theory and reality do not always tally. This is without doubt the dilemma of every practitioner. If a theory is to prescribe exactly what is to be done, then a large number of factors must be assumed to be fixed, stable, invariant and unalterable. This is never the case in an emergency call out and it is never the case in a classroom. Here, both teachers and students were using the method as a recipe without having appropriated the underlying theories. Dialogue, reflection and critical thinking require a breeding ground and stimulation. I believe that one important reason for the rejection behaviour is the fact that neither the fire service nor the educational setting at the time of the study was a natural place of growth for these skills. There was no living reading, writing, analysing, critical examining tradition to grow into, and the majority of the teachers had no pedagogic tools to support the students in a developed written text-based languaging. The study implies the need for teachers to be able to cope with the linguistic difficulties that might occur in the classroom when it comes to increasing the students' repertoires with learning from written and abstract texts, to motivate this kind of learning and to scaffold the students by acting as good models for developing language use. The good examples show, that it *is* possible to create motivation and support participation and open verbal co-creation. If the students were afforded more such opportunities to grow into a functioning verbalised educational practice and in addition were supported in a conscious active reflection of their own study, there would have arisen, I believe, several more fruitful transactions in the educational setting.

Note

1   Compare, for example, Halliday and Hasan (1989: 10), who define *text* as 'language that is functional [. . .] any instance of living language that is playing some part in a context of situation'.

References

Bruner, J. (1986) *Actual Minds, Possible Worlds*, Cambridge, MA and London: Harvard University Press.

Coser, L.A. (1974) *Greedy Institutions: Patterns of Undivided Commitment*, New York: Oxford University Press.

Göransson, A.-L. (2004) *Brandvägg: Ord och handling i en yrkesutbildning [Firewall: Words and Action in Vocational Training]*, Malmö: Malmö University.

Halliday, M.A.K. and Hasan, R. (1989) *Language, Context and Text: Aspects of Language in a Social-semiotic Perspective*, Oxford: Oxford University Press.

Hymes, D. (1986) 'Models of the interaction of language and social life', in J. Gumperz and D. Hymes (eds) *Directions in Sociolinguistics: The Ethnography of Communication*, Oxford and New York: Basil Blackwell.

Larsson, K. (1995) *Den skrivande människan* [*The Writing Human Being*], Lund: Studentlitteratur.

Madsén, T. (1999) 'Att skapa goda betingelser för lärande – meningsfull kommunikation och begreppslig progression' ['Creating good conditions for learning – meaningful communication and conceptual progression'], in *Rapport från Marienlyst: Värdegrund/ Ledarskap*, Högskolan Kristianstad, Centrum för kompetensutveckling, at: http://www. distans.hkr.se/kkmtrl.baslitteratur/progression.

McCormick, K. (1994) *The Culture of Reading and the Teaching of English*, Manchester and New York: Manchester University Press.

Säljö, R. (2000) *Lärande i praktiken: Ett sociokulturellt perspektiv* [*Learning in Practice: A Sociocultural Perspective*], Stockholm: Prisma.

Schön, D.A. (1987) *Educating the Reflective Practioner*, San Fransisco, CA and London: Jossey-Bass.

Uljens, M. (1997) *School Didactics and Learning*, London: Psychology Press.

Vygotsky, L. (1962) *Thought and Language*, Cambridge, MA: MIT Press.

Chapter 10

Reality bites

Bringing the 'real' world of work into educational classrooms

Nicky Solomon

The integration of work and learning is seen as essential in work environments and increasingly in educational institutions. In workplaces it is now taken for granted that while working we learn, and in secondary and post-compulsory education, employment and the production of workers are understood to be central to learning programmes. Indeed, *employability* and *engagement with employers*, a current focus of government education policy, highlight an agenda for educational institutions that encourages the integration of the business of work and employment with the outcomes of teaching and learning programmes. This integration has important pedagogical consequences for the practices of teachers and programme designers.

In this chapter drawing on the findings of an Australian research study, I focus on the pedagogical complexities that are emerging as the world of work is increasingly brought into our classrooms. The study, entitled 'Changing work, changing workers, changing selves: a study of pedagogies in the new vocationalism' (ARC 2002–2004), investigated various pedagogical approaches to vocational learning across various Tourism and Hospitality and Information Technology programmes in universities, further education colleges, senior high schools, community colleges and private providers.

The term *new vocationalism* (Grubb 1996; Symes and McIntyre 2000) is an important contextual and conceptual backdrop to the study, and to this chapter. It is a term that not only refers to the distribution of vocational learning across education sectors, but it also captures the idea that work in contemporary workplaces has changed in particular ways. Work is no longer understood to be just about technical knowledge and skills, but work also involves ongoing learning and involves the person (du Gay 1996). This is not any kind of person – rather, it is a person who has particular kinds of attributes and attitudes. In other words, there are new worker identities at work, and these identities are multiple and flexible, take on the idea that learning is lifelong, and have particular attributes, such as being a responsible team player, problem-solver, good communicator and self-initiator (Chappell et al. 2003).

The study examined how these new work requirements and worker identities were understood and enacted in classrooms. This led to a consideration of how the 'real' and 'authentic' world of work is played out across the various education sites and how the intersection of the two domains of practice – work and education – were managed. What are the 'real world' bits in educational programmes today and do they have a bite?

This chapter will examine these real world bit(e)s, by focusing on some vocational pedagogies that aim to reduce the distance between education and the 'real' world and between being a learner and being a worker. These pedagogies sit neatly within lifelong learning discourses as well as educational discourses that privilege the 'real' (Edwards et al. 2004). This privileging has a number of reasons. For many students, the term 'real' suggests relevance, jobs, and work skills; for some educators, the term sits comfortably with authentic learning and authentic assessment discourses, together with the current interest in situated knowledge and learning in situ; and for some higher education policy makers, the term 'real' is linked with their promotion of desired connections between education and work.

The 'real' world – bits of reality

In the study there were many examples of pedagogical practices that helped people and knowledge travel across work and education boundaries. These included familiar ones such as work placements and sandwich courses, where the clear structure and location of the pedagogical practices helped to delineate the varied experiences, realities and identities. In this chapter, however, the focus is on pedagogical practices where the boundary between the two domains of practice – learning and work – is not so clear. These are simulations and work-based projects. In these practices the teaching and learning activities involve a mix of experiences and realities.

In this section I will give an overview of simulations and work-based projects that were examined in order to provide a taste of their reality bits. This is followed by a detailed description of just one – a holistic simulation. While this kind of pedagogical practice was found in only one site, it is useful for the purposes of this analysis, as it is an example of vocational pedagogies that magnify the issues and complexities of attempts to conflate the two domains of practice.

Simulations

The current trend to bring work into classrooms and to make learning 'real' has encouraged an increase in this kind of pedagogical practice. Often, as found in the study, simulation activities are built into a teaching module and take the appearance of some kind of work practice. It is not a practice that students bring to the classroom from their own work experiences, but it is designed by the teacher. One example is in a university undergraduate Information Technology module where students worked on a computer network problem that required technical skills and ways of working as one would encounter in 'real work'. For example, a team leader was appointed, breakfast meetings were held in cafes, and meetings were structured in a business-like way.

Holistic simulations however are more adventurous kinds of simulations. In the study, the example is a private hotel school. It was a vocational level school operating as a hotel, with students shifting between different work roles, such as receptionist, housekeeper, waiter, etc. In this site the simulation is all-encompassing in an attempt to create a 'realistic work environment'. The practice is underpinned by a belief that education sites are not 'real' and that this is a problem. It was thought that education needs to be more relevant and authentic, in order to not only prepare people for work, but also to make them work-ready. Moreover, the educators in this programme felt that pedagogy can/should replicate the 'real' and that the current emphasis in the literature on situated learning approaches supported this practice.

Real work projects

Typically, this is a final (capstone) module where students work with an organisation to design and carry out a 'real' project that has useful and real outcomes for that workplace. It is not teacher-designed but it is generated through 'normal' work. Projects often produce a 'real' product to be used by a 'real' client, developed in negotiation with the client with the support of a mentor. This was found in a further education Information Technology programme and in a higher education Tourism undergraduate programme. The purpose of the project was to 'put to work' learning and knowledge from previous taught modules in the programme. Knowledge, here, is seen to reside within students and their accumulated knowledge and experience. As indicated by one of the lecturers, the project is not about collecting information. It is about problem solving, making informed decisions and producing professional relationships. In the introductory lecture, the lecturer informed the students: *We are not giving you knowledge . . . you will be responsible for generating the knowledge which can solve your project problem. [. . .] Your classes back [here] help you understand your real-work experience, and to see the bigger picture.*

While there were reality bit(e)s in each of these practices, as indicated earlier I will describe in detail the holistic simulation example.

Holistic simulation: a private hospitality site

As described in the brochure: 'The School provides a unique learning environment where students live and study on the campus as both guests and staff of a simulated fully operational hotel . . . and as students of a school.' This description of a simulated yet fully operational hotel where learners are students, guests and employees invites a longer commentary on the tensions around 'real and not real'. This commentary does not focus on the simulation as a pretence or on the effectiveness of this pretence but on the design and workings of this reality and what it produces in terms of experiences and identities. This commentary is organised around the researchers', teachers' and students' experiences of the simulation.

As its title and web description suggest, this hotel school is not a conventional educational institution but is a hybrid one – it is a school but it also represents itself as a fully operational hotel. Indeed the boundaries between other operational hotels and this one are considerably blurred. It was established as a hotel school in 1990 and describes itself as the 'oldest fully residential hotel school in Australia'. Indeed prior to this date the hotel school was a hotel and conveniently sits adjacent to other hotels in a busy tourist area near Sydney.

As a school, it has some of the usual features of a private post-compulsory school, with approximately 200 fee-paying students aged between 18 and 25 years old, 85 per cent of whom are international students from Asia and Northern Europe. The school offers vocational programmes across a range of Certificate, Diploma, and Advanced Diploma awards in the areas of operations and management in tourism and hospitality. After two and a half years of study students also attain a Swiss Diploma. And at the completion of a third year of full-time study they gain a Bachelor degree conferred by an external university, although the school will soon have accreditation as a higher education institution.

Researcher experience of the simulation

This account draws mainly on the researchers' observations over a period of months as the research team shadowed Bob, a programme coordinator and teacher and important person in the operationalisation of the hotel school. We shadowed Bob doing his everyday work as he interacted with the students as guests, as employees and in the classrooms.

The blurring of image and reality began as soon as we, the researchers, arrived. It looked like a hotel, with typical external signage, buildings and gardens. This impression was sustained by the furnishings in the reception area, by the many noticeboards with local 'what's on' information and by the fact that there was a reception desk where the staff wore reception staff uniforms. Later we learn that these front office staff are also the students and that these students are also at different times in the week or the semester in the operational work of other aspects of the hotel – including housekeeping, laundry work, waiting in the restaurants or cooking in the kitchen. A particular uniform accompanied each kind of work. However, unlike other hotels, this hotel also had classrooms and interestingly when in class, students wore 'school uniforms'. This is a confusing sign as it is usually one associated with primary and secondary school students rather than post-compulsory tertiary ones.

In order to sustain the simulation and the image of a 'fully operational hotel', where the students are not only staff but also guests, the office reception needs to have work to do. Requiring a reconciliation of room bills at the end of each week as if the guests-students were departing and then arriving generates this work. Each week therefore begins with a new account as if to mark the arrival of new or at least returning guests-students.

As might be expected in a hotel, and also in a school, it is a highly disciplined and hierarchical place. For example, students are called to attention in corridors if their uniform is not quite right or their name tags are missing. A commonly heard reprimand is 'guests can't see your name tag if it's under your jacket'. The teacher reminds us that there is 'no point in allowing students to be slack at the school and then get discipline in the *real* world workplace'. This is reflected also in the often repeated phrase, 'this is just like work often does in the industry', However this sits alongside other more school-like disciplinary practices. For example, students start with 100 points and lose points for infractions, such as drinking on the job and arriving late to class. If they miss a class, they are expected to make arrangements to 'make up' within two weeks or they will be asked to show cause. If they are inappropriately groomed in class, they are sent away to shave or change their clothes. This is about instilling in them the consequences of missing their shifts or being ungroomed in the workplace.

Name tags are de rigor not only for students/workers but also for teachers/ supervisors. Furthermore, during corridor exchanges hierarchical differences are affirmed in the various forms of address. Students and staff are called Mr or Mrs, while we are introduced as either Professor or Doctor. We are uncertain how to address the teachers, and whether or not we should act in the spirit of the simulation. Invariably, though, we fail to do so and use their first names. It seems as outsiders, only momentarily being in the inside, we are not completely caught up in the simulation, and we mix up the signs. However, when we disentangle ourselves from the simulation and behave as observers of the simulation, rather than participants, the hyper-reality seems to work. In the classrooms we experienced the place as a school, and while in the corridors and gardens we experienced the place as a hotel. Also Bob, the research team's guide during the research process, comes across as a teacher in the classroom, and as a hotel manager in the corridor.

The researcher's confusion, though, was highlighted during lunch in the hotel restaurant with the principal of the school and the teacher. In many ways lunch has many of the signs of other restaurants – a booking has been made, our name is crossed off the reservation list, we are shown to our table, a waiter hands out menus. The restaurant is full with other customers. These are the students (in school uniforms). However there are other signs in the restaurant that disrupt our experience of it as a 'real' restaurant. One such sign is the excessive nervousness of the waiter-student. This is no doubt encouraged by our presence and the watchful eye of Bob, who inevitably draws attention to any slip-up with the service. There are other hyper-reality signs. One appears during the serving of drinks. The waiter uses a corkscrew to open a bottle of wine and then proceeds to pour its contents into our glasses. But it is lemon and red cordial and not white and red wine. Another example of this hyper-reality is the menu. It looks like a menu except for one small detail, and that is the cost of each item, which is in an unfamiliar currency. It is not $A, $US or euros, but, as in some holiday resorts, the school uses its own currency. This currency does not have coins or notes, but has an accounting function.

One further incident illustrates some of the complexities around the combined positioning of these learner-workers, and the accompanying tensions and instability experienced by the students. During one of our classroom observations the class was interrupted by a 'real' employee of the hotel school asking for two students to 'step outside'. They did and indeed did not return. In due course those remaining in class were told the reason for this abrupt departure. A function was to be held that evening for some Austrian visitors. This 'real' event was to have 'real' wine (unlike our lunch). Apparently the wine was delivered two days ago and left at reception. At that time these two students were the front office workers. However the wine was not to be found and the 'suspect' students were asked to help track it down. Everyone, including the researchers, felt uncomfortable.

In Bob's classroom there are numerous examples of a secondary school class-room disciplinary regime. For example, students are chided for reading something other than class documents and students are required to ask permission to go to the toilet. At the same time, however, Bob often talks to students as if they are not in a secondary school, 'you are aspiring to a career in hotel management. . . . I don't see students sitting in this room, I see employees, potential employees, expected to reach benchmarks as per industry expectations.' Moreover, the teacher closes each lesson with the words 'thank you ladies and gentlemen'.

Teacher experience of the simulation

Bob, our guide, presented quite a complex picture of the school. These complexi-ties surfaced at various times during our interviews, casual chats and observations of the different aspects of his teaching and middle management work. Bob enjoyed the many identities related to his many roles but at the same time felt that these contributed to his own professional struggles and uncertainties.

This struggle, though, was not related to the simulated pedagogy. Rather, the concept of a simulated fully operational hotel learning experience sat very comfortably with Bob. He celebrates the 'real' experiences offered, presented within this pedagogical practice:

> There's scope for simulating quite closely a *real* context in the sense that next door here at the front desk, that's as live as it can be. You're answering a *real* switchboard. So you'll have the Director of Tourism, Training Australia ringing up wanting to speak to [the principal]. How much more *real* can you get than that? They are dealing with *real* money; they're dealing with a *real* guest complaining about why is that photocopying charged to my account?

Which from the experience point of view is conducive to, I guess, nurturing those dispositions, or developing those attitudes.

We were interested in the seemingly seamless identity shifts played out not only by the students-guests-workers but also by Bob as a manager-teacher. Bob made these identity shifts with apparent ease. His explanation is that in industry work, such shifts are just 'normal' – 'the same thing will happen in a hotel'.

When asked how he experiences the students – 'when they're out there at the front desk, do you experience them as learners, learner-workers, or as . . .' – Bob's immediate response is:

Learners. No, very much as learners. Very much as learners, but with the framework of the industry benchmarks. . . . As in these are the standards, this is what we expect in a hotel, whether it be grooming, appearance, words that come out of your mouth and so forth. I will coach you. We'll coach you. We'll coach and we'll develop that skill.

One of Bob's complaints, though, is related to this learner identity. He feels that students don't capitalise on the learning opportunities of the place, and have a mindset of: 'Well, I'm at school, you tell me what I need to know, don't tell me anything else, just tell me what I need to know.' Bob believes that is not the kind of learner that this hotel school is trying to produce. He believes the school provides opportunities for learners to take responsibility for their learning rather than being a learner who receives knowledge.

The 'reality' of the high fees each student pays creates a tension around the worker aspect of the simulation practice. As Bob says, 'You're constantly getting "well I'm paying 20,000 dollars" thrown in your face from that value point of view.' Bob knows that the reality of being a paid employee rather than a paying student contributes to different kinds of work performances. And it is this tension that legitimises the inclusion of a work placement component in all the programmes. Students complete two six-month semesters of work placement in Australia or overseas and during this placement students receive full award wages.

Overall, however, Bob's description of the school is a positive one. While he reveals some problems, he celebrates the simulated pedagogy and what it offers the students. However, while he can work easily with the identity shifts in the simulated fully operational hotel, he is uncertain about his own professional identity. His explanations for this draw on the fairly conventional divide between working in real work in industry and working in an educational institution.

Bob has moved between work in hotels and in schools for the last 15 years or so. He has a Bachelor of Further Education and Training and has been at the hotel school for the last six years. Recently he informed us that he has left to work in a 'real' hotel. However, in the interview he expressed concern about his employment chances in the 'real' world. This is based on his view that, 'the longer you stay out of the industry, how marketable are you really back in the real world?' Education and training distinctions come to the fore in his responses:

> I am feeling trapped . . . industry tends to think that having been back six years, that you're an educator, not a trainer. And that's a mindset, that's a perception type of thing.

> . . . as much as a place like this is comparable with an industry context, I think some operators tend to look at it as a school, and you wouldn't survive in the 'real' world. So that's the perception.

In response to a suggestion that this hotel school experience might be useful in working as a learning and development person in a hotel, Bob, says:

> Oh, very much so. I believe that. I believe that in myself. Whether the industry would recognise that is a question mark. From the point of view of you're . . . let's say, the school, it's education rather than training. I think there's a perception that you opt out to go into education. You can't hack it in the *real* world. So that's the perception. Sadly. I don't agree with it. I don't condone it but I think . . .

Currently Bob is doing a Masters in Educational Management. His reason for doing subjects in Human Resource Management is that he hopes they will give him 'some degree of leverage in making a transition back to a *real* world, not that this isn't *real*. The other world . . .'.

At the same time, he says that industry experience is integral to good teaching in this school and talks about teachers who haven't 'practised in that field of hotel operation'. His rationale for this is:

> The clientele we have here for the most part are looking for an applied experience. They're for the most part not greatly academically inclined and therefore want the real world application. And also the essence I guess of the qualification is that it's applied. . . . I couldn't imagine not being able to step into the room without that anecdotal, without that real life dimension.

Student experience of the simulation

Attention is now drawn to the student experience of this simulated fully operational hotel. In the observations they appeared to move in and out of the various identities with relative ease. In classrooms they behaved like students, some even displaying some typical behaviours of reluctant students. When working at reception they behaved like front office workers, although when waiting at our table they seemed less at ease. However, these appearances did not necessarily translate into satisfying learning experiences. During the focus group discussions quite a different picture emerged around their engagement with this pedagogy that attempted to conflate the real with the 'unreal'. Indeed, the discussions provided a site for expressing many issues around the unreality of the school compared to the real world of work.

Many students were unambiguous in their view that the simulation failed. Their reasons primarily focused on the fact that it wasn't real. For example, when asked whether they think that the simulation prepares or does not prepare them for work, a sample of the answers are:

It doesn't really . . . it's a waste of time.

I don't think it works.

I think what we know is simple compared with the real world.

You go out to the industry and you start doing the stuff and they go, 'we don't do that, just do it like a quicker way'.

There are actually real guests in the industry. I mean here it's your peers and stuff.

Other students however express more ambivalence, drawing attention to some of its strengths as well as limitations. For example:

I think the idea of the simulated environment is excellent and I think probably you would find the practical classes wouldn't work without it because you wouldn't take it as seriously. Not that possibly people do anyway. But I don't know. I mean it's worlds apart from the industry.

Group work activities are a feature of the classroom work, as in many classrooms today. Reasons for doing so are often related to a particular approach to teaching and learning, but in addition a frequently cited explanation is that teamwork is understood to be a characteristic of contemporary work and therefore everyone needs to learn how to work in a team. However, the *real* world of the classroom and its relationship to a *real* work rationale doesn't hold much weight for the students. As a *real* student, one aspect of that reality is achieving a good grade, which some feel is not possible with group work:

One of the problems that we've experienced this year with the whole simulated environment . . . with group work for example. Like our grades is dependent on these group works and you can't rely on yourself anymore. You have to rely on everyone else. If this was the industry you wouldn't have to take that someone didn't do their part of the job, because that person would be fired. But it doesn't work like that at the school.

> If you're working with a person, there's an assumed level of knowledge and experience that you're entering at, so then there's mutual respect and it's an environment where you want to help each other out . . . here, I mean, I mean in a sense, I don't think it's a very competitive environment, but in a sense I guess we're competing and it's . . . I don't know, it just doesn't work I don't think.

A number of the dissatisfactions such as these are expressed and reflect a confusion to do with the different realities of workplaces and schools, which are not overridden in the simulation. Some feel that this confusion is overcome during their work placements when 'real learning happens'. Some claim that the workplace 'helps [one] to become more responsible' and 'for me I'm just always thinking I come here and I pay money for doing this but if I go out for work I get money for doing this'. They seem to have clear ideas about the distinctions between being a consumer/customer and being an employee.

In school they don't think of themselves as workers. They are simply 'students', but in the workplace they see themselves differently:

> half a student and half a worker.

> you are an employee but also we are learning . . . yeah we learn something from there. Yeah still teach you if you do something wrong.

Summarising the simulation experiences

These are just some examples of the signs in the hotel school that have helped to produce a hyper-reality where the distinction between the real and unreal is blurred (Baudrillard 1983). Interestingly, in spite of this blurring in almost every pedagogic aspect of the site and the curriculum, distinctions between the real and unreal were nevertheless invoked and reproduced. And frequently these were used to highlight the fact that the hotel school was not a 'real' hotel but was a school and this school, in spite of itself, was experienced as all schools are, as a place that was not the real world, but a world that was preparing people for the real world.

The students in the hotel school have multiple identities and positions – as learners, workers, guests and consumers – along with the different identities and positions in their work placements – half workers-half students. They are located in different relations of power in each. They have to negotiate a multiplicity of identities in the simulated environment that they may not necessarily encounter in more traditional educational institutions or workplaces. Their identities in this site could be understood as unstable and perhaps this contributes to the unease and dissatisfaction. Perhaps, though, it could be said that the simulated hotel work produces confusion and disturbance that is not unlike the world outside and it is therefore a valuable learning experience.

The work of Nespor (1994) offers some useful insights into the problematics of simulation pedagogies. His particular attention is on undergraduate Physics and Management educational programmes, explaining the curriculum in these programmes as representational productions. He describes these educational programmes as 'obligatory passage points' that induct people into a particular disciplinary field. He does not see the programmes as preparation for later practice but as programmes interacting within the fields. Education in this way can be understood as space–time processes that use material spaces (such as buildings, classrooms) to bring students into contact with representations of other spaces and time – through the contents of textbooks and lectures that make 'absent' spaces 'present' in textual forms. In simulations, however, these absent spaces are drawn into the present through material forms rather than through representational reproductions.

Some concluding remarks

There are many teaching and learning practices in educational institutions that bring work into classrooms in an attempt to help people learn to be workers. This chapter, in examining one holistic simulation, focused on one such practice. While there are many pedagogical understandings and intentions around simulations which are not addressed in this chapter, from the above discussion of this practice it seems that there is a belief that a simulation experience attempts to educate students for the 'real world' of work and in doing so helps them to become 'real' workers. But as this discussion illustrates, the relationship between simulation and the real is problematic. Student perceptions of simulation is that it is 'unrealistic', compared with industry placement, or if they are employed, with the workplace. This student dissatisfaction with the simulation experience is not surprising. After all, simulations are not 'real' by their own definition – although, of course, they are just as real as anything else.

Therefore rather than understand simulation as an attempt to duplicate the world outside the classroom, it may be better to understand simulation on its own terms – as a discursive practice which produces its own world which is a hybrid of work and learning and whose conditions and problematics are peculiar to itself. This would shift the analysis from that of a failure of simulation to simulate the real and therefore how it might be improved in order to become 'more realistic', to an analysis of the simulated world itself, with its complex and contradictory terrain that is generated out of its constitutive conditions and what it purports to achieve. Perhaps this could be built into the pedagogical experience. Rather than being concerned that such an analysis would disrupt the hyper-reality (which is in any case inevitable), a consideration of the knowledges, identities and power relations within the particular reality that is being produced could be productive.

If we understand lifelong learning as a response to the features of contemporary life, characterised by continuous change, uncertainty, the erosion of traditional life trajectories, the need to negotiate one's life more reflexively and the pluralisation of individual and collective identities, then simulation pedagogies and indeed vocational pedagogies in classrooms provide an opportunity for learners not only to engage with change processes but also to become reflexive. Edwards et al. (2002: 533) see reflexivity as 'the capacity to develop critical awareness of the assumptions that underlie practices'. They suggest that through self and social questioning (reflexivity) people are able to engage with and (en)counter contemporary uncertainties.

Given the appeal of the rhetoric of the 'real' in educational contexts in terms of its promise for jobs, and real work skills, we need to further interrogate the work that the term 'real' currently does and in doing so consider the reasons why 'simulations' and other vocational pedagogies are, in many educational sites, a frequently used pedagogical practice. The current focus on the 'real' and 'vocational utility' has a visceral urgency. Indeed it is difficult to resist, but it is also important for educators to see that it also involves a privileging in which education may be backgrounded unless there is an engagement and an analysis of situational and domain differences. Such an engagement may offset some of the reality bites!

References

Australian Research Council Research Study (2002–2004) *Changing Work, Changing Workers, Changing Selves: A Study of Pedagogies in the New Vocationalism*, Canberra: DEST, Australian Government.

Baudrillard, J. (1983) *Simulations*, New York: Semiotext(e).

Chappell, C., Rhodes, C., Solomon, N., Tennant, M. and Yates, L. (2003) *Reconstructing the Lifelong Learner: Pedagogy and Identity in Individual, Organisational and Social Change*, London: RoutledgeFalmer.

Edwards, R., Nicoll, K., Solomon, N. and Usher, R. (2004) *Rhetoric and Educational Discourse: Persuasive Texts?*, London: RoutledgeFalmer.

Edwards, R., Ranson, S. and Strain, M. (2002) 'Reflexivity: towards a theory of lifelong learning', *International Journal of Lifelong Education*, 21(6): 525–536.

du Gay, P. (1996) *Consumption and Identity at Work*, London: Sage.

Grubb, W.N. (1996) 'The new vocationalism in the United States: returning to Dewey', *Educational Philosophy and Theory*, 28(1): 1–23.

Nespor, J. (1994) *Knowledge in Motion: Space, Time and Curriculum in Undergraduate Physics and Management*, London: Falmer Press.

Symes, C. and McIntyre, J. (2000) *Working Knowledge: New Vocationalism and Higher Education*, Milton Keynes: Open University Press.

Chapter 11

The effects of social and organisational mediation on the student learning experience

An introduction to the SOMUL project

Rob Edmunds, Muir Houston and Ruth Watkins

This chapter presents an overview of a collaborative ESRC TLRP project that explores how the social and organisational aspects of the university experience may mediate student learning. The research particularly focuses on how variations in the organisational and social mediation of the institutional and disciplinary environments may impact on the student experience. The student biography is also considered to be a key component when exploring mediating factors on student learning and its outcomes. The nature of the research design means that a range of theoretical perspectives have been deployed and attempts will be made to integrate aspects of these into a coherent, multidisciplinary framework that employs a multi-method approach to data collection and analysis. Empirical data on the student learning experience, and the social and organisational settings of this experience, have been collected across three main discipline areas (Biosciences, Business Studies and Sociology) at five distinct Higher Education Institutions (HEIs). Purposive sampling was employed and where possible HEIs were chosen to reflect and represent the social and organisational diversity that exists in contemporary higher education. The project was initiated at the beginning of 2004 and will reach completion at the end of 2007. This chapter outlines the aims of the project, summarises the underpinning theoretical frameworks, describes the project design and methodology and presents some preliminary findings.

Introduction and aims of the SOMUL project

Over the last decade there have been significant changes in higher education, with an increasingly diverse student population, a proliferation of 'non-traditional' degree programmes, a blurring of subject boundaries and a teaching and learning agenda that has been increasingly driven by a quality framework. A product of this agenda is the formal articulation, standardisation and benchmarking of both intra-disciplinary and inter-disciplinary learning outcomes. This research focuses on improving our understanding of what the formal and informal learning outcomes actually are for a student within higher education and what are the significant factors that impact on these outcomes. It is also engaged with questions of the nature and comparability of these learning outcomes both within and between different disciplines and across a diversity of institutions. As summarised in Brennan and Jary (2005), the research aims for the SOMUL project include:

- Collecting data on student perceptions of academic, personal and professional identity and on the student learning experience across the three distinct discipline areas set within contrasting HEIs.
- To identify how variations in institutional organisation, curriculum design, the social and spatial context of study and informal learning experiences mediate student conceptions of their learning and identity.
- To use this data to improve our understanding of the nature and characteristics of higher education learning outcomes (as perceived by the students themselves) and how these are facilitated. This offers the potential for recognising and articulating a more holistic view of learning outcomes in higher education and enhancing both the formal and informal learning process.

Relevant literature and theoretical framework

The focus of the research and its multi-method approach require that it draw upon a wide range of developmental and sociological literatures and theoretical frameworks. The literature is summarised in Brennan and Jary (2005), who indicate that the work is framed within three broad areas of literature, including that associated with theories of learning in higher education, academic identity and cultures and sociologically-based work that explores the impacts of these on the student learning experience.

Early work on theories of learning includes Perry (1970, 1981) and Belenky et al. (1986), whose work was based upon a Piagetian model of development, suggesting that students go through a linear learning sequence; a progression from a simplistic to complex perspective on the status of knowledge. This work has been further developed by Marton (1976, 1984), who created the distinctions of 'deep' and 'surface' learning and Säljö (1979), who explored conceptions of learning and learning outcomes. Other work of relevance to the project includes Morton and Booth (1997) and Baxter Magolda (1992). There is, therefore, a well-established literature where learning and learning outcomes are viewed as both cognitive processes and products which are heavily influenced by formal education (Pascarella and Terenzini 1991) and can be measured at different levels. Contemporary research (e.g. Richardson 2000) has further developed this work with a focus on student learning across a broad range of contexts. How these conceptions of learning and learning outcomes may be mediated by social and organisational factors are an important strand of the project.

The concept of 'identity' (personal, academic and professional) is central to this research as it explores learning outcomes within distinct subject areas. Discipline areas within higher education have been recognised as having distinct communities defined by epistemological, cultural and social differences (Henkel 2000; Becher and Trowler 2001) and expressed and maintained through shared languages, practices and values (Kogan 2000). However, this framework and associated concepts have been constructed from the perspectives of academics who are usually already well integrated into their discipline area. There is little data available on the student experience of these communities and the impact that the strength of these communities may have on student identity and learning. This is of particular interest now that many students learn within modular systems that cut across traditional subject boundaries and/or participate in inter-disciplinary degree programmes. Bernstein's work (e.g. 1975) on the classification of academic disciplines (e.g. 'subject loyalty' and concepts of 'open' and 'closed' curricula) and their impact on students is of particular relevance to the project, where we are attempting to elucidate the ways in which the organisation of the curriculum and the influence of identity and culture mediate students' conceptions of learning outcomes.

Relevant sociological studies include a broad range of work and approaches and include some significant literature reviews, including Pascarella and Terenzini (1991, 2005), who present a more holistic view of the student experience and its impact on the outcomes of higher education. Work has focused on the breach between what the intended outcomes of teaching are and the actual learning outcome as perceived by the student (Brennan and Jary 2005). This then raises questions about the learning outcomes that manifest themselves within the affective domain (part of the 'hidden curriculum' as described by Snyder 1971) and include changes in attitudes, values, beliefs, morals and development of personal qualities and self-esteem (Pascarella and Terenzini 2005). The diversity of the student experience outside formal education (Becker et al. 1961, 1968) has been recognised for a long time and more recently this has been developed further to investigate the learning that takes in informal settings within higher education and also the workplace (Terenzini et al. 1996). The importance of the individual and what they bring to the construction of both identity and culture have also been highlighted (e.g. Becher and Trowler 2001). In contrast, the role of the institution in determining academic cultures and identities (Dubet 1994) has been identified, and the links this has with the role of higher education in 'elite reproduction' have been explored (e.g. Bourdieu 1996).

The integration of the literature from these three broad areas has been critical in providing the theoretical framework for this project and a number of working concepts and a language through which the project has developed (see Brennan and Jary 2005, for more detail). The main concepts that the research rests upon include levels of learning (deep/surface) and the construction of learning outcomes and how these impact on student identity through time (Brennan and Jary 2005). The theoretical frameworks and these concepts have been significant in shaping the study design and research instruments.

Design of study

Five case studies were identified in each subject (in collaboration with the Higher Education Academy) to reflect and represent the range of HEIs within what is a highly differentiated education sector. Within these case studies, three distinct disciplinary areas have been studied: Biosciences, Business Studies and Sociology. These represent a natural science ('hard/pure' – Biglan 1973; Becher and Trowler 2001), a vocational discipline (Business Studies – 'soft/applied' – Biglan 1973; Becher and Trowler 2001) and a social science ('soft/pure' – Biglan 1973; Becher and Trowler 2001). Detailed overviews of these subject areas have been produced (Biosciences: Houston and Wood 2005; Business Studies: Edmunds and Richardson 2005; Sociology: Jones et al. 2004). Sampling was therefore purposive, with cases chosen to reflect social and cultural variations, and organisational diversity of curricula (specialist provision or combined curricula, availability of full-time and part-time study; further details are available in Brennan and Jary 2005).

The term 'learning outcomes' as used in this project has been conceptualised in three ways: as a product of cognitive development, as a change in identity, and as changes in concepts of self (Brennan and Jary 2005). This conceptualisation enables changes in learning outcomes to be operationalised and measured over time and the factors that mediate these changes (particularly social and organisational) to be elucidated. Data collection has employed both qualitative and quantitative methods. Table 11.1 indicates methods of data collection and their links to key variables critical to the project. Participants have included both entering (first year through to third year) students and exiting students (i.e. final year – EX1, Table 11.1) through to the year after graduation (EX2, Table 11.1).

Questionnaires included sections on demographic data, institutional and course choice, and also instruments adapted from existing scales and inventories. Mental models of learning were drawn from the Vermunt's (1998) 'Inventory of Learning Styles' (ILS). Three scales were used: construction of knowledge, intake of knowledge, and use of knowledge. Construction of knowledge refers to how connections within the subject matter are made using a number of different sources, intake of knowledge contains items that ask about how well the information needs to be prescribed for the student, and use of knowledge is concerned with questions about the practical use of what is learned. Approaches to learning (surface versus deep) were explored through ten items drawn from the Enhancing Teaching-Learning Environments project's ASSIST inventory (ETLa no date). This inventory distinguishes learning subject facts from aiming to develop a deeper understanding of the underlying structure of the knowledge. Items to investigate learning orientations were adapted from the 'Shortened Experiences of Teaching and Learning Questionnaire' (ETLb no date) and a 'Personal and Educational Development Inventory' (PEDI; Lawless and Richardson 2004) was used to investigate cognitive skills, mathematical skills, self-organisation and social skills. In addition to these, the questionnaires included scales specifically

Table 11.1 Key variables and data collection

Key variables		Data Collection							
		Q		FG	I		SI	D	O
		Ex1	Ex2	Ex	Ex1	Ex2			
Diversity before HE									
Educational	Type of schooling	O							
	Achievements	O							
	Post-school study (nature and timing)	O							
Personal	Social and ethnic background	O							
	Age	O							
	Gender		O						
	Place		O						
	Achievements								
Diversity in HE									
HE experience	Knowledge codes						O	O	
	Student culture	O	O	O	O	O	O	O	O
	Departmental culture			O	O	O	O	O	O
	Course aims/programme specification						O	O	
	Teaching methods and SSR						O	O	O
	Institutional structures and cultures						O	O	O
	Architecture and geography								O
	Institutional status and type						O	O	O
HE experience (personalised)	Intensity of engagement			O	O	O			
	Curriculum choice				O	O			
	Study methods				O	O			
	Reasons for study	O			O	O			
	Stage in life course				O	O			
	Living arrangements	O			O	O			

continued

Table 11.1 (continued)

Key variables		Data Collection							
		Q		FG	I		SI	D	O
		Ex1	Ex2	Ex	Ex1	Ex2			
Parallel	Amount and nature of paid work	O	O		O	O			
	Domestic life	O			O	O			
	Other commitments	O			O	O			
Diversity of outcomes									
Personal	Remembered knowledge		O			O	O	O	O
	Skills		O			O			
	Competencies		O			O			
	Critical thinking		O						
	Loyalties/identities			O	O	O			
	Confidence/aspiration				O	O			
Social	Social reproduction		O			O			
	Social mobility	O	O			O			
	'Knowledge society' (human capital)		O			O			

Q = Questionnaire; FG = Focus groups; I = Student interviews; SI = Staff interviews; D = Documents;
O = Observation; EX1 = final year cohort, EX2 = same cohort, I year post-graduation.

designed for the project, including a section based on subject benchmark statements and a section on personal change. The reliability and validity of the inventories has been tested (Richardson and Edmunds 2007) and is discussed below.

The questionnaires were administered to two cohorts of students on two occasions. The first group received questionnaires in their first and third year of study, while a second group were surveyed in their final year (EX1, Table 11.1) and approximately 18 months after leaving university (EX2, Table 11.1). This allowed the university experience from first year through to post-university to be captured within the timescale of the project. The questionnaire content was slightly modified at each stage to reflect the progression of the student. For example, for the exiting and post-graduation students, additional questions were included to encourage reflection upon their learning experiences, how they had changed since the first year, their achievements and future aspirations.

Qualitative methods included collecting documentary and observational evidence from each site (Table 11.1). Detailed field notes were taken on each visit in order to record impressions of significant environmental, social and cultural features of the learning environment (e.g. infrastructure, organisation of space, communication between students/staff, social facilities etc. Interviews (involving staff and students) and focus groups were also a primary source of data. Interviews for first year students concentrated very much on the social contexts of study, whereas later interviews concentrated very much on the changes in student perceptions and the factors that have influenced these changes. Interviews were semi-structured to allow comparisons to be made between the discipline areas. All student interviews were transcribed and team meetings facilitated theme and code identification. Themes related to the schedules and included: aspects of choice and guidance; the degree of engagement with the discipline and the department; aspects of student life and integration; socio-economic conditions; personal change and identity formation; and future expectations. Data was managed and coded through the use of QSR NVivo (V2.0).

Interviews were also conducted with staff to gain an overview of staff perceptions of curriculum organisation, intended learning outcomes, factors influencing the curriculum and their perspective on student motivation and engagement. In addition, staff career trajectories were investigated. This involved discussing the academic trajectory which had led staff to their present position and a discussion of the academic and administrative dimensions of their current post. Further, for each case one interview involved the participation of a senior academic whose perspective on the development of the subject area, both within the particular case-study institution and more generally, was invaluable.

Student focus groups were organised to facilitate discussion on perceptions of the student experience within their particular institution and department and their conceptions of the subject area, culture and identity. For the entering cohort, the emphasis was very much on their expectations and initial experiences of student culture and the academic environment. For the exiting cohort, discussions concentrated on student and departmental cultures; the intensity of student engagement and changes over time; and changing or developing personal loyalties and identities (Table 11.1).

Comments on initial quantitative and qualitative data sets

At this stage of the project an initial analysis of the final year student questionnaire (administered to students in 2004–2005) had been undertaken (EX1, Table 11.1). Factor analysis was carried out in order to identify underlying constructs, which are briefly discussed below. Cronbach's coefficient alpha was used to determine the reliability of the scales identified. These are commented upon below. The mean factor scores were then compared by multivariate analysis of variance, using the independent variables of subject and institution within subjects.

Mental models of learning

Responses were received from 493 students on 12 items. Factor analysis found that items loaded on three factors corresponded to the original scales used. Factors for 'construction of knowledge', 'intake of knowledge' and 'use of knowledge' were identified. The three scales achieved values of Cronbach's alpha that suggested adequate reliability. Further analysis found significant variation across the three subjects and across the institutions within subjects, as shown in Table 11.2.

Business Studies students achieved significantly lower scores on 'construction of knowledge' and significantly higher scores on 'intake of knowledge' than Biosciences or Sociology students; the two latter groups did not significantly differ from one another. Regarding 'use of knowledge', Business Studies students obtained significantly higher factor scores than Bioscience students, who, in turn, had higher scores than the Sociology students. Also found were significant institutional variations in 'construction of knowledge' and 'intake of knowledge' for Business Studies, but not the other two subjects. There were significant institutional variations in 'use of knowledge' for Biosciences, but not the other two subject areas.

Approaches to studying

This section received 495 student responses. Factor analysis identified three factors. The first two corresponded to the deep and surface approach found in the original scales. The additional two items were unrelated to either a deep or surface approach and unlike the 'deep' and 'surface' factors did not achieve a value of Cronbach's alpha that would be satisfactory from a psychometric perspective. Accordingly, this third factor was dropped from the analysis. Table 11.3 indicates a significant variation across the three subject areas and institutions within subjects.

Business Studies students had significantly lower scores on 'deep approach' and reliably higher scores on 'surface approach' compared with Biosciences or Sociology. The latter two subject areas did not reliably differ from each other. Reliable institutional variation existed in 'deep approach' for Business Studies, but not the other two. There were no institutional variations across the three subjects in 'surface approach'.

Personal and educational development

Five hundred and one students provided responses. Factor analysis identified the four underlying constructs of the scales used (PEDI; Lawless and Richardson 2004): cognitive skills, mathematical skills, self-organisation, and social skills. Further analysis found that, again, there was significant variation across the three subjects and significant variation across institutions within subjects. See Table 11.4.

Table 11.2 Mean factor scores: mental models of learning

	Business Studies	Biosciences	Sociology
Construction of knowledge[a]	3.90[b]	4.23	4.16
Intake of knowledge[a]	3.87[b]	3.62	3.69
Use of knowledge[a]	4.10	3.91[b]	3.54

[a] Significant variation across subjects ($p < 0.05$).
[b] Significant variation across institutions within subjects ($p < 0.05$).

Table 11.3 Mean factor scores: approaches to studying

	Business Studies	Biosciences	Sociology
Deep approach[a]	3.55[b]	3.75	3.84
Surface approach[a]	2.69	2.44	2.35

[a] Significant variation across subjects ($p < 0.05$).
[b] Significant variation across institutions within subjects ($p < 0.05$).

Table 11.4 Mean factor scores: personal and educational development

	Business Studies	Biosciences	Sociology
Cognitive skills[a]	3.06	3.23	3.48
Mathematical skills[a]	2.83	2.97[b]	1.92[b]
Self-organisation	3.13[b]	3.26	3.33
Social skills[a]	3.13[b]	2.93[b]	2.85

[a] Significant variation across subjects ($p < 0.05$).
[b] Significant variation across institutions within subjects ($p < 0.05$).

Business Studies students obtained significantly lower scores in 'cognitive skills' than Bioscience students, who in turn had significantly lower scores than Sociology students. For 'mathematical skills', Sociology students obtained reliably lower scores than both Business Studies and Biosciences students, though the latter two did not differ from each other. On 'social skills', Business Studies students had significantly higher scores than Biosciences or Sociology students, although the latter two did not differ from each other. On 'self-organisation', there was no significant difference in scores amongst the three groups. Regarding institutional variations, there were significant institutional differences in 'mathematical skills' within the subjects of Biosciences and Sociology, significant variation in 'self-organisation' for Business Studies students and significant variations in 'social skills' for Business Studies and Bioscience students, but no institutional variations in 'cognitive skills'.

Learning orientations

Factor analysis identified three components: 'intrinsic orientation', 'qualification orientation', and 'social orientation'. However, internal consistency, as measured by Cronbach's alpha, was not satisfactory, reducing the validity of these scales in this instance. However, as with the other scales used, the mean factor scores indicate a significant variation across the three subjects and a significant variation across the institutions within subjects (Table 11.5).

Table 11.5 Mean factor scores: learning orientations

	Business Studies	Biosciences	Sociology
Intrinsic orientation[a]	2.82[b]	3.25	3.18
Qualification orientation[a]	3.16	2.84[b]	2.91
Social orientation	2.90[b]	3.02[b]	2.96[b]

[a] Significant variation across subjects ($p < 0.05$).
[b] Significant variation across institutions within subjects ($p < 0.05$).

Benchmark statements and personal change

Of the remaining sections of the questionnaire considered here, one section measured responses to benchmark statements while the other investigated the concept of personal change. The benchmark statements were overall endorsed by all the students. Subsequent discriminant analysis found that even with all the items, students' responses only weakly determined their subject of study. Factor analysis of the personal change section did not find an underlying structure beyond one factor. Rather, this scale appears to represent an undifferentiated sense of personal change.

Overall the scales reported above have been found to distinguish between students taking different subjects and between students from different institutions. Three of the four scales based on existing instruments have been found to have reliable internal consistency and so have proved satisfactory from a psychometric point of view. It would therefore seem likely that different conceptions of learning can be measured within the SOMUL project. The challenge will be to combine the large quantitative and qualitative data sets and determine the effect of different social and organisational mediators on these concepts. Data analysis is still at a relatively early stage and so the following discussion is a brief insight into the convergence of both the qualitative and quantitative data.

Programme choice

From the questionnaire returns for final year students, it appears that those in the Biosciences were more likely than their counterparts in both Business Studies and

Sociology not to be on the degree programme for which they originally applied. During individual interviews, a number of potential influencing factors were identified. Firstly, the Biosciences may be a second choice for those who fail to be accepted to medicine. Data from UCAS (2006) suggest that around 10 per cent of those accepted in the Biosciences had originally applied to medical schools. In addition, the opportunities offered by a common core (leading to perhaps six or eight individual degree programmes) offer students the flexibility to change their mind at the end of the first year.[1] Finally, at institutions with higher entry requirements, some students saw the Biosciences as an alternative route into medicine, allowing access at post-graduate level.

Class contact time

Once students are at university, one aspect of the work/study/life balance which becomes apparent is the amount of reported contact time. As can be seen in Figure 11.1, the number of reported contact hours was highly variable within each of the three subjects, with the number of reported contact hours tending to be higher in biosciences than in the other two subject areas. This difference was confirmed on a number of occasions in interviews with final year Bioscience students and in staff interviews, where it was recognised that the time demands for final year students in the Biosciences was significant. Indeed, students often raised the issue of their perceptions of the amount of time spent in class when compared with the contact time of fellow students within other subject areas. A related point concerns the role of paid work. A number of Bioscience students reported that they had consciously

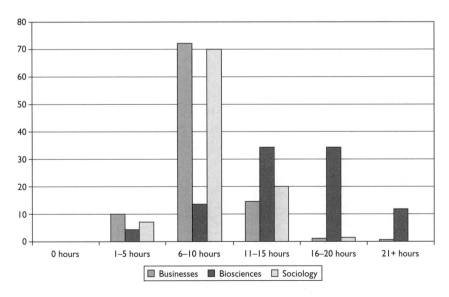

Figure 11.1 Self-reported contact time by subject area for final year student.

made a decision not to work in their final year simply due to the demands of the course.

Commuting and residential students

Another issue arising from the data is the experience of commuting and residential students in terms of academic and social integration. In Houston and Lebeau (2006) interview data provided an example of how for two Bioscience students at the same institution (Case study Bio_8), the social experience contrasted markedly between the commuting and the residential student. The commuting student took no part in social activities within the university and predominantly socialised with her existing peer network at home. This was in contrast to the behaviour of the residential student, who was a member of sports teams and university societies and whose social life revolved around the university. However, what was of interest was that in their final year, both reported a similar daily commitment to being on campus for academic reasons.

In contrast, and perhaps related to the amount of paid work which Business Studies students report, the experiences of two Business students (at a different institution; Case study BS_1) were quite different. For one residential, inter-national student, problems with accommodation and isolation resulted in a fragmented or individual social experience, whereby work and study took up the majority of free time. For the commuting student, the demands of work and study again left little time to avail themselves of opportunities to socially integrate and their social life remained centred around partner and family. Individual experiences of social and academic engagement are therefore highly variable both within and between disciplines and the challenge of the project is to explore how these experiences impact on the learning outcomes for the student.

Post-graduate expectations

Expectations around employment and possible post-graduate study were found to vary between disciplines. Relative to Biosciences and Sociology, Business Studies students were more likely to report the expectation that they would be in employment after graduation. Less than half of the Business Studies students reported that further study was a possibility. Interview data suggested that many Business Studies students considered they would move directly from graduation to employment. This is corroborated by the HESA (2005) first destination data, which indicate that 70 per cent of Business Studies students are in employment a year after graduation. The students also expected that any further training or study would take place within their employment ('training on the job'), reflecting the vocational perceptions of this discipline.

Sociology students, however, were particularly uncertain about their future prospects. This could perhaps be anticipated as Sociology is located halfway between the two other disciplines on both the soft/hard and pure/applied axes

(Biglan classification) – neither vocational nor scientific. Sociology is less polarised than the Biosciences and Business Studies: 74 per cent of Business Studies students are in employment a year after graduation and 43 per cent of Biosciences students participate in further studies. The figures for Sociology are, respectively, 55 per cent (employment) and 23 per cent (further study) and Sociology gets the highest percentages in the unemployed/not available for employment categories (HESA 2005).

In line with these trajectories, Sociology students in their final year express the greatest uncertainty in the way they relate their studies to their future career plans. Seventy-three per cent of the Sociology students considered their degree would be key to obtaining employment, compared with an average of 87 per cent of students across all subjects. The uncertainty and indecisiveness of the Sociology students could be interpreted as a flexible attitude to the wide range of options offered (or imposed) by the non-vocational nature of their course. However, this stance appears to echo the common view expressed by Sociology lecturers that their subject is, and should remain, non-vocational. This is reflected in the fact that for many Sociology students, views on future prospects hardly change between first to final year, suggesting limited impact of professional development programmes within the Sociology curriculum. Therefore, the non-vocational element of Sociology could be regarded as a strong component of the subject identity and a distinctive element of the Sociology syllabuses.

However, within this general trend there are institutional patterns emerging from the data, particularly for students taking broad-based Sociology degrees. In the post-1992 institutions, Sociology students are less likely to engage with post-graduate study and have better defined professional plans. The 'sociology experience' for these students appears to have negligible impact on their future plans. This should not be over-interpreted in terms of 'college effects' because new universities tend to have smaller numbers of distinct Sociology courses and for combined courses the professional finality is more evident. However, the perceptions of students on 'straight' Sociology degrees of the utility of their degree and its professional prospects show no significant institutional variations. It is also interesting to note that the data suggest that overall Sociology students tend to define their learning experience and its impact in a more holistic way (than, for example, the Business Studies students), placing more emphasis on the general skills acquired (creative and critical thinking, independence of mind) than on technical skills.

Whilst this section has only briefly mentioned aspects of the quantitative and qualitative data, it is suggested that it shows how different data sources can be combined to provide triangulation, detail and a greater understanding of the issues under investigation. The qualitative work is a critical component of this project and initial analysis indicates that much of the data corroborates the quantitative results. Early data analysis (as noted in both quantitative and qualitative sections above) indicates that differences between and within disciplines are apparent and some explanations have been provided to suggest how these may have come about.

Further analysis is ongoing to provide a more detailed account of similarities and differences between the student experience and student learning, both across and within subjects. Emergent findings from this analysis suggest that although there are subject and institutional differences in 'what is learned at university', similarities are also being revealed. This in some way adds support to the contention that while there has been an increase in the diversity of students and their expectations, and motivations for study may have changed, there are still some commonalities in the way students experience higher education. Using the conceptions and key variables described previously, the detailed data from all sources will be analysed to identify 'what is learned' at university and what are the mediating influences on these learning outcomes.

Conclusions

This research comes at an important time, when there is an increasing interest in the way that students learn, what they learn and also the recognition that student learning is not confined to formal educational settings. This is within the context of an evolving higher education system that has become increasingly diversified, but where perhaps approaches to pedagogy, learning and learning outcomes have remained essentially static. The preliminary results show that three of the four scales used within the project have been found to have reliable internal consistency in this context and it would seem likely, therefore, that different conceptions of learning can be measured within the SOMUL project and variations within disciplines and across institutions have already been identified. The examples given from the qualitative data provide an additional insight into the student experience and the themes are providing rich data to support the questionnaire returns. The challenge for the project is to now combine the large longitudinal qualitative and quantitative data sets in order to identify and evidence changes in learning outcomes through time and the factors that mediate these changes. The project is particularly interested in determining the effects of different social and organisational mediators on the concepts of learning and learning outcomes as perceived by students. The results of this project will make a significant contribution to evidence-based policy at a number of levels and strong links with collaborators will ensure effective and efficient data dissemination.

Acknowledgements

The authors of this paper acknowledge the contribution of other members of the project team: J. Brennan, D.W. Jary, Y. Lebeau, J.T.E. Richardson and M. Osborne. The ESRC/TLRP grant number is RES-139-25-0109. Acknowledgements are also due to collaborators, including the members of the Higher Education Academy (in particular of its Subject Centres in our main fields of study – Biosciences, etc.), the Quality Assurance Agency for Higher Education, and the Open University and the University of Stirling (who are hosting the project). Special thanks are also due to participating institutions, departments, staff and in particular to the students.

Note

1 A formal common core was in operation at least in first year in three out of five of the Bioscience cases.

References

Baxter Magolda, M.B. (1992) *Knowing and Reasoning in College: Gender-related Patterns in Students' Intellectual Development*, San Francisco, CA: Jossey-Bass.

Becher, T. and Trowler, P. (2001) *Academic Tribes and Territories: Intellectual Enquiry and the Cultures of Disciplines*, Buckingham: SRHE/Open University Press.

Becker, H.S., Geer, B. and Hughes, E.C. (1968) *Making the Grade: The Academic Side of College Life*, New York: Wiley.

Becker, H., Geer, B., Hughes, E. and Strauss, A. (1961) *Boys in White: Student Culture in Medical School*, Chicago: University of Chicago Press.

Belenky, M.F., Ckinchy, B.M., Coldberger, N.R. and Tarule, J.M. (1986) *Women's Ways of Knowing: The Development of Self, Voice and Mind*, New York: Basic Books.

Bernstein, B. (1975) *Class, Codes and Control, Volume 3*, London: Routledge and Kegan Paul.

Biglan, A. (1973) 'The characteristics of a subject matter in different academic areas', *Journal of Applied Psychology*, 57: 195–203.

Bourdieu, P. (1996) *The State Nobility*, Cambridge: Polity Press.

Brennan, J. and Jary, D. (2005) *What Is learned at University? The Social and Organisational Mediation of University Learning: A Research Project*, Working Paper 1, York: Higher Education Academy and Open University/CHERI.

Dubet, F. (1994) 'Student experience in mass higher education', *Revue Française de Sociologie*, XXXV.

Edmunds, R. and Richardson, J.T.E. (2005) 'Business studies: an overview of undergraduate studies in the UK', report for SOMUL, ESRC-TRLP, Milton Keynes: Open University.

ETLa (no date) *Approaches and Study Skills Inventory for Students (ASSIST)*, at: http://www.ed.ac.uk/etl/questionnaires/ASSIST.pdf.

ETLb (no date) *Shortened Experiences of Teaching and Learning Questionnaire (SETLQ)*, at: http://www.ed.ac.uk/etl/docs/SETLQ.pdf.

Henkel, M. (2000) *Academic Identities and Policy Change in Higher Education*, London: Jessica Kingsley.

HESA (2005) Custom dataset for the SOMUL project, supplied by Information Provision Team, Higher Education Statistics Agency, Cheltenham.

Houston, M. and Lebeau, Y. (2006) *The Social Mediation of University Learning*, Working Paper 3, York: Education Academy and Open University/CHERI.

Houston, M. and Wood, E. (2005) *Biosciences: An Overview of Undergraduate Studies in the UK*, report for SOMUL, ESRC-TRLP, Milton Keynes: Open University.

Jones, R., Jary, D and Rosie, A. (2004) *Sociology: An Overview of Undergraduate Studies in the UK*, report for SOMUL, ESRC-TRLP, Milton Keynes: Open University.

Kogan, M. (2000) 'Higher education communities and academic identity', in I. McNay (ed.) *Higher Education and its Communities*, Buckingham: Open University Press.

Lawless, C.J. and Richardson, J.T.E. (2004) 'Monitoring the experiences of graduates in distance education', *Studies in Higher Education*, 29(3): 257–282.

Marton, F. (1976) 'What does it take to learn? Some implications of an alternative view of learning', in N. Entwistle (ed.) *Strategies for Research and Development in Higher Education*, Amsterdam: Swets & Zeitlinger, pp. 32–42.

Marton, F. (ed.) (1984) *The Experience of Learning*, Edinburgh: Scottish Academic Press.

Marton, F. and Booth, S. (1997) *Learning and Awareness*, Mahwah, NJ: Lawrence Erlbaum.

Pascarella, E.T. and Terenzini, P.T. (1991) *How College Affects Students: Findings and Insights from Twenty Years of Research*, San Francisco, CA: Jossey-Bass.

Pascarella, E.T. and Terenzini, P.T. (2005) *How College Affects Students, Volume 2: A Third Decade of Research*, San Francisco, CA: Jossey-Bass.

Perry, W.G. (1970) *Forms of Intellectual and Ethical Development in the College Years: A Scheme*, New York: Holt, Rinehart & Winston.

Perry, W.G. (1981) 'Cognitive and ethical growth: the making of meaning', in. A. W. Chickering and Associates, *The Modern American College: Responding to the New Realities of Diverse Students and a Changing Society*, San Francisco, CA: Jossey-Bass, pp. 76–116.

Richardson, J.T.E. (2000) *Researching Student Learning: Approaches to Studying in Campus-based and Distance Education*, Buckingham: SRHE/Open University Press.

Richardson, J.T.E. and Edmunds, R. (2007) *A Cognitive-development Model of University Learning*, SOMUL Working Paper No. 4, York: Education Academy and Open University/CHERI.

Säljö, R. (1979) 'Learning about learning', *Higher Education*, 8: 443–451.

Snyder, B. (1971) *The Hidden Curriculum*, New York: Alfred A. Knopf.

Terenzini, P., Springer, L., Pascarella, E.T. and Nora, A. (1996) 'First generation college students: characteristics, experiences and cognitive development', *Research in Higher Education*, 37: 1–22.

UCAS (2006) *Annual Datasets*, at: http://www.ucas.ac.uk/figures/ads.html.

Vermunt, J.D. (1998) 'The regulation of constructive learning processes', *British Journal of Educational Psychology*, 68: 149–171.

Chapter 12

What are the implications of an uncertain future for pedagogy, curriculum and qualifications?

Leesa Wheelahan

Introduction

What kind of curriculum, pedagogy and qualifications do we need for an uncertain future? This chapter seeks to answer these questions by engaging with the influential ideas of Ronald Barnett (2004a), who called for an 'ontological turn' in curriculum and pedagogy away from a primary focus on knowledge and skills to a 'pedagogy for human being'. A 'pedagogy for human being' seeks to develop the human qualities and dispositions needed to thrive in a future that is not merely uncertain, but radically unknowable. On the face of it, Barnett's approach is a welcome alternative to the traditional 'generic skills' approach in tertiary education, an approach which is often criticised because it seeks to develop abstract and decontextualised skills in the absence of the communities of practice that invest these skills with content and meaning (Bernstein 2000: 59). Barnett's criticism is different. He describes generic skills as a cul-de-sac, because they are premised on certain and knowable skills to navigate an uncertain world (2004a: 256). Barnett argues that disciplinary knowledge and skills are still important, but less so than they used to be in an age of certainty. More important now is a pedagogy that disturbs 'human beings as such' (ibid.: 257).

There is much to agree with in Barnett's approach, particularly his notion that we should seek to develop a 'pedagogy for human being', and that generic skills are a cul-de-sac. However, this chapter argues that a 'pedagogy for human being' must be contextualised by a vocation, which means that knowledge and skills are important because they help to develop the human qualities and dispositions sought by Barnett. This chapter is primarily a theoretical exploration of these issues. The chapter argues that unless the notion of vocation is used to ground Barnett's 'ontological turn' in the curriculum, the danger is that the attributes and dispositions he seeks will result in disconnected and fragmented identities, which find expression in market oriented capacities and patterns of consumption (Bernstein 2000: 59), rather than an intrinsic sense of inner calling, or (as sought by Barnett) an authentic self. This chapter outlines Barnett's argument, uses critical realism to critique his analysis, argues for the importance of a vocation, and considers the curricula implications that follow.

Barnett's argument

Barnett draws on the concept of reflexive modernity to argue that the process of change in late modernity is distinguished from change in earlier eras 'by its character, its intensity, its felt impact' (Barnett 2004a: 248). While I think that perhaps he goes beyond the concept of reflexive modernisation in arguing that the world is radically unknowable under conditions of 'super-complexity', his argument has much that is familiar. The pace of change is accelerating, and perpetual and pervasive change results in anxiety and stress, and 'an inner sense of a destabilized world. It is a destabilization that arises from a personal sense that we never can come into a stable relationship with the world' (ibid.: 251). One must choose between multiple descriptions of the world, and know at the same time that these choices are fallible, open to challenge, and likely to change: 'Our hold on the world is now always fragile' (ibid.: 251). This means that there always an 'epistemological gap' between our knowledge of the world and our knowing that we must act in the world. In other words, we must act even in the face of uncertainty, because certainty is not possible, and we need to develop confidence and capacity to do so.

Barnett argues that the constant flux of change means that our identities are now fluid and problematic. As the external moorings of identity slip away from us, individuals must find a new basis for being in the world, and Barnett says they must find the source in themselves. Consequently, he argues, the world order is one 'which is characterized by ontological dispositions' (ibid.: 248). This has implications for education. The basis of Barnett's ontological turn in, and the outcomes sought from, curriculum and pedagogy is 'being-for-uncertainty' (ibid.: 258): He explains:

> Being-for-uncertainty does not especially know much about the world nor have at its disposal a raft of skills to deploy in and on the world. Being-for-uncertainty stands in certain kinds of relationships to the world. It is disposed in certain kinds of way. It is characterized, therefore, by certain kinds of disposition. Among such dispositions are carefulness, thoughtfulness, humility, criticality, receptiveness, resilience, courage and stillness.
>
> (Barnett 2004a: 258)

He proposes a 'mode 3' knowledge in contrast to mode 1 and mode 2 knowledge. The distinction between mode 1 and mode 2 knowledge was made most famous by Michael Gibbons and his colleagues (Nowotny et al. 2001). Mode 1 knowledge is disciplinary based, often 'pure' research, conducted in universities by disciplinary specialists within a hierarchical framework that specifies the rules for knowledge creation, what counts as knowledge and who can contribute to it. Mode 2 knowledge, on the other hand, is categorised by 'a distinct set of cognitive and social practices' suitable for cross-disciplinary, problem-oriented, applied and less hierarchical research that occurs at the site of application, and which is, as a consequence, 'more socially accountable and reflexive' than is mode 1 knowledge (Gibbons 1997: 3). Nowotny et al. (2001: 39) argue that society and science have changed because of (among other things) the inherent generation of uncertainty. They argue that the traditional boundaries between society, science, politics, culture and the market have become blurred, with each transgressing on the other, and co-mingling with each other (Nowotny et al. 2001: 4). They call this a mode 2 society that requires a mode 2 knowledge, knowledge that is also transgressive and no respecter of traditional, disciplinary boundaries and universities as privileged sites of knowledge creation.

Barnett (2004a: 251) argues that while mode 2 knowledge is an advance on mode 1, because it is problem-focused, creative, bounded by uncertainty, and calls for a 'creative knowing *in situ*', that it too is limited. This is because in focusing on problems, mode 2 knowledge presupposes that problems can be identified and solutions found, given enough creativity. This is flawed because, Barnett (ibid.: 251) argues, 'this is a world in which solutions cannot be designed, in the sense that a problem has been entirely satisfactorily met; there are always repercussions, unintended consequences and loose ends.'

Barnett says that mode 2 knowledge is capable of taking students on an episte-mological journey, but is not enough to provide an ontological basis for being. Nor are generic skills the solution. While they appear to transcend problems of perpetual change by seeking to develop skills that can be applied across many contexts, and are premised on recognition of the limited shelf life of knowledge and skill, Barnett argues that they are a dead end. This is because generic skills are premised on a certainty that these skills can be known, resulting in tightly specified outcomes used as the basis for teaching and assessment. This does not assist students to develop the dispositions they need for conceptual and ontological uncertainty (ibid.: 256).

Against mode 1 and 2 forms of knowledge, and against generic skills, Barnett argues for mode 3 knowledge as the basis of the curriculum and pedagogy. He says that this 'is a curriculum that is aimed at the transformation of human being; nothing less' (ibid.: 256–257). Pedagogy itself must be characterised by uncertainty, with knowledge loosely framed, provisional and open-ended, and curriculum must be designed so that it insists students confront and engage with the uncertainties and dilemmas in their field of knowledge, but in ways in which 'human being itself is implicated' (ibid.: 257). He says this pedagogy must engage 'students as persons, not merely as knowers', and that while the disciplinary field is still present, its relative importance recedes because 'More to the fore here are educational processes that disturb human being as such' (ibid.: 257). As for knowledge, he argues that this has now become a process of active knowing, rather than something that is external to individuals. Active knowing produces episte-mological gaps because 'our very epistemological interventions in turn disturb the world, so bringing a new world before us' (ibid.: 251).

There is much in Barnett's account that I agree with, particularly the notion that generic skills are a dead-end, that learning must engage the whole person because it is not enough to focus on knowledge and skills, and that the dispositions he argues as needed for being-in-the-world should be an explicit goal of education. However, I think that Barnett's argument is underpinned by a fundamental incoherence, which leads him to posit individuals who are divorced from the social relations, professional and knowledge communities, *and knowledge* which give their lives meaning, and which help to shape their identity.

Why a theory of ontology is needed

Barnett presents an ontological *description* of the world, but he does not explicitly ground his argument for an ontological turn in pedagogy in a *theory* of ontology. Nonetheless, his approach is grounded in an *implicit* theory of ontology, because it is not possible to make claims about social reality without making some assumptions about the nature of reality (Archer 1995).

Barnett's argument for super-complexity is not necessarily synonymous with the argument for reflexive modernisation. Claiming that the world is radically unknowable and unpredictable is quite different to arguing that the pace of change has accelerated (even exponentially), that the 'risks' we now face are those manufactured by society rather than as a consequence of nature, that authority and tradition are no longer a reliable guide to action, and that the basis of our identities has become more fluid and reflexive (Beck et al. 1994; Field 2002). Moreover, the distinction is not between the knowable and the unknowable, because the world has always been unpredictable, but this does not mean it is *radically* unknowable.

Barnett's super-complexity seems to be based upon super-relativism, while not being post-modernist. It is not post-modernist because he is seeking an ontological mooring to ground an 'authentic self'. In contrast, post-modernism argues that there is no authentic self. For example, Usher et al. (1997: 103) describe the post-modern self as: '... an artefact socially, historically and linguistically produced. ... The post-modern story of the self is that of a decentred self, subjectivity without a centre or origin. ....' Barnett seeks to rescue subjectivity and the self, whereas post-modernism seeks to dissolve it. Moreover, Barnett (2004b: 68) recognises that he is making universal claims whereas post-modernism eschews such claims. He posits a universal role for teaching and for universities amidst super-complexity, whilst confronting what he sees as the limits of traditional notions of the university and of academic knowledge. The *purposes* of the university are to *add* to uncertainty by producing challenging new frameworks to interpret the world, to help 'us to monitor and evaluate that uncertainty', and to enable 'us to live with that uncertainty' at the level of the individual and society (ibid.: 71).

However, Barnett's argument about the universal role of the university is still, nonetheless, premised on radical relativism. He argues that the cause of uncertainty and anxiety arises from multiple and competing *descriptions* of the world. It is the *descriptions* that 'multiply and conflict with each other' (Barnett

2004a: 250). There is now no basis for choosing between descriptions, because 'amid supercomplexity, the world is not just radically unknowable but is now indescribable' (ibid.: 252). This does not allow for the possibility of *testing* some of those descriptions through our *practice* in the world, as a basis for *evaluating* different and competing descriptions. As Sayer (1998: 122) explains, 'it does not follow from the fact that [because] all knowledge is fallible, that it is all *equally* fallible'.

Barnett's approach seems to be based on methodological individualism and idealism. It is methodologically individualist because a world in which nothing can make sense (because that's what a radically unknowable world must be) is a world in which events and objects are discrete and their connections contingent, as are the outcomes that result, or at least a world in which we can never know the nature of these connections. It also leads to methodological individualism because the emphasis is on securing an ontological premise for the *individual*; not relationally, but in terms of dispositions which inhere in the individual. Finally, it is idealist because the world is reducible to descriptions, and it seems to lead to Cartesian dualism, in which all that can be certain (in the end) is the self.[1]

Realist, relational theories of ontology provide a more promising basis for developing curriculum and pedagogy. For example, critical realism makes claims about the nature of reality in distinguishing between the real world and our knowledge of it, arguing that what exists does not depend on what we think about it or know about it. However, while the natural world exists independently of our conceptions of it, and the social world is *relatively* independent of our conceptions, our knowledge of both is fallible and provisional because our experience of the world is always theory laden (though not theory *determined*) (Sayer 2000). Bhaskar (1998: x–xi) explains that critical realism is premised on 'a clear concept of the continued independent *reality* of being . . . the *relativity* of our *knowledge* . . . and *judgemental rationality*'. In other words, while our knowledge about the world is relative, there are grounds for choosing some theories over others, grounds that we must be able to defend through recourse to evidence.

Critical realism argues that the world is complex and stratified. It is a *relational* philosophy because it examines the interplay between different objects and strata, arguing 'that the world is characterised by emergence, that is, situations in which the conjunction of two or more features or aspects gives rise to new phenomena, which have properties which are irreducible to those of their constituents, even though the latter are necessary for their existence' (Sayer 2000: 12). For example, even though societies comprise lots of individuals and could not exist without them, adding up all the individuals who live in a society does not express the totality of that society. Society is *more* than the sum of its parts, and the nature of society reacts back to affect the individuals and other factors (such as material and social resources) that make society possible.

Critical realists argue that what is needed in both the natural and social sciences is to identify the *underlying causal mechanisms* that give rise to events in the world. What we see is not all there is, and the limits of what we can see are continually reshaped by science and our practices. The world is far more complex than is the knowledge we have of it, and more complex than our experiences of events, and so we need to go beyond empirical descriptions to understand the complexities that produce events and our experiences (ibid.). The world is a complex, open system characterised by the constant interplay of different kinds of causal mechanisms (for example, social class and gender in the social world). This means that the outcomes that ensue are neither wholly random, nor wholly predictable. The world is not radically unknowable (and the converse, perfect and certain knowledge is not possible), and outcomes that ensue are not entirely random and contingent. Otherwise all knowledge would be impossible (Archer 1995).

This provides a basis for the curriculum because it shifts from teaching students immutable truths (as in traditional curriculum models based on eternal truths) to providing a grounding in knowledge that recognises the provisional nature of that knowledge, while providing students with the capacity to *test* such knowledge. It encourages the development of a critical and open-minded way of thinking about knowledge and the aspect of the world that it describes.

The overwhelming consensus around constructivist theories of curriculum (echoed by Barnett) downplays the importance of knowledge in the curriculum and increasingly emphasises knowledge that is contextual, situational and immediately applicable (Cullen et al. 2002). However, such accounts underplay the extent to which contextual and situational knowledge is an emergent property of individual agency, collective agency, the material and social world and existing, codified knowledge.

A realist and relational ontology regards knowledge as social product that emerges through our practice in the world. We use the knowledge that others have produced before us to understand the world and what to do next, and in the process we transform that knowledge because we are applying it in a new and different way, in a new and different context. In other words, existing knowledge is the outcome of prior agential practice. If individuals are to *use* and *transform* this knowledge they must embody it (to a greater or lesser extent) and integrate it with their tacit understandings of the world. Tacit knowledge or expertise includes the knowledge, concepts, ideas and experiences that we have internalised. Bransford and Schwartz (1999: 69–70) refer to this as 'knowing with', and explain that people 'know with' their previously acquired concepts and experiences. . . . By 'knowing with' our cumulative set of knowledge and experiences, we perceive, interpret, and judge situations based on our past experiences.'

I think the notion of emergence is very useful for understanding processes of learning, because the individual is always in a process of *becoming* through engaging in the world through their practice (Beach 1999). It is *relational*, and therefore rejects individualistic notions of skill and skill development. It is *holistic*, because it recognises that the capacity to exercise skill and use knowledge productively relies on the full development of the person – a person who has the capacity to live within and make connections between their personal, working and civic lives. It also provides an ontological basis for understanding the world as the outcome of processes that are neither wholly random nor wholly predictable. This means that knowledge is not about *prediction* but about *understanding*. Knowledge consequently is always revisable, but there are grounds for judging some theories and concepts as more reliable than others. Two implications ensue: the first is that processes of learning must be active, as this is the only way in which knowledge can become embodied and changed in the process; and the second is that curriculum must emphasise the provisional nature of knowledge while providing students with the tools for testing, evaluating and judging knowledge claims.

The importance of a vocation

Bernstein argues that the selection of knowledge for curriculum and the way that knowledge is mediated through pedagogic practice always occurs on the basis of assumptions about human nature and the place of the individual in society. He argues that the current human capital discourse within the 'official' education and training field is based on a new concept of work and life in which every area of life is perpetually transformed, and that the concept of trainability is now the key principle governing the construction of curriculum and pedagogy (Bernstein 2000: 59). Rather than specific knowledge and skills, the new paradigm calls for 'generic' skills. He explains that the process of perpetual re-formation, 'is based on the acquisition of generic modes . . .' that can be used in a variety of contexts (ibid.: 59).

Human capital theory emphasises trainability because it has substituted the market for vocations, in which the knowledge and skills needed to operate within markets take priority over knowledge and skill needed for vocations. Because the *market* has become the naturalised regulator of human relations (and not vocations or occupations), education and training seeks to produce the market individual, or the economic citizen (Marginson 1997). These marketable skills and knowledges are thus decontextualised from the vocations in which they were originally embedded. This is reflected in the increasing dominance of 'employability skills' in all sectors of education in countries such as Australia, particularly vocational education and training (VET). Australia has developed a new set of employability skills that must be 'front and centre' of all VET qualifications as they are redeveloped (Department of Education Science and Training 2005: 160). These employability skills are more tightly tied to the world of work than were the previous generic 'key competencies', and reflect an unproblematic view of work, in which all work together in harmonious ways for the greater good of the enterprise. Questions about the nature of work and power have no place.

However, Bernstein (2000: 59) explains that the generic capacities to be taught and 'trained' cannot be considered independently of the vocation for which individuals are preparing, because it is this that provides individuals with their *identity* and the *context* they need to make sense of these 'meta-thinking' and 'meta-learning' strategies. He explains that individuals develop the capacity to 'respond' to training as a consequence of developing a specialised identity that allows 'the actor to project him/herself *meaningfully* rather than relevantly, into this future, and recover a coherent past' (ibid.: 59). The notion of trainability is, he argues, based on notions of *individual* workers who psychologically construct knowledge and skills they need as a consequence of training, knowledge and skills that can be used in any context. He argues that the opposite is true, because 'This identity arises out of a particular social order, through relations which the identity enters into with other identities of reciprocal recognition, support, mutual legitimisation and finally through a negotiated collective purpose' (ibid.).

Bernstein argues that because the concept of 'trainability' is devoid of social content and divorced from vocations that were the basis of identity, there is now no framework in which actors can recognise themselves, except through the 'materialities of consumption, by its distributions, by its absences. Here the products of the market relay the signifiers whereby temporary stabilities, orientations, relations and evaluations are constructed' (Bernstein 2000: 59). Vocations shape identities through a negotiated collective purpose, and this fosters the development of an orientation to a field of practice and to the *knowledge* privileged within that field. In contrast, the concept of trainability divorces knowers from knowledge, and 'from their commitments, their personal dedications' (ibid.: 86). Bernstein says that commitments and personal dedications:

> . . . become impediments, restrictions on the flow of knowledge, and introduce deformations in the working of the symbolic market. Moving knowledge about, or even creating it, should not be more difficult than moving and regulating money. Knowledge, after nearly a thousand years, is divorced from inwardness and literally dehumanised.
>
> (ibid.)

He says in this way, knowledge 'is separated from the deep structure of the self . . .' (ibid.).

While Barnett is arguing against generic skills as a paradigm, he also divorces individuals from the field of knowledge or the field of practice in which they can recognise themselves and develop their identity. His argument is overly individualistic, because the outcomes he seeks can only be expressed through individual psychological constructions. The dispositions he seeks are worthwhile goals of education, but they cannot be developed in the absence of a framework which gives them meaning and context. Unless reworked notions of a person's calling or vocation are again made explicit goals of education, then the only enduring context in which individuals will be able to recognise themselves is in material consumption and marketised (and fragmented) identities.

Dewey (1997: 456) explains that the concept of vocation encompasses the role of that occupation in society, the values that underpin it and the knowledge and skills that are needed to engage in problem solving. Paradoxically, the notion of a vocation becomes *more* important in the context of rapid change. A vocation is predicated on change, and on active engagement by practitioners in creating change. A vocation goes beyond the technical requirements of an occupation and includes '. . . the development of artistic capacity of any kind, of special scientific ability, of effective citizenship, as well as professional and business occupations, to say nothing of mechanical labor or engagement in gainful pursuits' (ibid.: 307).

On the face of it, this approach may seem to be directly counter to prevailing views about the nature of education and globalisation, in which individuals need to prepare for several careers, and in which skills must constantly evolve to keep pace with technological change. The 'generic' view holds only if education and training for work is restricted to narrow notions of specific skill acquisition. People will need to learn several skill sets throughout their lives, but this does not make a vocation. A vocation is the framework in which an individual connects knowledge, skills, attributes, dispositions and values with a deep knowledge and understanding of their profession, and uses this 'connectedness' to define themselves (their identity in their vocation), and as implicit (or tacit) and explicit guides to action in their practice. A vocation provides the framework in which individuals can develop their identities, recognise themselves, and develop the dispositions that Barnett seeks – a way of being in the world that connects different aspects of our lives as a way of navigating uncertain futures.

Implications for qualifications, curriculum and pedagogy

Young (2003) argues that qualifications, curriculum and pedagogy need to be oriented around the vocation or occupation and the communities of interest that underpin that vocation, while insisting on the irreducible role of knowledge in the curriculum. Knowledge and skill is reworked, developed and extended within context of vocations, and the shared practices that ensue provide the credibility, authority and basis of trust for qualifications. The 'communities of interest' that underpin qualifications include employers, unions and professional associations, but also education providers and teachers.

The concept of communities of interest is useful for exploring the different contexts of learning that students need to engage in if they are to engage in holistic learning processes. Learning that is entirely based in the workplace or in an education institution is inadequate – both are needed, and students need to be able to make connections between them. This provides the scaffolding students can use to consider codified knowledge – it is not to be learnt for its own sake or as dead knowledge, but as an intellectual tool to be used in practice. *How* students learn to use, test and evaluate that knowledge and create new knowledge must be the focus of the curriculum. Qualifications need to be emergent outcomes that engage students in an orientation to their vocation, to the knowledge, skills and practices of that vocation, and provide a basis for an emergent identity for the student within their vocation.

Conclusion

Barnett's call for an ontological turn in curriculum and pedagogy so that students can develop the dispositions they need for being-for-uncertainty is useful because it forces us to consider the outcomes we seek from education. Being-for-uncertainty needs an anchor, and I've argued in this chapter that this anchor can be provided by the notion of a vocation. A vocation is not reducible to a set of skills – it is a way of being in the world that allows us to make sense of a world that is constantly changing. The knowledge and skills needed in a vocation will change as the world changes. An orientation to a field of practice, to a sense of calling and an 'authentic self' is more likely to result in the dispositions of 'carefulness, thoughtfulness, humility, criticality, receptiveness, resilience, courage and stillness' that Barnett (2004a: 258) seeks.

Note

1   See Curzon-Hobson (2002), who argues the opposite to the argument I've put here. He argues that Barnett's approach leads to the capacity to explore relationships because it is embedded and an 'I–Thou' pedagogic relation, rather than an 'I–It' pedagogic relation. However, radical unknowability is just that, including the nature of our relationships.

References

Archer, M. (1995) *Realist Social Theory: The Morphogenetic Approach*, Cambridge: Cambridge University Press.

Barnett, R. (2004a) 'Learning for an unknown future', *Higher Education Research and Development*, 23(3): 247–260.

Barnett, R. (2004b) 'The purposes of higher education and the changing face of academia', *London Review of Education*, 2(1): 61–73.

Beach, K. (1999) 'Consequential transitions: a sociocultural expedition beyond transfer in education', in A. Iran-Nejad and P. D. Pearson (eds) *Review of Research in Education*, 24: 101–139.

Beck, U., Giddens, A. and Lash, S. (1994) *Reflexive Modernization*, Stanford, CA: Stanford University Press.

Bernstein, B. (2000) *Pedagogy, Symbolic Control and Identity*, 2nd edition, Oxford: Rowman & Littlefield Publishers.

Bhaskar, R. (1998) 'General introduction', in M. Archer, R. Bhaskar, A. Collier, T. Lawson and A. Norrie (eds) *Critical Realism: Essential Readings*, London: Routledge.

Bransford, J.D. and Schwartz, D.L. (1999) 'Rethinking transfer: a simple proposal with multiple implications', in A. Iran-Nejad and P. D. Pearson (eds) *Review of Research in Education*, 24: 61–100.

Cullen, J., Hadjivassiliou, K., Hamilton, E., Kelleher, J., Sommerlad, E. and Stern, E. (2002) *Review of Current Pedagogic Research and Practice in the Fields of Post-compulsory Education and Lifelong Learning*, London: Tavistock Institute.

Curzon-Hobson, A. (2002) 'Higher education in a world of radical unknowability: an extension of the challenge of Ronald Barnett', *Teaching in Higher Education* 7(2): 179–191.

Department of Education Science and Training (2005) Training package: development handbook, Canberra: DEST.

Dewey, J. (1997) *Democracy and Education: An Introduction to the Philosophy of Education*, New York: Free Press.

Field, J. (2002) *Lifelong Learning and the New Educational Order*, 2nd edition, Stafford: Trentham Books.

Gibbons, M. (1997) *What Kind of University? Research and Teaching in the 21st Century*, Beanland Lecture, Melbourne: Victoria University of Technology.

Marginson, S. (1997) *Markets in Education*, St Leonards: Allen & Unwin.

Nowotny, H., Scott, P. and Gibbons, M. (2001) *Re-thinking Science: Knowledge and the Public in an Age of Uncertainty*, Cambridge: Polity Press.

Sayer, A. (1998) 'Abstraction: a realist interpretation', in M. Archer, R. Bhaskar, A. Collier, T. Lawson and A. Norrie (eds) *Critical Realism: Essential Readings*, London: Routledge.

Sayer, A. (2000) *Realism and Social Science*, London: Sage.

Usher, R., Byrant, I. and Johnston, R. (1997) *Adult Education and the Postmodern Challenge*, London: Routledge.

Young, M. (2003) 'Comparing approaches to the role of qualifications in the promotion of lifelong learning', *European Journal of Education*, 38(2): 199–211.

Chapter 13

Lifelong learning on individual accounts

The impact of individual learning accounts on workers of low educational levels

Albert Renkema

Introduction

The image of the employee who stays with the same company during his or her entire occupational career appears to be becoming outdated. Individual workers no longer have a career for life that develops vertically in one organisation. Employees are supposed to be willing and able to take a more flexible stance towards their career in order to remain attractive in the labour market. The paradigm of lifetime employment seems to be making way for the principle of lifetime employability. As a consequence, educational policy makers and human resource professionals in labour organisations are becoming increasingly interested in the employability of individual workers. In order to meet the objectives of the Lisbon strategy to maintain the position of the European Union as a competitive knowledge economy, governments of the member states are becoming more aware of the necessity of creating appropriate conditions to facilitate the individual worker's endeavour to stay employable (European Commission 2000). The European Commission has repeatedly called attention to the need to stimulate participation in training and educational activities of adults. Since the end of the 1990s, the Dutch government has attempted to encourage lifelong learning by introducing regulative policy measures aimed at strengthening the position of individual learners and, accordingly, stimulating the articulation of educational demand. Mechanisms for co-financing lifelong learning are measures which focus explicitly on the individual citizen or worker (OECD 2003, 2004). Following experiences with Individual Learning Accounts (ILAs) in the United Kingdom, at the beginning of this century, the Dutch government supported a number of (labour) organisations in society to explore modalities for implementing an instrument to provide individual workers with an amount of money for training activities, to which employee, employer and third parties could contribute in either time or money. These modalities are known as experiments with Individual Learning Accounts.

A number of large employers and organisations of social partners (i.e. employer organisations and trade unions united in the Labour Foundation) expressed interest in this initiative. This is not surprising, considering that trends in human resource management in labour organisations run parallel with initiatives that seek to emancipate and activate the individual learner (Renkema 2006a). Companies are now more and more confronted with dynamic and competitive environments, which have led to internal restructuring and *delayering* of the organisation and rapid changes in skill requirements. Walton (1999) stresses the notion of partnership between line managers and employees because of the increasing focus on the individual responsibility for work-based and career-based training. Employees make a new kind of commitment between themselves and the organisation. An ILA is supposed to stimulate the initiative of employees, because it assumes partnership between employer and employee with respect to decisions about training and development (Kidd 1996).

According to Payne (2000), the ILA is located in a line of thought that portrays the individual worker as goal-oriented and expecting a reward. Individuals are viewed as self-entrepreneurs who 'run their own life as a small business' (Wagner 1994: 164). However, ideas about employees, who are entrepreneurs of their own working and learning process and are pro-active in making well-reasoned educational decisions during their career, seem rather to refer to more highly educated employees in knowledge-intensive labour organisations (Van der Kamp 1997). What is more, evidence shows that the British ILA system mainly attracted more highly educated citizens (Thursfield et al. 2002). Therefore, in this chapter the question is asked whether ILAs will stimulate educational intentions to engage in lifelong learning amongst employees with lower levels of education. For this study, research focused on two sectors of industry participating in the Dutch experiments with ILAs in which workers with secondary vocational level[1] qualifications or less are employed: small and medium-sized enterprises (SMEs) in the technical installation sector and care organisations for the elderly (Renkema 2006b).

Conceptual framework

An ILA aims to encourage workers to regulate their learning decisions, which implicitly involves the establishment of training intentions on the basis of a rational decision-making process. Hodkinson and Sparkes (1995), however, pointed out that the idea of technically rational choices does not have value when analysing decision-making processes of employees in the framework of instruments such as ILAs. They assume that the decision-making process about how to spend an ILA does not always follow a linear sequence; it can also be a response to circumstantial opportunities. Information that provides the basis for decision making can be both objective and subjective, or culturally determined. Therefore, both individual decision-making processes as well as processes in the social environment of the individual worker are incorporated within the research model.

In order to study the effects of ILAs on training intentions, Ajzen's (1991) *Theory of Planned Behaviour* was applied as the point of departure for their effect evaluation. According to the Theory of Planned Behaviour, motivation is reflected in intentions to execute a certain action. Figure 13.1 suggests that behavioural intentions are predicted by underlying determinants, such as attitude, perceived behavioural control and normative beliefs. Attitude refers on the one hand to certain beliefs about how much *fun* or how interesting learning and engaging in training activities is, according to the individual (affective attitude), and on the other hand to the extent to which the individual regards learning as useful or profitable (instrumental attitude). The construct of perceived behavioural control contains, on the one hand, perceived self-efficacy and on the other, perceived controllability. Perceived self-efficacy relates to beliefs of the individual about his or her ability to engage in learning activities and about the perceived ease in bringing these activities to a satisfactory end. Perceived controllability relates to beliefs about whether a behaviour is under the individual's control, or whether the individual can make his or her own decisions.

Furthermore, the Theory of Planned Behaviour incorporates the influences of other people in the individual's environment. According to Ajzen (1991), people who are important to the individual play a significant role in the establishment of subjective norms with regard to performing a certain behaviour. Other authors doubt if subjective norms are relevant predictors of behaviour for all behavioural domains (Courneya et al. 2000). They raise the question as to whether social norms are significant factors for behaviour that is not completely undertaken out of free will. For some activities of a less volitional character, social support might be a more important predictor of intention (see also Maurer and Rafuse 2001).

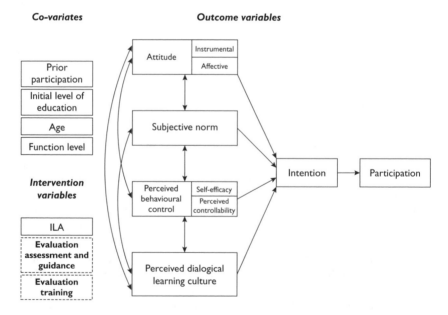

Figure 13.1 Research model.

Therefore I define a construct with which I attempt to encapsulate supportive communication in the immediate work environment. On the basis of a study about the voucher experiment in the technical installation sector, conducted by Meijers (2003), I have developed the concept of a dialogical learning culture: the rate to which the respondent perceives whether (a) he or she is appreciated by the employer and colleagues as a person and as a professional; and whether (b) there is room on the workfloor to discuss (personal and professional) development within and outside of the current workfloor. In this study 'workfloor' refers to social interactions with co-workers and immediate supervisors in the immediate work environment of the individual worker. Within the framework of an ILA, workers are provided with assessment of competency needs and guidance during the decision-making and the learning process.

In this study, I distinguish between two aspects of the intervention that do not directly relate to the concept of the ILA. Several authors conclude that individual workers, especially those with little learning experience, need coaching and guidance in order to articulate individual educational needs (Payne 2000; Bosley et al. 2001). Therefore, the evaluation of coaching and guidance is an intervention variable that should be taken up in the research model. Studies of both Dutch and British ILA schemes recognise that ILAs have given individuals the opportunity to engage in learning activities. For many low-skilled employees with low educational levels in the Dutch experiments, this would have been the first educational experience for many years. Therefore, positive evaluation of training might have a significant influence on further intentions to engage in lifelong learning. In those cases where the effects of the ILA on educational intention are evident, the influence of these two evaluations will be assessed. Finally, educational intention and its underlying predictors are likely to be influenced by a number of independent co-variates such as the respondent's age, level of initial education, prior participation in schooling activities and the functional level at which he or she is currently employed.

Design and methodology

In this section, I describe the research design and methodology utilised in order to measure the effects of ILAs on the variables just described. First, I compare the two studies with respect to relevant characteristics and give attention to the differences between the execution of two ILA experiments. Then, I expound on the type of research conducted and the research design. Finally, I discuss the methods of data collection and data analysis.

Background of the ILA experiments

The main difference between the two types of organisation relates to their corporate training policy. Before the ILA experiment, the organisations for elderly care regularly held off-the-job and on-the-job training for its workers. All five participating organisations have a fully outlined and operative training policy; while in the technical installation companies a purely economically-driven and short-term perspective determines interaction between the organisation and individual workers. The organisations for elderly care are much larger in terms of total numbers of employees, and a training advice infrastructure is present in the form of Personnel and Training Advisors. In their training policies, immediate supervisors do not have a crucial role.

The initiative for the experiments with ILAs in the technical installation sector was launched by the sector training fund[2] who wished to enhance long-term training policy, particularly in SMEs. In these types of companies the employer (who is also the manager and immediate supervisor) is responsible for the outline and execution of personnel and training policy. Another important difference between the two sectors of employment is that technical installation companies contain mainly male workers, and the elderly care organisations mainly female.

Typical to both experiments was that a broad variety of courses and training was possible. Workers could choose courses that varied from work task-related training to courses in personal effectiveness. However, in both experiments a connection to the job was strongly recommended. In the technical installation companies, for instance, worker and immediate supervisor had to come to a formal agreement on how to spend the budget available. The technical installation sector used standardised Personal Development Plans (PDP) in the ILA experiment. In the framework of the ILA experiments employers, in particular those with SMEs, were coached by external employability advisors to set up PDP meetings with workers.

In the elderly care experiment, workers had an initial contracting meeting with the Personnel and Training Advisor, in which they talked about the possibilities of the ILA and the learning needs of the worker. The immediate supervisor could advise the Personnel and Training Advisor and the worker about how to spend the budget, but this advice was not binding. Further guidance after the initial meeting was optional. The ILA instrument was complementary to the already existing training facilities within the organisations.

Research design

For the two experiments, two different sampling methods were used. Both studies started when the actual experiments with ILAs were already running and respondents were already – not randomly – assigned to the experiment. Respondents in the elderly care organisations subscribed themselves to the experiments out of free will; so did companies in the technical installation sector. Individual workers employed in these companies were compelled to participate in the experiment. Therefore, both studies were constructed on the basis of a quasi-experimental design. In this study, the participants in the experiment form the experiment group. A control group was constructed in both sectors that resembled the experiment group with respect to variables such as age and functional levels specific to this study. The control groups in the elderly care study were constructed within the same organisations participating in the experiment. Because this study focused on small technical installation companies, it was not possible to construct control groups within the same organisations that participated in the experiment. That is why control companies were selected that matched the participating companies with respect to variables such as company size, company structure and corporate training policy.

In the study there were two measurement periods. The first measurements took place six months after the initial meetings about the ILA between worker and training advisor in elderly care organisations, and between worker and employer in the SMEs. Immediately after the experiments with the ILA, a second measurement was conducted. These measurements were conducted through closed questionnaire surveys and in-depth interviews with employers and workers in both sectors. The control groups in the technical installation sector were constructed independently from the experiment with the ILA. Therefore, it was not expected that these companies would change their training policy dramatically during the experiment and it was decided to approach these companies once only.

In this study various individual characteristics were taken into account: age, prior participation in training activities, and functional levels. The functional levels that can be distinguished in the study are derived from the level categories pertaining to secondary vocational education in the Netherlands. The first two levels refer to assistant-in-training and assistant functions. Workers working on the third level operate autonomously as a mechanic, installer or nurse. Most respondents in both the control group and the experiment group had a third level position. Fourth level positions contain co-ordinating functions such as foremen, planners and co-ordinators.

Data collection and analysis

For the study, the experimental group of the technical installation sector consisted of 63 workers in total and the control group of 46 workers. In the elderly care sector, there was an experimental group of 112 workers and a control group of 103 workers.

In the first and second measurements, data were collected through questionnaires which mostly contained (five-point) ordinal Likert scales and semantic differential scales. In the second measurement, in-depth interviews were also conducted with 14 respondents in the experimental groups (ten elderly care workers and four technical installation workers). These interviews consisted of questions based on the behavioural determinants identified by the Theory of Planned Behaviour, and questions about their perception of the dialogical learning culture. Furthermore, we interviewed the four immediate supervisors in technical installation com-panies and the five Personnel and Training Advisors in elderly care organisations about the course of the experiments and their observations with respect to the educational intentions of the workers and the dialogical learning culture.

Apart from examining the relative importance of the several behavioural determinants through multiple regression analysis, in this study we used both parametric tests[3] and non-parametric tests[4] to assess the significance of differences in these determinants between the experimental group and the control group. Apart from matching strategies, we used statistically equated constructed controls. Through co-variance analysis, effects of ILAs on educational intention and the behavioural determinants – attitude, self-efficacy and perceived dialogical learning culture – were explored, checking for variables that statistically influence these dependent variables. The outcomes reported in this chapter are significant at a reliability level of 99 per cent, unless otherwise indicated. The study in the technical installation sector was considerably smaller and included fewer older workers than the required number of 30. Therefore, for specific analysis in this group we employed non-parametric tests of significance. For the analysis of the interviews we employed a qualitative codification method.

Results

Tables 13.1 and 13.2 present the regression analysis of the Model of Planned Behaviour in the two work environments. The concept of perceived dialogical learning culture, constructed for this study, was automatically removed from both regression models. In both studies, perceived dialogical learning culture did not seem to have any influence on training intention. Apart from dialogical learning culture, the item constructed to measure perceived controllability was removed from the models. Therefore we can assume that the model does not fully apply to the comprehension of educational intention. I elaborate on the findings with respect to dialogical learning culture in the discussion section of this chapter.

Effects of ILAs in technical installation companies

In the first measurement wave, there was a significant effect of ILAs on educational intention after controlling for age and prior participation ($p < 0.05$). Co-variance analysis in the first measurement wave revealed that the co-variate, age, and prior participation in post-initial education related significantly to educational intention. The experimental condition of respondents accounted for only 5 per cent of the variation of educational intention, whereas age and prior participation together accounted for 28 per cent of the variation (age accounts for 27 per cent and prior participation for 10 per cent). Separate analyses of the three intention items revealed that the experimental group only scored higher on the item that referred to concrete plans to engage in training activities. In the second measurement wave there was no significant effect of ILAs on educational intention after controlling for age and prior participation.

There was a significant difference in prior participation to post-initial training between the age groups. The questionnaire contained an item with a reference period of the last five years. The participation percentage decreased for older

Table 13.1 Regression model: educational intention of technical installation workers

	First measurement wave			Second measurement wave		
	r	β	R	r	β	R
Instrumental attitude						
Affective attitude	0.60**	0.36**		0.52**	0.39**	
Perceived behavioural control	0.55**	0.23*		0.49**	0.24**	
Subjective norm	0.45**	0.25**	0.66**	0.45**	0.26*	0.71**

* Correlation significant at reliability level of 95%; ** correlation significant at reliability level of 99%.

Table 13.2 Regression model: educational intention of elderly care workers

	First measurement wave			Second measurement wave		
	r	β	R	r	β	R
Instrumental attitude	0.52**	0.29**				
Affective attitude	0.53**	0.25**		0.55**	0.32**	
Perceived behavioural control	0.29**	0.17*		0.52**	0.31**	
Subjective norm			0.59**	0.34**	0.23**	0.64**

* Correlation significant at reliability level of 95%; **correlation significant at reliability level of 99%.

employees (< 0.05). This indicates that in the last five years, older employees have participated to a significantly lesser extent in post-initial education and training activities than younger employees.

The group of older employees who had an ILA scored significantly higher on educational intention in the first measurement (p < 0.05). In both measurement waves, in the group of older employees who responded the first and the second time, older employees with an ILA scored significantly higher on educational intention than their older colleagues without a voucher.

Because this study does not conduct an initial measurement, the questionnaire included a retrospective item within which respondents could assess on a Likert scale the extent of their agreement with the statement: 'Before the ILA experiment, I would never have thought about learning.' With this item it was intended to analyse whether respondents in the experimental group observed a change in their educational intention through the ILA. A one-way ANOVA test revealed a significant difference between the mean scores on this scale (p < 0.05). A Bonferroni *post-hoc* test shows that the oldest and the youngest age groups differ significantly (p < 0.05). On the scale, constructed in the direction from positive to negative (totally agree – totally disagree), the older age group scores are significantly lower than those of the younger.

Furthermore, the relationship between educational intention and the evaluations of employees on training experiences with the ILA was scrutinised. Notable is the correlation between the affective attitudes of account holders over 46 years of age and their evaluation of the coaching and guidance of the immediate supervisor and their evaluation of the courses followed with the voucher. Therefore, we could assume that positive experiences with courses and with coaching from the immediate supervisor have a positive influence on the extent to which older employees regard learning and training as *fun* or *interesting*.

Interviews with employees and employers demonstrated that the voucher experiment did influence the way in which schooling, performance and development was initially a subject of conversation on the workfloor. Nonetheless, during the experiment the attention to learning was weakened, despite regular attempts on the part of employers to put out a feeler about the subject. Between the two measurements the mean score on dialogical learning culture dropped significantly. We also observed that direct supervisors tended to leave out information about the individual aspect of the learning account. Some supervisors in interviews explained that they informed their workers about a collective financial bonus that every individual employee could spend on training, rather than about an individual voucher.

Effects of ILAs in the organisations for elderly care

In contrast to technical installation employees, prior participation in post-initial learning activities was equally divided over and within the age groups. There was no significant statistical relationship between age and prior participation in post-initial schooling activities in the last five years. These findings are illustrated by the interviews with the respondents in the elderly care organisations. Seven out of ten respondents interviewed were older than 41 years of age and had recently followed vocational training or were engaged in labour reintegration programmes. Six of these commented that they had started vocational training trajectories later on in life. Although their reasons for taking up learning vary, the stories coincide with respect to the decision to either re-enter the labour market or to work more hours in current employment when their children became more independent. There were nevertheless significant correlations between functional level and prior participation in post-initial training. In both measurement waves, educational intention related significantly with the level at which workers were employed.

There was no significant difference between scores on educational intention of the experimental group and control group in either of the two measurement waves. This means that the ILA project did not seem to have a categorised effect on the training intention of employees in the elderly care sector. In none of the functional level groups could an effect of the ILA on educational intention be found. When different scores on attitude between the control group and the experiment group as a whole were analysed, there were significant differences of score on attitude between those groups, controlling for level of education and prior participation. This also applies to the scores on affective attitude. In the second measurement wave there was a significant difference in scores on affective attitude between the control group and the experiment group ($p < 0.05$). A paired sample t-test did not reveal differences in attitude scores between the two measurement waves.

In spite of these results with respect to educational attitude, interviews with respondents in elderly care organisations illustrate that the attitude to engage in learning activities is more likely to depend on certain aspects of their biographical narratives, rather than experiences with an ILA. As outlined above, a majority of the respondents interviewed commented that they started vocational training trajectories later on in life. These respondents commented that they felt more engaged with learning at an older age, because they themselves chose this specific vocation. For example, one respondent commented: 'If you get the chance to follow a course at an older age, then you really work for it. You know what it is worth and that you have to do something for it.'

Like in the technical installation experiment, we found significant differences with respect to controllability scores between elderly care workers in the experimental group and the control group. Account holders in particular relied on their own insights and that of colleagues when making a decision regarding schooling. Respondents reported in the interviews that through the ILA experiment they discussed issues related to training and development more than previously, particularly among colleagues. This finding was, however, not sustained by the outcomes of the quantitative measure of dialogical learning culture. Furthermore, although account holders could draw on coaching provided by the Personnel and Training Department of the organisation, they preferred the support of colleagues to the official coaching facilities more distant from the workfloor.

Discussion

In the conceptual framework I debated that the idea of technically rational choices does not have value when analysing decision-making processes in the framework of instruments such as ILAs. This study confirmed that the decision-making process of employees with low levels of education is not so much determined by a rational needs assessment, but influenced by a complexity of subjective factors, such as subjective norms, educational attitude, perceived self-efficacy, and situational factors such as prior learning experiences and the influence of others. This study also confirmed that these underlying factors are difficult to influence directly through a (temporal) social intervention such as an ILA.

In the elderly care experiment, for example, ILAs did not have any effect on the long- or short-term intentions of employees to engage in learning activities. The experiment with the ILA itself probably did not provide these workers with significant educational experiences. In this sector of employment, educational intention and attitude is likely to relate to certain aspects of the biographical narratives of workers. The choice for career development activities later on in life most likely had a positive effect on motivation towards learning and education. Therefore, the experiment with an ILA itself did not have much effect on educational motivation. Individual learning vouchers in the technical installation companies, however, seem to have had a modest positive effect, especially on the educational intention of older workers. Their affective attitude seemed to relate to positive experiences with respect to coaching provided by the employer, and to positive experiences with courses paid by the learning account. The vouchers gave older workers in particular the opportunity to think about learning and development in their work.

For the implementation of a mechanism such as an ILA it is important to take into account the role of coaching and guidance. The question is who will be responsible for organising and carrying out coaching trajectories. The role of the immediate supervisor with respect to training decisions within the framework of an ILA engenders a dilemma. On the one hand, an ILA can easily be employed for the benefit of the employer if the immediate supervisor can exercise influence on learning decisions. This study showed that some employers conceal important information from employees about the individual aspects of the instrument. On the other hand, this study confirms that coaching and guidance should be close at hand. More distant impartial coaching is not effective; employees with a lower level of education experience this distance as a barrier to making use of the guidance available. What is more, Bosley et al. (2001) argue that in the framework of the ILA system, the proactiveness of such a coach (or 'case manager') is more important than impartiality. In order to overcome this dilemma, social partners should switch focus to the individual employee as a target group. Investment in individual coaching and guidance facilities seems to be appropriate. Social partners could, for instance, play an important role in stimulating sector-specific networks for small companies.

Although there is evidence that coaching and guidance can stimulate the decision-making process in the framework of an ILA, this study revealed that dialogical learning culture neither relates to intention nor to any other behavioural determinant expounded in this study. It became clear that a concept that encompasses interactive features of the direct work environment might not be relevant for individual decision-making processes for formal training activities. The emphasis of the instrument such as an ILA is on the individual learner and on participation in formal education. In this respect, the ILA is in line with the human capital approach, which focuses on the individual agent, as opposed to the social capital theory, which emphasises that learning is embedded in social networks and culture. The ILA system is not primarily set up to encourage social capital within organisations. There is no evidence either that learning culture directly relates to individual decisions about formal (or non-formal) training activities. An individual worker can have the feeling that he or she can develop themself on the workfloor, that he or she is recognised as a professional, and that training and competence development is a regular issue of conversation on the workfloor, but that does not necessarily affect educational intention. The rate at which there is room for dialogue on the workfloor, however, might be an important premise for the establishment of commitment to informal workplace learning processes. Although ILAs are exclusively linked to formal educational activities, I would argue that the system could contribute more effectively to widening participation in life-long learning. An ILA can be employed on the basis of individual educational needs which emerge from assessment and recognition of learning other than that formally acquired.

Notes

1   Secondary vocational education in the Netherlands consists of four levels. Level one is comparable to level two of the International Standard Classification of Education (ISCED). The levels two up to four are comparable to ISCED 3. The Dutch government indicated level two of secondary vocational education as the minimal level required in order to enter the labour market. Most respondents in this study are educated at level two or three of secondary vocational education.
2   Sector training funds are sector-based foundations in which employer organisations and trade unions of a particular sector of industry are united. Sector training funds provide finance for sector-based initiatives for training and employability.
3   That is, the two-tailed t-test for independent samples and the t-test for paired samples.
4   That is, the Wilcoxon test for the difference between two related samples, and the Mann-Whitney test for the analysis of two independent samples.

References

Ajzen, I. (1991) 'The Theory of Planned Behavior', *Organizational Behavior and Human Decision Processes*, 50: 179–211.
Bosley, S., El-Sawad, A., Hughes, D., Jackson, C. and Watts, A.G. (2001) *Guidance and Individual Learning Accounts*, Derby: Centre for Guidance Studies, University of Derby.
Courneya, K.S., Plonikoff, R.C., Hotz, S.B. and Birkett, N.J. (2000) 'Social support and the Theory of Planned Behavior in the exercise domain', *American Journal of Health Behavior*, 24: 300–308.
European Commission (2000) *A Memorandum on Lifelong Learning*, Brussels: European Commission.
Hodkinson, P. and Sparkes, A.C. (1995) 'Markets and vouchers: the inadequacy of individualist policies for vocational education and training in England and Wales', *Education Policy*, 10: 189–207.
Kidd, J.M. (1996) 'Career planning within work organisations', in A. G. Watts (ed.) *Rethinking Careers Education and Guidance: Theory, Policy and Practice*, London and New York: Routledge.
Maurer, T.J. and Rafuse, N.E. (2001) 'Learning, not litigating: managing employee development and avoiding claims of age discrimination', *Academy of Management Executive*, 15: 110–121.
Meijers, F. (2003) 'Scholing en vouchers: een stand van zaken' ['Training and vouchers: state of affairs'], in P. W. J. Schramade and J. G. L. Thijssen (eds) *Handboek Effectief Opleiden*, Gravenhage: Delwel.

OECD (2003) *Mechanisms for the Co-finance of Lifelong Learning. Second International Seminar: Taking Stock of Experience with Co-finance Mechanisms*, London: OECD.

OECD (2004) *Co-financing Lifelong Learning: Towards a Systemic Approach*, Paris: OECD.

Payne, J. (2000) 'The contribution of Individual Learning Accounts to the Lifelong Learning Policies of the UK government: a case study', *Studies in the Education of Adults*, 32: 257–275.

Renkema, A. (2006a) 'Individual learning accounts: a strategy for lifelong learning?', *Journal of Workplace Learning*, 18: 384–394.

Renkema, A.G. (2006b) *Individual Learning Accounts: A Strategy for Lifelong Learning?*, Hertogenbosch: Cinop.

Thursfield, D., Smith, V., Holden, R. and Hamblett, J. (2002) 'Individual Learning Accounts: honourable intentions, ignoble utility?', *Research in Post-compulsory Education*, 7: 133–146.

Van der Kamp, M. (1997) 'Dissertatie besproken, een transformatie van de ontwerpmethodologie' ['Dissertation discussed, a transformation of the Design Methodology'], *BBO-Bulletin*, 5: 7–9.

Wagner, P. (1994) *A Sociology of Modernity: Liberty and Discipline*, London and New York: Routledge.

Walton, J. (1999) *Strategic Human Resource Development*, Harlow: Financial Times/ Prentice Hall.

Chapter 14

Essential skills training in Canada for under-literate workers

'Vocational representations' of sectoral committee and training context actors

Chantal Ouellet, Isabelle Medeiros,
Marjolaine Thouin and Nicolas Dedek

Context and research problematic

This chapter presents the context, problematic, theoretical framework, methodology and results of a research study now underway in the Canadian province of Quebec into the training offered to lesser-educated and under-literate workers employed in various economic activity sectors.

Globalisation and the value-added economy have contributed to a weakened demand for non-qualified or semi-qualified workers in the various activity sectors of advanced industrialised economies. As such, there is reason for concern regarding the prospects of less-educated individuals (Statistics Canada and HRDC 2001; MÉQ 2002). Indeed, Quebec, one of Canada's ten provinces (and three territories), is home to almost 1.5 million individuals between the ages of 15 and 64 who hold no diploma and who have attended school for fewer than 13 years. Furthermore, as many as 41 per cent of these individuals have fewer than nine years of schooling (MÉQ 2002). Such individuals suffer from a lack of basic training and many find themselves increasingly marginalised in a labour market that is both demanding and volatile. According to the results of recent national and international studies, participation rates in training increase in relation to higher education levels – and that pattern is even more marked with respect to employer-sponsored training (Statistics Canada and HRDC 2001; OECD 2002, 2003). Today, political actors at both the provincial and the federal levels have made basic or essential skills training a priority.

With respect to employer-sponsored training, our own explorations, as well as a case study involving three companies that offered basic skills training to its employees (Ouellet 2005) and studies conducted by our research partner, the Literacy Foundation (Léger Marketing 2002), reveal large disparities among different sectoral committees, companies and managers, both in relation to their training efforts and as regards the various regions of Quebec where such actions are focused. Certain sectors demonstrate proactiveness, whereas the efforts of others are all but non-existent. Moreover, the various actors involved – managers, unions, trainers and workers themselves – have highly differing representations of essential skills training. They show divergences, not only amongst one another, but also in relation to the definitions offered by governmental actors who view essential skills training as a priority (e.g. Quebec's Ministry of Education). Managers, for instance, understand the term basic training to refer to training *in the task*, which is far removed from, for example, how Quebec's Ministry of Education (MÉQ 2002) and the federal department of Human Resources and Development Canada (HRDC) interpret essential skills training: i.e. reading text, document use, writing, oral communication, numeracy, computer use, thinking skills, working with others, and continuous learning. These essential skills are ranked at different levels on a scale from 1 to 5, according to different trades and occupations, and according to the different tasks inherent to each.

Labour training in Quebec, within the different economic activity sectors, is planned and organised, among others, by the intervention of workforce sectoral committees – *authoritative* bodies composed of business, labour and government representatives. These committees, as shown in Figure 14.1, are pivotal insofar as raising awareness and implementing initiatives related to essential skills training with the various decision makers. Yet our observations (Ouellet 2002, 2005) and investigative research data, as well as studies carried out by the Literacy Foundation (Léger Marketing 2002), highlight large disparities among the different sectoral committees as regards both their training efforts and the contexts in which these take place. Moreover, the way in which essential skills training is perceived by certain actors (managers, workers, trainers, etc.) and the way in which they take part in training reveal great divergences, which has an incidence on actions taken in this regard.

We may further note that the contexts of basic skills training, just as the training programmes and the pedagogical approaches they engender, are closely tied to such differing representations or visions of the phenomenon. In the course of our various investigations, we have observed that the contexts of essential skills training (e.g. offered in the workplace by the employer, followed in school commissions on the employee's initiative and financial incentives for independent training), are strongly linked to certain social attitudes and motivated by specific representations of the actors involved, whether they be managers, trainers or workers. For example, in companies where training is little valued and where there is no shortage of qualified labour, financial compensation is reserved only for those workers willing to seek training outside of the workplace, whereas in companies where training is deemed more important it is offered in the workplace, along with numerous incentives (Ouellet 2005). In such a context, it is complicated for a non-governmental organisation such as the Literacy Foundation to engage in awareness initiatives aimed at essentials skills training.

Thus, the research described here, which involves workforce sectoral committees comprising workers as well as management, union and government representatives,

The 26 workforce sectoral committees in Quebec	
1. Aerospace	14. Textiles
2. Forest management	15. Metallurgy
3. Sawn timber	16. Maritime fishing
4. Rubber	17. Plastics
5. Chemicals, petrochemicals and refining	18. Doors and windows, furniture and kitchen cabinetry
6. Retail commerce	19. Agricultural production
7. Food distribution	20. Pharmaceuticals and biotechnological products
8. Graphic communications	21. Automotive services
9. Culture	22. Personal care
10. Social economy and community action	23. Information and communications technology
11. Environment	24. Tourism
12. Industrial metal manufacturing	25. Food processing
13. Electrical and electronics	26. Road transportation

Figure 14.1 List of Workforce Sectoral Committees.

aims to allow us to understand how such committees arrive at their action plans. By studying the representations of the actors who make up the committee, we have sought to provide precise indications as to areas of opposition and consensus, and of the difficulties and implementation approaches liable to emerge from these representations. Understanding the representations of the various actors involved will allow for a better appreciation of their visions and methods of engagement in relation to essential skills training, which will ultimately create opportunities to hone awareness strategies and enhance reference services for managers as well as workers wishing to engage in such training.

In order to better understand the phenomenon of essential skills training in the workplace, far from constituting a monolithic bloc, the following objectives were pursued with respect to the target groups of directors of the various sectoral labour training committees, human resources officers and worker representatives:

1 To ascertain their representations of essential skills training.
2 To identify the essential skills training contexts favoured within different sectors of economic activity, according to the options available (e.g. workplace versus educational establishments).
3 To analyse the relations between the representations (or social attitudes) of these actors and the training contexts favoured within each sector.

4   For each economic activity sector, to distinguish practicable means of raising awareness about essential skills training in light of the observed representations.

Theoretical framework

Investigations of representations deployed in vocational situations (Bataille et al. 1997; Blin 1997) have established that subjects and groups position themselves according to their work, more through an appropriation of the situation – through the meanings they attribute to it and the systems of social representations they connect to their vocational activities – than on the basis of the situation's objective characteristics. Workplace behaviour, as well as agreed-upon initiatives, appears to be closely linked to the way in which the vocational situation is perceived in its complexity, and to the significance that the actors and groups attribute to it. Thus Piaser (1999) and Blin (1997) have developed an approach to vocational representations. For these authors, vocational activity is founded in part on a more or less coherent, and more or less conscious, system of representations of what the vocation and its activity is on the part of those who practise it. Such a set of vocational representations correspond to a vocational model. Each model is characterised by aims, beliefs, conceptions, values, action schematics and attitudes that drive the favoured vocational approach and orient the choices inherent to actions and decisions.

Representations must therefore be analysed as product and process, subjacent to practices implemented in vocational contexts by socially situated individuals – in other words, one must question the way in which subjects represent their vocations and their associated activities to themselves in a particular context of exercise (ibid.: 80).[1]

Thus, vocational representations are social representations developed through vocational action and communication and are specified by contexts, by the actors belonging to groups, and by objects that are relevant and useful to the exercise of vocational activities (Blin 1997). This approach to vocational representations shows the interest in analysing the process of positioning groups within the same population of vocational actors and studying the way in which representations and vocational practices hinge on one another. Vocational representations are informed by the vocational context in which they develop, and are communicated and shared. As such, the context constitutes an essential parameter for studying vocational representations.

Moreover, these same vocational representations are linked to the degree of subjects' and groups' engagement and involvement in their vocational activity, and are susceptible to mutation based on modifications to the conditions of activity or changes in status. For Moliner (1993), representational development of a vocational object occurs when, for structural or economic reasons, a group of individuals faces a polymorphous object which, in order to be controlled, presents a challenge in terms of identity or social cohesion. In this light, we view essential skills training as a vocational object, in particular for the various members of the sectoral labour training committees, given the challenge it presents. These actors position themselves in turn in a socio-economic context which puts pressure on them in relation to the social and vocational object that essential skills training constitutes. Such training is, furthermore, a polymorphous object (given its different types and differing conditions of application) which is uncontrolled, weakly controlled or variously controlled according to the group or the vocational field of belonging. Finally, controlling this object constitutes a challenge in terms of identity or social cohesion. Like social representations, vocational representations are made up of a collection of elements, also termed cognitions, including informative, cognitive, ideological and normative elements (beliefs, values, attitudes, opinions, images, etc.) (Jodelet 1989). Consequently, we have adopted Blin's (1997) definition and consider that: 'vocational representations, ever specific to a vocational context, are defined as sets of descriptive, prescriptive and evaluative cognitions revolving around objects which are meaningful and useful to the vocational activity, and which are organised in a structured way that offers meaning as a whole' (ibid.: 89).[2]

Methodology

To carry out our investigation, which aims to provide indications as to representations, training contexts and possible means of enhancing awareness of essential skills training – a qualitative research exercise – the following methodological considerations have been applied. The first steps involve conducting a documentary analysis of documents produced by the sectoral committees, such as their mandates and their training and promotion activities, as presented on their internet sites. Also analysed are annual reports overviewing their activities. Second, based on information gathered through the documentary analysis, semi-structured individual interviews were conducted with 23 directors of workforce sectoral committees on: the training needs of the sector; training programmes and the pedagogical approaches used; difficulties encountered; the various actors' responsibilities; and measures required to increase participation in essential skills training, etc. Interviews were held face to face or via telephone.

Thematic content analysis is the chosen approach for the documentary analysis. The technique used to analyse the interviews is inspired by the work of Maget (1962) in studying cultural behaviours and that of Jodelet (1989) with respect to social representations and mental illness. Various successive stages of thematic codification have been executed with the help of qualitative analysis software. Such an approach allows for the extraction of: (1) themes; (2) associations; and (3) the relationships between different concepts. To identify the categories and prototypes of descriptors in the text during content analysis, we relied on the software program N'Vivo, which we have utilised in prior studies.

Results and discussion

Representations of essential skills

Essential skills, as promoted by the Canadian federal government body responsible for labour training, specifically refers to the nine following competencies: reading text, document use, writing, oral communication, numeracy, computer use, thinking skills, working with others, and continuous learning. One of the aims of this research study was to identify the representations (or perceptions) of essential skills held by workforce sectoral committee directors and to verify not only what terms they use in discussing the topic and what connotations are advanced by those terms, but also to what extent such terms and their connotations conform to the nine essential skills above. A content analysis of the interviews revealed that nearly half of respondents (n = 10/23) employ, simultaneously and interchangeably, one or two terms to refer to these concepts and that the remainder (n = 13) employ three or more. As for the terms used, the most frequently cited is *basic skills* (n = 13), followed by (n = 11) a specific term referring to a particular skill (e.g. working with others, reading text, oral communication, etc.). The term *essential skills* is used by only a third of respondents, with a frequency comparable to the term *be able to*.

Furthermore, over 24 different terms were cited at least once by each of the respondents in referring to essential skills, including: knowledge, aptitudes, attitudes, general skills, specific skills, necessary skills, technical skills, desired skills and literacy. These results reflect a state of confusion, possibly brought about by the concurrent promotion and usage of equivalent or non-equivalent terms by the various government bodies and services at the provincial and federal levels. For instance, Quebec's Ministry of Education, in its Government Policy on Adult Education and Continuing Education and Training (MÉQ 2002), talks about *basic training*; certain government services, as well as school boards which develop training programmes, refer to *basic skills*; and the federal department responsible for labour training – although education is under provincial jurisdiction – speaks of *essential skills*. The concurrent usage of these terms is thus, in the current context, perfectly understandable. At the same time, it engenders confusion, which in turn constitutes many 'filters' to a clear and precise understanding of just which skills are to be promoted in the workplace, from the standpoint both of those calling for an essential skills approach and of those who would be taught. This situation consequently makes complex any effort towards promoting and raising awareness of such skills training. Just who should be made aware of what exactly? Such is the challenge faced by the governmental and non-governmental bodies charged with fostering awareness among the various actors, employers in particular, of the importance of training.

The value placed on essential skills as a whole was also examined within the framework of this research. For the majority of respondents, essential skills training ranks as important or very important for their sector of economic activity.

Only a minority consider it moderately important or not very important. Our study also sought to understand the importance attributed to each of the nine essential skills by the various workforce sectoral committees. To enable this, each respondent was asked to rank each of the skills from 1 to 9 in order of importance. Initially, the results as regards employees in all sectors and at all education levels indicate that trends emerge when the top three positions are grouped together. Thus, it is *working with others* that ranks first, followed by *oral communication* and then *thinking skills*, which ties for importance with *continuous learning*. As for the next three positions, no clear trend is apparent. However, the last three places show that *writing* is the least valorised skill for a quarter of respondents, with *computer use, continuous learning* and *reading text* all qualifying, in one form or another, as less valued skills. Finally, according to the sectoral committee directors, skills with greater value and closely associated with important training requirements include: *oral communication, working with others* and *thinking skills*. These same skills are at the centre of newer management strategies that focus on human resources as an added value of the organisation.

Several further distinctions are observable with respect to under-educated workers. Here, the highest-ranked skills are, as one might expect, *numeracy, reading text* and *oral communication*. For these workers, as for all workers regardless of their level of education, no clear trend is apparent for the fourth to sixth positions. However, it is interesting to note that the lowest-priority skill for less-educated workers is also *writing*, followed by *computer use* and *continuous learning*.

When it comes to overall responsibility for the essential skills training portfolio, most believe it belongs with governmental organisations, and that it is equally incumbent on both local and regional bodies. Only a minority believe that the federal government is primarily responsible for this dossier, whereas a majority point to provincial authorities (e.g. *MELS* [Quebec Ministry of Education, Leisure and Sports], *Emploi-Québec* [Quebec Ministry of Employment and Social Solidarity] and sectoral committees). At the local and regional levels, it is the labour unions, employers and employees who ought to carry this portfolio. Responsibility for training employees in essential skills should be shared by the employer and employee, according to the majority of respondents (n = 18/23); a minority believe that it is solely up to the employee to train himself or herself. Yet, for less-educated workers in particular, a greater number of respondents believe the employee alone is responsible for acquiring training, although the majority (n = 15) still see it as a shared responsibility.

Contexts of essential skills training

The results of our documentary analysis of the internet sites of sectoral committees indicate that all 26 committees have a training mandate. All are actively involved in training initiatives in the workplace (learning, apprenticeship or mentoring programmes); in vocational training at the secondary, collegiate and university levels; and in continuous development training in general. Their actions consist primarily in reviewing, developing and implementing programmes in co-operation with Quebec's Ministry of Education and in contributing to the development of learning programmes in the workplace. More specifically, the types of training which they contribute to developing that touch workers with more than nine years of education, as well as the tools which accompany those workers, are varied: work–study alternance; course or learning manuals; CD-ROMs or videos for independent study or skills-improvement; competency-profiling guides; and trainers' manuals and interactive training via electronic media or the internet.

More specifically regarding essential skills training, while the great majority (n = 18/23) view this area as important, it is offered only in a little over half of the sectors (n = 14/23). The skills emphasised in these training programmes are the so-called basic ones (reading text, writing, numeracy), as well as oral communication (n = 11), followed by working with others (n = 8), computer use (n = 5) and continuous learning (n = 4). As regards the 14 sectors that offer essential skills training, the majority of companies, according to the perceptions of the sectoral committee directors, rely on the public training network (school boards and *cégeps* [colleges of general and vocational education]). Private consultants, community organisations, internal company services and sectoral committees are occasionally solicited, but less often and for more specific training needs. In this context, companies in more than half the sectors favour training in the workplace, that is, within the company itself; in almost a third of sectors, skills training is also delivered in adult education centres located nearby. Finally, a minority of respondents reported using offsite locations to deliver essential skills training to workers in their sector.

The principal catalyst for the implementation of essential skills training in a majority of sectors is the realisation of a training need following a sectoral-level diagnostic needs analysis (n = 9/14). The development of professional or vocational standards in certain sectors also required upgrading employees through essential skills training. Finally, the establishment of a youth integration programme in one sector, the fierce competition in another and a cultural shift towards continuous training in a third were also cited as motivating the development of essential skills training.

As for the sectors which do not offer essential skills training (n = 9/23), their rationales are diverse. Four respondents state that they have observed no need for such training. Three report that they have proposed plans which were not accepted by the companies or the joint members of the sectoral committee in question, and three others confirm that it is not a matter of current priority for their sector. The organisational and workflow complexity of two sectors and one's high level of worker education are further reasons cited. A final respondent indicated that limited resources precluded the possibility of essential skills training in that particular sector at the time of questioning.

A summary of preferred approaches for delivering essential skills training in those 14 sectors where it is offered, once again brings to the fore each one's specificity. Four sectors support mentoring and coaching techniques to impart learning. Four respondents in other sectors state their preference for training in small groups. The wide range of additional alternate approaches testifies to the uniqueness of each sector: problem-solving, learning modules, individualised learning, traditional learning, the use of authentic documents and the use of diversified approaches. Three individuals did not respond to the question.

The difficulties encountered by those sectors which have put in place essential skills training (n = 14/23) were manifold. The organisation of training was cited by respondents as being the greatest challenge; contributing factors included working hours (shifts), transportation for participating employees, the employment cycles of seasonal workers, the time required, employee remuneration, lack of flexibility on the part of school boards in their training programmes and schedules, company motivation and choosing the right moment to implement training. Next came questions of financing and the costs associated with essential skills training (n = 4). Merely attempting to convince companies to train their workers in essential skills was also cited as a major difficulty, certain company directors seemingly having doubts as to the returns on such training, as well as a lack of awareness of existing programmes designed to facilitate its implementation. The lack of know-how in certain sectors was a challenge encountered not just in terms of training implementation, but especially in obtaining financing. One sector noted the range of different needs from worker to worker, which made it difficult to ensure homogeneous groups. Two sectors reported experiencing no difficulties in implementing this type of training.

Favoured methods of raising awareness

Nearly half of respondents report promoting essential skills training in their marketing materials, although the majority (n = 8/10) refer to it by other terms. The remainder state that they do not promote such training. Several reasons are offered, including: the fact that it is not a priority for that sector; that the sector is not ready for continuous training, favours basic or technical skills training, or lacks resources.

The sectoral committee directors point to various methods of enhancing awareness. Half of respondents cite the importance of first demonstrating not only the need for essential skills training, but also its potential impact on finances and profit generation. From their perspective, messaging must be focused on solutions and on sensitising companies to the current and ongoing implications of globalisation for the various sectors. A second approach, referred to by half of respondents, entails a sector-by-sector process adapted for the specificities of each one. Some highlight the benefits of using 'success stories' and exemplary practical case studies; others speak of developing 'tools' and raising awareness not only of these, but also of programmes already in existence; others underline the importance of making additional financial resources available for this type of training. A further method mentioned by half of respondents involves providing better support for existing organisations – these individuals point to their own committees as specific examples of such bodies. To a lesser extent, respondents propose leveraging a range of media for purposes of generating awareness, while broadcasting their message as frequently as possible. Two respondents believe the key lies in mobilising teachers, influencers and students of secondary-level learning programmes to recognise the importance of acquiring these essential skills prior to entering the labour market.

Conclusions

The representations held by sectoral committee directors of essential skills form a 'plural' concept. The majority associate them with basic skills (reading text, writing and numeracy at levels 1 and 2), which differs greatly from the representation held by the government ministry promoting such training. Even though their mandate drives them to prioritise skills which are specific to their sector, the great majority of directors consider essential skills to be important. Nevertheless, training in these skills would appear to be available in only slightly over half of sectors. Those sectors that do consider essential skills training to be important would like to be made better aware of it, would like to offer it, or already do offer it but are also experiencing challenges. This latter group is able to provide suggestions for overcoming obstacles. As for those that do not consider such training important, they do not see the benefit in being made better aware and do not feel directly concerned by the question. Their representation thus has an effect on the degree of involvement of these actors, as well as on the contexts of training.

The majority of companies would appear to turn to the public training network of school boards and vocational colleges. Various private training services providers are also called upon, but to a lesser extent. Responsibility for the essential skills training portfolio should, it is believed, be assumed by actors and organisations as much at the local and regional levels as at the provincial level, but only to a very small degree by the federal government. Responsibility for acquiring training in essential skills should be shared between the company and the worker, although less-educated workers see themselves as bearing a disproportionate share. It would appear to be in the context of a labour shortage that implementing essential skills training becomes a priority. In such contexts, the sectors would prefer to retain employees with good social attitudes.

Finally, this 'plural' representation of essential skills makes it difficult to promote and raise awareness around the importance of training in such skills. From the point of view of efficiency, using the media is not a preferred method of enhancing awareness for respondents by comparison to a series of direct and *personalised*, sector-specific contacts, demonstrating the need and interest of the part of each sector, as well as supporting those organisations already working to this end.

Acknowledgements

This research is conducted in partnership with the Literacy Foundation and has been subsidised by the Social Sciences and Humanities Research Council/Human Resources and Skills Development Canada.

Notes

1 Free translation.
2 Free translation.

References

Bataille, M., Blin, J.-F., Jacquet-Mias, C. and Piaser A. (1997) 'Représentations sociales, représentations professionnelles, systèmes des activités professionnelles', *L'Année de la recherche en sciences de l'éducation*: 57–86.

Blin, J.-F. (1997) *Représentations, pratiques et identités professionnelles*, Paris: L'Harmattan.

Jodelet, D. (1989) *Les représentations sociales*, Paris: PUF.

Léger Marketing (2002) *Enquête sur les indices indicateurs à la formation de base en entreprise: Perception de la formation spécialisée et de la formation de base par les gestionnaires*, Fascicule no 2 Montréal: Fondation pour l'Alphabétisation.

Maget, M. (1962) *Guide d'études directes des comportements*, Paris: CNRS.

Ministère de l'Éducation Québec (MÉQ) (2002) *Politique gouvernementale d'éducation des adultes et de formation continue*, Québec: MÉQ.

Moliner, P. (1993) 'Cinq questions à propos des représentations sociales', *Cahiers internationaux de psychologie sociale*, 20: 5–13.

OECD (2002) *Regards sur l'Éducation. Les indicateurs de l'OCDE 2002*, Paris: OECD.

OECD (2003) *Au-delà du discours. Politiques et pratiques de formation d'adultes*, Paris: OECD.

Ouellet, C. (2002) *Représentations professionnelles de la formation continue chez les travailleurs peu scolarisés du secteur manufacturier*, 70e Congrès de l'ACFAS, Université Laval, Québec.

Ouellet, C. (2005) 'Pratiques et représentations de la formation chez des ouvriers ayant suivi une formation en compétences de base', Thèse de doctorat en Éducation, UQAM, Montréal.

Piaser, A. (1999) 'Représentations professionnelles à l'école. Particularités selon le statut : enseignant, inspecteur', Thèse de doctorat inédite, Université de Toulouse Le Mirail.

Statistique Canada et Développement des Ressources humaines Canada (1997) *Enquête sur l'éducation et la formation des adultes de 1994*, Ottawa: Statistique Canada et Développement des Ressources Humaines Canada.

Statistique Canada et Développement des Ressources Humaines Canada (2001) *Un rapport sur l'éducation et la formation des adultes au Canada. Apprentissage et réussite*, Ottawa: Statistique Canada et Développement des Ressources Humaines Canada.

Chapter 15

Adult education, museums and critique

Towards new methods of researching the field

Sotiria Grek

Introduction

This chapter focuses on methodological problems – and potential solutions – in researching adult education in museums and galleries. In particular, I discuss the methodological framework of a doctoral study which investigated the significance, reasons and impacts behind museums' shift from the more traditional – mainly transmission-based – pedagogies to the new discourse around learning in the 'post-museum' (Hooper-Greenhill 2000). The research examined the possibilities of such a shift unfolding in the urban context of Dundee, a city of many museums and galleries,[1] a long history of adult education and a vibrant community life.

Prior to the analysis of the methodological schema, a brief overview of the theoretical background is introduced. A mixed methods research approach was followed, combining both quantitative with qualitative tools. Nonetheless, the focus of this chapter is on the qualitative methods applied, namely critical ethnography and critical discourse analysis. Both of them have explicit ontological and epistemological assumptions, examined in relation to the specific context under consideration.

Theoretical framework

Whilst there have been substantial efforts to theorise learning in museums and analyse it on the basis of current educational theories (Hooper-Greenhill 1999), these are arguably built on the increasing pressures on museums to identify their constituencies and widen their publics. This is the relatively new reality museums face, in order to secure their share in the competitive market of the leisure and culture industry (Lawley 2003). The two most common theoretical approaches are constructivism (Falk and Dierking 1992; Durbin 1996; Roberts 1997; Hein 1998) and hermeneutics (Hooper-Greenhill 2000). Both theoretical perspectives value understanding as a process based on experience and prior knowledge. Although this study does not ignore post-modernist museum theory (Hooper-Greenhill 1997), it criticises both the constructivist and the hermeneutic paradigms for their failure to grasp the asymmetrical relations of power in the construction of meaning. The weakness of these models is that they do not recognise that:

- knowledge does not merely originate from or relate to individual constructs, but is also an ideological tool, consciously or unconsciously communicated through museum narratives,
- social processes are not equal; apart from tradition and the relative prior knowledge, there are material and objective conditions directly affecting people's experiences and perceptions,
- museum education is not ahistorical, apolitical and taking place in a void; it is substantially affected, both in the policies and in the practices employed, by the wider political, economic and educational policy agendas.

Critical research, according to Horkheimer and Adorno (1972), is never satisfied with simply increasing knowledge. It is political, in the sense that it becomes a transformative endeavour. 'Thus critical researchers enter into an investigation with their assumptions on the table, so no one is confused concerning the epistemological and political baggage they bring with them in the research site' (Kincheloe and McLaren 1994: 140). A critical theory framework requires the utilisation of research methods that can offer a critique of the agents' understandings, an explanation of the reasons those understandings are being employed, and possibly an alternative interpretation of the agents' identity – their capacities and real interests (Fay 1987).

The methodological framework under discussion was developed for a study which examines museum education policies and practices; it attempts to show how dominant learning discourses, deriving from the governmental modernising and managerial agenda, have entered the museum field and created unforeseen tensions. Despite the claim for a 'new museology'[2] (Vergo 1989) that would dismantle the museum from its authoritative and didactic standing and the sincere efforts of many museums and galleries in the UK towards this direction, the 'post-museum' (Hooper-Greenhill 2000) faces difficult times, competing demands and cumulative pressures for scholarship, education, accountability, social inclusion, representation, participation, regeneration; the list can go on and on.

Museums used to – and some of them still do – portray a version of the world that belonged to the few. They showed what was considered precious and rejected the ordinary, the popular, the vulgar and the 'low'. People from all walks of life, but primarily from higher educational and financial backgrounds (Bourdieu and Darbel 1991), would visit them, knowing more or less what to expect – visitor demographics, according to recent research (Museums, Libraries and Archives Council (MLA) 2004), have not changed dramatically.[3] Thus, what is the impact of the discourses around learning, access, inclusion, participation and the like as core 'performance indicators' for museums? Was this an internal, self-generated development in the museum world itself? Was it subject to the new post-modernist thinking of relativism and the celebration of the subject? Or, was it due to the latest trends of transforming the public sphere into the market arena of competitive forces? Instead of searching for definitive answers, the paradoxes museums once more face (Kawashima 1997) point towards a questioning rather than a conclusive approach.

Therefore, I would suggest that the work of Antonio Gramsci and Pierre Bourdieu is particularly useful in order to formulate new questions regarding the educational role of museums. In what follows, I argue for a mixed methods enquiry, as a fruitful framework for researching education in the museum field. Further, I discuss critical ethnography and critical discourse analysis as the main qualitative research tools applied. Gramsci and Bourdieu, although not extensively referred to here due to space limitations, have accompanied me in this process all along.

Methodology

Overcoming the dichotomy? The application of a mixed-method research design

Mixed-method research combines the use of both qualitative and quantitative methods, either by following a pattern of applying them in sequence and thereby feeding the findings of one strand to the other, or following a more synchronised combination of both (Brewer and Hunter 1989; Greene and Caracelli 1997; Morgan 1998; Newman et al. 1998; Sandelowski 2000; Tashakori and Teddlie 1998, 2002). Despite merging traditionally different methodological models, epistemologies and value stances, research has shown the generative potential of the mixed methods inquiry for a more complete understanding of educational phenomena (Green and Preston 2005).

More specifically, through a mixed-method examination of the museum field, both its particular and general attributes can be investigated; the researcher enquires on patterned regularities that are to be found in visiting trends, but also pursues more sophisticated close-ups of the contextual complexities of the specific cases under investigation. The application of such a research design can assist the examination of both the macro-structural contexts the museum sector is part of and, at the same time, engage with the diversity and difference of more topical issues.

In studies where narrative accounts are not accompanied by contextual information, meanings are sometimes interpreted merely on the basis of the actors' own interpretations (Nilsen and Brannen 2002). In a way, such approaches follow a similar logic to the dominant museum education theory, which examines visitors' 'meaning-making', without attempting to contextualise, exemplify or even challenge it in regard to the socio-economic conditions that define it. Hence, agency is often attributed to actors without reference and link to the resources available to them. In this way, no continuity is sustained between individual experiences and social reality.

On the contrary, this study attempted to explore both the socio-historical context within which museums operate, *and* the distinctive ways with which they adopt or oppose dominant trends and discourses. Therefore, despite my closer affiliations with what has been broadly described as ethnographic research, quantitative data is seen as adding value to the study, offering an analysis of visiting trends. Regarding the particular case of Dundee, this framework offers an overview of the visitation patterns and the characteristics of the visitors in the city's museums, under the light of which narrative accounts of interviewees' learning experiences are analysed. Similarly, the qualitative data informs the statistical information, in an attempt to either strengthen some of the research findings through triangulation, or find contradictions and question their generalisability.

On the other hand, there has been critique against mixed-method research. Most of it concentrates on the different epistemological assumptions of the quantitative and qualitative paradigms; namely, that their different research cultures and traditions could never converge (Brannen 1992). Creswell (2003) supports the view that there are limits to mixed methods applications, first, because the use of primary data collection is declining, and second, due to confidentiality issues. However,

> The aim of methodology is to help us understand, not only the products of scientific inquiry but the process itself. A multi-method strategy should be adopted to serve particular theoretical, methodological and practical purposes. Such a strategy is not a toolkit or a technical fix. Nor should it be seen as a belt and braces approach. Multi-method research is not necessarily better research. Rather it is an approach employed to address the variety of questions posed in a research investigation that, with further reading, may lead to the use of a range of methods.
>
> (Brannen 2005: 182)

Instead of treating them as monolithic, this study finds in the mixing of quantitative and qualitative methods the permeable domain, where the 'messiness' of the museum encounter, its tensions, ambiguities and ambivalences are to be revealed.

Quantitative tools

In terms of the quantitative strand, primary data collection was conducted, using a questionnaire that included seven areas of investigation: namely, frequency of visit; area of living; gender; age; occupation; education; and ethnicity. The sampling of the population was random and the questionnaire survey lasted for five months (March–July 2005). Approximately 300 questionnaires were gathered from each site.[4] Data cross-tabulations produced statistically significant observations regarding the visitors' social background. Such a comparative, structural analysis allowed for a concrete contextual basis on which to analyse participants' contributions regarding the educational offer of their city museums.

Qualitative tools

Critical ethnography

Whilst more conventional forms of ethnographic work follow the interpretivist paradigm of looking at '. . . cultural scenes, microcultures . . .' in order to '. . . provide the kind of account of human social activity out of which cultural patterning can be discerned . . .' (Wolcott 1999: 67–68), critical ethnography adopts an ontology of political commitment, adding the 'so what?' question to the interpretation of ethnographic findings. In other words, it enriches the 'thick description' (Geertz 1973: 7) of social sites with the dialectics of the possible, moving from 'what is' to 'what could be' (Thomas 1993: 4). In terms of epistemology, rather than adopting a 'disinterested' approach, critical ethnography is political, acknowledging as its primary politics the need to privilege the voice of the researched (McLaren 1992). Nevertheless, commitments of this kind have received strong criticism from academia; Hammersley, for example, criticises emancipatory models of inquiry, arguing against social change as the ultimate purpose of research and claiming that the terms emancipation and oppression 'as slogans . . . may be appealing but as analytical concepts they are problematic' (2004: 482).

Critical ethnography has an interest in exploring those particular phenomena that social agents take for granted and 'observes . . . what is largely familiar as if it were alien' (Lüders 2004: 224). However, it is often the case of ethnographic studies focusing exclusively on the lifeworlds of their subjects, thus ignoring the relationship between this world and the predominant system. In the face of this, Paul Willis, together with others at the Centre for Contemporary Cultural Studies (University of Birmingham), has insisted on the need to consider the theoretical background which cannot be directly derived from the field of inquiry. Willis (1997) gave this approach the acronym TIES: Theoretically Informed Ethnographic Study. According to Willis, critical ethnography adapts ethnographic writing to take into account issues of political economy and enlarged vistas of representation. Nevertheless,

> While it has achieved respectability and is now part of the qualitative tradition within universities, the question remains as to whether it has had any significant impact beyond the seminar room. . . . Our point is that academic success and respectability is one thing, changing the world is quite another.
>
> (Jordan and Yeomans 1995: 399)

Therefore, in order to pursue a critical project which starts from and works with research participants' knowledge, this research design was based on Jordan and Yeomans' (1995) proposal for linking critical ethnography with Johnson's concept of 'really useful knowledge' (1988).

Johnson (ibid.) analysed an early nineteenth-century radical movement for establishing alternative, counter-hegemonic forms of education, as having four broad objectives: (a) resist formal education; (b) promote self-education; (c) focus on 'education, politics, knowledge and power' (Johnson 1979: 5); and (d) seek educational practices which would offer the learner everyday knowledge.

Jordan and Yeomans (1995), following Gramsci's notion that social relations are always pedagogical in nature, seek to apply a 'really useful' critical ethnography, where educational research and expertise is a resource available to all, rather than the few. As they support, 'at the end of the day/night shift, the ethnographer's material location is often at odds with those whom they research' (1995: 400). Similarly, Crowther and Martin (2005) stress that the purpose of critical research in the radical tradition of 'really useful knowledge' is education for social transformation; essentially, Johnson's notion of 'practical' knowledge emphasised the need for education to be integrated with the experience and interests of everyday people. For instance, one of the study participants commented on this absence of a link between ordinary people's stories and museum narratives:

> Well, they are not schools in that sense, and I wasn't schooled enough so I always thought when I came in the museum 'yi shood be interested in this, yi shood get somethin oot of this instead of always lookin for a pint of beer . . .' [. . .] People here are kinda toffee-nose and how can I describe it . . . they speak in this so un-Dundee way. Well, you don't fit in, but I guess everyone is the same. You really find yourself daunted and it is not because of them, it is because of you.
>
> (P – male interviewer, 68 years old,
> not frequent museum visitor)

In order to avoid 'data decay' and truly engage with the researched in disclosing relations of power and creating knowledge for conscientisation (Freire 1973), researchers could impart the skills of a critical questioning of the world; 'making the everyday world problematic for ourselves is not enough; making it problematic for those we leave behind in the field should be the point' (Jordan and Yeomans 1995: 401). Critical ethnography assists both the researcher and the researched question practices that at a first glance might seem as increasing inclusiveness and participation in the museum. For example, an interviewee summarised his involvement in the consultation process about the refurbishment of the McManus Galleries, the local authority museum in Dundee, as follows:

> The discussions were aboot what we thought, what we wanted from the museum after the refurbishment of the two years. And there were ex-architects, ex-journalists, artists from DC Thompson, ex-academics and a few members from retired groups, all very higher education people, and we were the only ones who were there, the rough end, yi ken? . . . There are always upper or upper-middle class people in those committees and they think in that manner, they want to see jewels and crowns. If the jewels and crowns were

connected with the workin people then that's fine, they would be interested in them, they would say we bought these things. But what do they say? We paid for these things.

(AK – male, 66 years old, frequent museum visitor)

Further, the application of an ethnographic framework which purely examines the 'reality' of exhibition interpretation in the micro-environment of a gallery, could easily lead to missing out the wider 'reality' which lies in structures transcending the specific interaction. Bourdieu speaks about 'strategies of condescension': to use simple language, interactive displays, and 'fun' exhibits, could sometimes consist in deriving more power and authority 'in the very act of symbolically negating that relation, namely, the hierarchy of the languages and of those who speak them' (2002: 128). Indeed, interviewees in the study were asked about their views on the hands-on media, touch screens and other multimedia facilities offered in the museums. Many of them seemed to look at these developments with a sceptical mind:

Sometimes all these arcades kind of make it work against what you really want. It is kind of overdoing it, putting too much into it, especially with older people. They sometimes don't understand the use of these things. Younger people find them more interesting.

(O – female, 48 years old, frequent museum visitor)

In conclusion, like any other tool, critical ethnography can present the researcher with hurdles in the field, the most profound being the claim of the ability to see things others miss. The ramifications of such a powerful knowledge claim have to be taken into account and constantly interrogated (Springwood and King 2001); this is what Kincheloe and McLaren mean, when they talk about the need for 'research humility' (1994: 151). Other criticisms focus around issues of 'validity'; there is scepticism regarding the objectivity of critical ethnographers' work. As Anderson suggests, 'their agenda of social critique, their attempt to locate their respondents' meanings in larger impersonal systems of political economy, and the resulting conceptual 'front-endedness' of much of their research raises validity issues beyond those of mainstream naturalistic research' (1989: 253).

Dingwall has criticised critical researchers for not allowing any space for the opposing argument: 'Are the privileged treated as having something serious to say, or simply dismissed as evil, corrupt or greedy without further inquiry?' (1992: 172) Nevertheless, critical ethnography, instead of looking for scapegoats, examines the field of human interaction – namely, the discursive, ideological or institutional spaces of education and culture. The objects of the critical gaze are to be found in the interface of a diversity of forces, rather than specific instances or people.

Critical Discourse Analysis

The theoretical origins of Critical Discourse Analysis (CDA) lie in Louis Althusser's theories of ideology, Mikhail Bakhtin's genre theory, and the philosophical traditions of Antonio Gramsci and the Frankfurt School (Titscher et al. 2000). It is a research tool which examines the ideological use of language, by analysing texts to investigate their interpretation, reception and social effects (Wodak 2004). CDA, like critical ethnography, has been criticised for its open political commitment (Toolan 2002). Henry Widdowson, for example, has strongly argued against it, by claiming that it constantly sits on the fence between social research and political activism, and also arguing against the term 'discourse' as being both 'vogue and vague' (1995: 158).

CDA as an established paradigm in linguistics, however, sees 'language as social practice':

> Discourse is socially constitutive as well as socially conditioned – it constitutes situations, objects of knowledge, and the social identities of and relationship between people and groups of people. It is constitutive both in the sense that it helps to sustain and reproduce the status quo, and in the sense that it contributes to transforming it. Since discourse is so socially consequential, it gives rise to important issues of power.
>
> (Fairclough and Wodak 1997: 258)

Even though CDA deals principally with language, Fairclough emphasised the need to incorporate visual images and sound, as other semiotic 'texts' (1995); a similar synthesis of script and icons is applied by museums in constructing their exhibition narratives. Regarding the mode of analysis used, there are three dimensions of every 'discursive event':[5] the *textual level*, where content and form are analysed; the level of *discursive practice*, i.e. the socio-cognitive aspects of text production and interpretation; and finally, the level of *social practice*, related to the different level of institutional or social context.

CDA is applied in the study discussed, in order to examine documentation data derived from the museums under investigation, i.e. mission statements, educational policies, promotional leaflets, and any other related material. Fairclough talks about *interdiscursivity*, examining how discourses and genres blend, forming bridges between texts and contexts; he gives the example of documentary texts, where information and entertainment are combined (Titscher et al. 2000). Similar examples can be found in the ways a market discourse has 'interdiscursively' penetrated the language of education and culture:

> Dundee has long recognised that its cultural activities have the *capacity* to fulfil a crucial role in improving the *quality* of life of its citizens and tackling social exclusion. They promote a positive *image* of the city, contribute to

economic regeneration, retain *skills*, attract *jobs*, provide *opportunities* for voluntary and community participation and stimulate lifelong learning.

(Dundee City Council Cultural Strategy 2002–2006: 3, my emphasis)

Clearly, what is found here is a growing tendency to move to a stronger investment in the construction of an entrepreneurial identity (Fairclough 1993). Increasingly, cultural policies, and especially museum education policies, are adopting a promotional genre of language. According to the document quoted above, the Dundee City Council Cultural Strategy, '. . . is arranged under three Aims, seven Strategic Objectives, twenty-one Key Areas and over one hundred Action Points' (Dundee City Council Cultural Strategy 2002–2006: 5). Such 'listing' syntax of language is reader-friendly, but it is also reader-directive: any argumentative links are lost in such a monologue, where no space is left for the counter-argument. Instead, a clear divide is set between 'those who are making all these assertions and those who are addressed at – those who tell and those who are told, those who know and those who don't' (Fairclough 2001: 229). According to Bourdieu:

> Linguistic exchange . . . is also an economic exchange which is established within a particular symbolic relation of power between a producer, endowed with a certain linguistic capital, and a consumer (or a market), and which is capable of procuring a certain material or symbolic profit. In other words, utterances are not only (save in exceptional circumstances) signs to be understood and deciphered; they are also signs of wealth, intended to be evaluated and appreciated, and signs of authority, intended to be believed and obeyed.
>
> (2002: 129)

Likewise, exhibition narratives, which use not only language but also images and objects – and therefore might even require specific deciphering of aesthetic norms – are not purely informative. The poetics of exhibitionary language send across a unique communicating style, laden with social value and symbolic efficacy. CDA could therefore unveil the hidden 'curricula' involved in 'meaning-making' in museums; it deconstructs the different layers of meaning by imposing a critical questioning of the visual communication. Adapting Fairclough's model of text and discourse analysis (1992), the following schema for exhibition interpretation appears – see Figure 15.1.

By starting from the analysis of a specific display, the researcher can move to the interpretivist model of looking at how people actively produce meanings and make sense of them on the basis of shared ideas and pre-knowledge. Finally, the analysis widens to a macro-sociology of education, by examining the socio-historical conditions that govern meaning production and learning processes in museums. Every phase of analysis is embedded in the previous one, emphasising their interdependence and allowing the researcher to move back and forth between the three strata of examination. According to Fairclough, there are two types of interpretation:

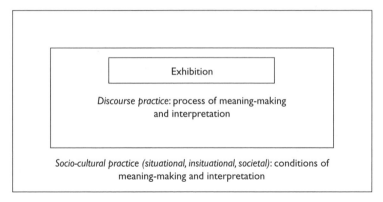

Figure 15.1 Method of analysis: from Description (exhibition analysis) to Interpretation (learning process analysis) to Explanation (sociological analysis).

Interpretation-1 is an inherent part of ordinary language use: make meaning from/with spoken or written texts. People make meanings through an interplay between features of a text and the varying resources which they bring to *Interpretation-1 [. . .] Interpretation-2* is a matter of analysts seeking to show connections between both properties of texts and practices of *Interpretation-1* in a particular social space. Notice that *Interpretation-1* is part of the domain of *Interpretation-2*; one concern of *Interpretation-2* is to investigate how different practices of *Interpretation-1* are socially, culturally and ideologically shaped.

(2002: 149)

This research used critical discourse analysis in order to go beyond looking at the 'interpretive repertoires' (Hooper-Greenhill and Moussouri 2001) people use during their museum encounters, to an *Interpretation-2* model of analysis; a focus on the explanatory connections between museum exhibitions, education and social relations of power – on questions of ideology.

Conclusion

Research which assumes the non-ideological nature of education can have a significant ideological effect in sustaining hegemonic practices. On the one hand, mixed-method research designs combine narrative interpretations with structural analysis, casting light on the 'bigger picture' museums are part of. On the other hand, critical ethnography and critical discourse analysis are research methods with an overt political standpoint; the fact that other methods do not recognise or acknowledge *their* equivalent commitments does not in any way mean that they are more objective or that such commitments do not exist (Fairclough 2002). This study looked at ideologies as those assumptions built into museum practices which sustain relations of domination. Research always entails interests, hypotheses, inclusions and exclusions – this work recognises its own 'partiality'. I would suggest that a type of research that only looks at the subjective ways adults make meaning in museums, without examining the socio-historical context of this learning, is also partial. Indeed, according to Elspeth King, former curator at the People's Palace in Glasgow (1974–1990):

> It is essential that any genuinely popular education should reconnect with the hidden histories before they are merchandised as heritage or simply forgotten. The alternative is 'a slavery of intellect and a servility of attitude' which would be a betrayal of the historic struggle for freedom and dignity.
>
> (1999: 186)

Notes

1   Hereafter I will be using the term 'museum' to refer to both museums and galleries.
2   For a critique of the 'new museology', see also Ross (2004).
3   In fact, they do not really seem to have changed at all. According to 'Renaissance in the Regions', the governmental project for supporting English museums, delivered by the Museums, Libraries and Archives Council, museum visiting is 'heavily biased towards ABC1s (76 per cent of museum visitors versus 51 per cent of the population), that is, the upper- and the upper-middle classes, and people educated to bachelor or post-graduate degree level (42 per cent versus 17 per cent)' (MLA 2004: 3).
4   These are: the McManus Galleries and Museum, Dundee Contemporary Arts, Verdant Works and Discovery Point Antarctic Museum.
5   Meaning, 'instance of language use' (Titscher et al. 2000: 147). Ernesto Laclau (1981) has also commented: 'By "the discursive" I understand nothing which in a narrow sense relates to texts but the ensemble of phenomena of the social production of meaning on which society as such is based. It is not a question of regarding the discursive as a plane or dimension of the social but as having the same meaning as the social as such. . . . Subsequently, the non-discursive is not opposite to the discursive as if one were dealing with two different planes because there is nothing societal that is determined outside the discursive. History and society are therefore an unfinished text.'

References

Anderson, G.L. (1989) 'Critical ethnography in education: origins, current status, and new directions', *Review of Educational Research*, 59(3): 249–270.

Bourdieu, P. (2002) 'Price formation and the anticipation of profits', in M. Toolan (ed.) *Critical Discourse Analysis: Critical Concepts in Linguistics*, London: Routledge, pp. 125–148.

Bourdieu, P. and Darbel, A. (1991) *The Love of Art: European Art Museums and their Public*, Cambridge: Polity Press.

Brannen, J. (1992) *Mixing Methods: Qualitative and Quantitative Research*, London: Avebury.

Brannen, J. (2005) 'Mixing methods: the entry of qualitative and quantitative approaches into the research process', *International Journal of Social Research Methodology*, 8(3): 173–184.

Brewer, J. and Hunter, A. (1989) *Multimethod Research: A Synthesis of Styles*, Thousand Oaks, CA: Sage.

Creswell, J.W. (2003) *Research Design: Qualitative, Quantitative and Mixed Methods Approach*, Thousand Oaks, CA: Sage.

Crowther, J. and Martin, I. (2005) 'Is there any space left for "really useful knowledge" in the knowledge society?', in A. Bron et al. (eds) *Between the Old and New Worlds of Adult Education*, Wroclaw: ESREA.

Dingwall, R. (1992) 'Don't mind him – he's from Barcelona: qualitative methods in health studies', in J. Daly, I. McDonald and E. Willis (eds) *Researching Health Care: Designs, Dilemmas, Disciplines*, London: Routledge, pp. 161–175.

Dundee City Council (2002) *Dundee City Council Cultural Strategy 2002–2006*, Dundee: Dundee City Council.

Durbin, G. (ed.) (1996) *Developing Museum Exhibitions for Lifelong Learning*, London: Stationery Office.

Fairclough, N. (1992) *Discourse and Social Change*, Cambridge: Polity Press.

Fairclough, N. (1993) 'Critical discourse analysis and the marketisation of public discourse: the universities', *Discourse and Society*, 4(2): 133–168.

Fairclough, N. (1995) *Critical Discourse Analysis: The Critical Study of Language*, London: Longman.

Fairclough, N. (2001) 'The discourse of New Labour: critical discourse analysis', in M. Wetherell, S. Taylor and S. J. Yates (eds) *Discourse as Data: A Guide for Analysis*, London: Sage in association with the Open University, pp. 229–266.

Fairclough, N. (2002) 'A reply to Henry Widdowson's "Discourse Analysis: A Critical View"', in M. Toolan (ed.) *Critical Discourse Analysis: Critical Concepts in Linguistics, Volume III: Concurrent Analyses and Critiques,* London: Routledge, pp. 148–155.

Fairclough, N. and Wodak, R. (1997) 'Critical discourse analysis', in T. A. van Dijk (ed.) *Introduction to Discourse Analysis*, London: Sage, pp. 258–284.

Falk, J. and Dierking, L. (1992) *Learning from Museums: Visitor Experiences and the Making of Meaning*, Lanham, MD: AltaMira Press.

Fay, B. (1987) *Critical Social Science: Liberation and its Limits*, Cambridge: Polity Press.

Freire, P. (1973) *Education: The Practice of Freedom*, London: Writers and Readers Publishing Cooperative.

Geertz, C. (1973) *The Interpretation of Cultures*, New York: Basic Books.

Green, A. and Preston, J. (2005) 'Editorial: Speaking in tongues – diversity in mixed methods research', *International Journal of Social Research Methodology*, 8(3): 167–171.

Greene, J.C. and Caracelli, V.J. (1997) *Advances in Mixed-Methods Evaluation: The Challenges and Benefits of Integrating Diverse Paradigms*, San Francisco, CA: Jossey-Bass.

Hammersley, M. (2004) 'Hierarchy and emancipation', in C. Seale (ed.) *Social Research Methods: A Reader*, London: Routledge, pp. 478–485.

Hein, G. (1998) *Learning in the Museum*, London: Routledge.

Hooper-Greenhill, E. (1997) 'Museum learners as active post-modernists: contextualising constructivism', *Journal of Education in Museums*, 18(1): 1–4.

Hooper-Greenhill, E. (1999) *The Educational Role of the Museum*, London: Routledge.

Hooper-Greenhill, E. (2000) *Museums and the Interpretation of Visual Culture*, London: Routledge.

Hooper-Greenhill, E. and Moussouri, T. (2001) *Making Meaning in Art Museums 1: Visitors' Interpretive Strategies at Wolverhampton Art Gallery*, Leicester: Research Centre for Museums and Galleries.

Horkheimer, M. and Adorno, T. (1972) *The Dialectic of the Enlightenment*, New York: Herder and Herder.

Johnson, R. (1979) 'Really useful knowledge: radical education and working-class culture, 1790–1848', in J. Clarke, C. Critcher and R. Johnson (eds) *Working Class Culture: Studies in History and Theory*, New York: St Martin's Press.

Johnson, R. (1988) 'Really useful knowledge, 1790–1850: memories for education in the 1980s', in T. Lovett (ed.) *Radical Approaches to Education: A Reader*, New York: Routledge and Kegan Paul.

Jordan, S. and Yeomans, D. (1995) 'Critical ethnography: problems in contemporary theory and practice', *British Journal of Sociology of Education*, 16(3): 389–408.

Kawashima, N. (1997) *Museum Management in a Time of Change*, Warwick: University of Warwick, Centre for the Study of Cultural Policy.

Kincheloe, J.L. and McLaren, P.L. (1994) 'Rethinking critical theory and qualitative research', in N. Denzin and Y. Lincoln (eds) *Handbook of Qualitative Research*, Thousand Oaks, CA: Sage.

King, E. (1999) 'Not on the curriculum: the story of Scottish working class material culture', in J. Crowther, I. Martin and M. Shaw (eds) *Popular Education and Social Movements in Scotland Today*, Leicester: NIACE, pp. 186–192.

Laclau, E. (1981) *Politik und Ideologie im Marxismus. Kapitalismus-Faschismus-Populismus*, [*Politics and Ideology in Marxism: Capitalism, Fascism, Populism*] Berlin: Argument.

Lawley, I. (2003) 'Local authority museums and the modernising government agenda in England', *Museum and Society*, 1(2): 75–86.

Lüders, C. (2004) 'Field observation and ethnography', in U. Flick, E. Kardoff and I. Steinke (eds) *A Companion to Qualitative Research*, London: Sage.

McLaren, P. (1992) 'Collisions with otherness: travelling theory, post-colonial criticisms, and the politics of ethnographic practice – the mission of the wounded ethnographer', *Qualitative Studies in Education*, 5(1): 77–92.

Morgan, D.L. (1998) 'Practical strategies for combining qualitative and quantitative methods: applications to health research', *Qualitative Health Research*, 8: 362–376.

Museums, Libraries and Archives Council (2004) *Renaissance in the Regions: National Report*, London: MLA.

Newman, I., Benz, C.R. and Ridenour, C. (1998) *Qualitative–Quantitative Research Methodology: Exploring the Interactive Continuum*, Carbondale: Southern Illinois University Press.

Nilsen, A. and Brannen, J. (2002) 'Theorising the individual-structure dynamic', in J. Brannen, A. Nilsen, S. Lewis and J. Smithson (eds) *Young Europeans, Work and Family Life: Futures in Transition*, London: Routledge.

Roberts, L.C. (1997) *From Knowledge to Narrative: Educators and the Changing Museum*, Washington, DC: Smithsonian Institution Press.

Ross, M. (2004) 'Interpreting the new museology', *Museum and Society*, 2(2): 84–103.

Sandelowski, M. (2000) 'Combining qualitative and quantitative sampling, data collection and analysis techniques in mixed methods studies', *Research in Nursing and Health*, 23: 246–255.

Springwood, C.F. and King, C.R. (2001) 'Unsettling engagements: on the ends of rapport in critical ethnography', *Qualitative Inquiry*, 7(4): 403–417.

Tashakkori, A. and Teddlie, C. (1998) *Mixed Methods: Combining Qualitative and Quantitative Approaches*, Thousands Oaks, CA: Sage.

Tashakori, A. and Teddlie, C. (eds) (2002) *Handbook of Mixed Methods in Social and Behavioral Research*, Thousand Oaks, CA: Sage.

Thomas, J. (1993) *Doing Critical Ethnography*, London: Sage.

Titscher, S., Mayer, M., Wodak, R. and Vetter, E. (2000) *Methods of Text and Discourse Analysis*, London: Sage.

Toolan, M. (2002) 'What is critical discourse analysis and why are people saying such terrible things about it?', in M. Toolan (ed.) *Critical Discourse Analysis: Critical Concepts in Linguistics, Volume III: Concurrent Analyses and Critiques*, London: Routledge, pp. 219–241.

Vergo, P. (ed.) (1989) *The New Museology*, London: Reaktion Books.

Widdowson, H.G. (1995) 'Discourse analysis – a critical view', *Language and Literature*, 4(3): 157–172.

Willis, P. (1997) 'TIES: Theoretically Informed Ethnographic Study', in S. Nugent and C. Shore (eds) *Anthropology and Cultural Studies*, London and Chicago: University of Chicago Press, pp. 185–192.

Wodak, R. (2004) 'Critical discourse analysis', in C. Seale et al. (eds) *Qualitative Research Practice*, London: Sage, pp. 197–213.

Wolcott, H.F. (1999) *Ethnography: A Way of Seeing*, Thousand Oaks, CA: Sage.

Chapter 16

Blogs and wikis as disruptive technologies

Is it time for a new pedagogy?

Rita Kop

Introduction

Questions have been raised in recent years about the tenability of the classical views of knowledge and learning in a rapidly changing world (Lyotard 1984; Glaser 1999; Lewis 1999; Lankshear et al. 2000; O'Hara 2002). Technological change has been a driver for change in adult education as it has introduced a new flexibility, with a range of new developments, including the introduction of virtual learning environments, knowledge banks, and the use of handheld and mobile devices in the learning space. The dramatic increase in the use of peer-to-peer software such as blogs, wikis and personal spaces amongst young people in society and their consequent introduction in the formal educational environment have caused excitement and concern amongst learning technologists as they seem to provide new options for communication and network building which could change our educational institutions forever.

Much discussion has taken place about the impact of the introduction of virtual learning systems on education. The changing position of educational institutions such as universities due to the changed sense of space, place and identity in a virtual learning environment has been lamented as a loss, as universities were seen as places where people came together, where minds met and where new ideas were conceived as nowhere else in society. Proponents of the use of peer-to-peer technology in education (Lamb 2004; MacCallum-Stewart 2004) have argued that tools such as wikis and blogs could fulfil exactly this role, as the openness of these media and the willingness of people to share in such experiences encourages a similar discussion of ideas and collaborative development of thoughts and knowledge. The added advantage of the online tools lies in their globally positioned communication forums and instantaneous forms of publication, which provides immediate responses on a scale unimaginable in the traditional university.

This chapter will analyse the changing nature of knowledge creation and communication in adult education and will examine if emergent tools, such as wikis and blogs, could play a part in meaningful knowledge creation in an educational context. It will explore the challenges that online educators face and the innovations that emergent technology could offer.

The concept of knowledge in a technology rich world

Current theories of knowledge have moved away from the ideas of Plato (Lewis 1999) that knowledge is a justified belief, reaching the 'truth' through intelligence and reason, where knowledge would be achieved through dialogue with others in order to reach understanding. Other forms of knowledge have been identified, including 'practical knowledge' and 'bodies of knowledge' (O'Hara 2002). Downes (2003: 1) states that 'knowledge is the product of producing order out of a chaos of experience', while Guy (2004: 142) argues that 'the debate – indeed the war – over what counts as knowledge is intrinsically linked to who gets to say what counts as knowledge' and that the people who were the authority on knowledge throughout the ages might have only shown one part of the knowledge picture because of the context in which they operated.

How then is knowledge changing? Jean-Francois Lyotard, in *The Postmodern Condition* (1984: 4), put forward a convincing argument for the inevitability of changed knowledge in a changing world. His book analyses the status of knowledge and the way it has transformed under influence of technology. He points to the commodification of knowledge: the way in which acquiring knowledge is no longer an end in itself, but how it has become a commodity that can be bought and sold and has exchange value. The validity of knowledge has become judged by the way it relates to the performance of society. Lyotard (ibid.: 9) questions 'who decides what knowledge is, and who knows what needs to be decided. In the computer age the question of knowledge is now more than ever a question of government', while in the past the university would be the authority in matters of knowledge.

Current views of knowledge take this thinking one step further and pose that people create knowledge themselves. Lave and Wenger (2002) and Cobb (1999) emphasise constructivist and socio-cultural perspectives, and aim to leave behind a curriculum dominated by the teacher as expert in her discipline, and embrace a curriculum in which the student takes control of his own learning, making connections with his own experiences and knowledge in co-operative activities with fellow-learners. Initially the tutor might be the expert, but by engaging the learners in participation in problem-solving activities, information-gathering exercises and communication with peers, experts facilitate their move from the periphery to the centre of the community of practice. Knowledge is no longer transferred, but created and constructed. Active participation in collaborative learning activities, rather than passively receiving knowledge from the teacher, are key in these theories and have been embraced by developers of e-learning (Salmon 2004; Lafarierre 2006). The crux to active knowledge construction and understanding of new concepts in this view is online collaboration (Mayes 2002; Laferriere 2006; Salmon 2004). Moreover, as Mayes (2002: 169) suggests, 'activity, motivation and learning are all related to a need for a positive sense of identity shaped by social forces'. In the words of Lyotard (1984: 15): 'A self does not amount to much, but no self is an island; each exists in a fabric of relations that is now more complex and mobile than ever before.' An individual lives in a network of inter-related nodal points where he meets and communicates with others.

Some observers suggest that to get the best out of the new media, we should stop mimicking a face-to-face environment and let go of the traditional classroom ways of teaching and learning altogether and look at teaching in a new light (Lee 2000; Bereiter 2002; Lankshear and Knobel 2003). According to Lankshear and Knobel (2003), about school classrooms:

> All sort of contrived practices have been created in order to find ways of accommodating new technologies to classroom 'ways'. It has wasted the potential of new technologies to provide bridges to new forms of social and cultural practice.

One way to adapt the technology used in the institution would be to take notice of the ways in which learners use technology outside a formal educational environment (Scardamalia and Bereiter 1994; Lee 2000). Lee (2000: 3) identifies in the teenagers of today a way of 'chaotic' learning, 'happily venturing into the unknown, and learning as they "do" and discover. . . . The "Net" users appear at ease handling a variety of tasks at once, and moving from one activity to another in a seemingly random manner . . . not only make extensive use of the electronic networks, but network with like minded folk across the world in their learning.' Furthermore, as Gulati (2004) and Selwyn and Gorard (2004) argue, for Information and Communications Technology (ICT) assisted-learning to really become effective, formal learning needs to be complemented with informal online learning as students will need opportunities to relate what they learn to their own context in order to create knowledge.

New developments in communication technologies

Over the past five years, the internet has moved on from being a resource of infor-mation (Web 1.0) to emerge as an instrument of communication and networking (Web 2.0). Informal social software, such as blogs (web-logs), instant messaging, wikis (collaborative websites), networked social spaces, including MySpace and YouTube, allow for peer-to peer interaction and are all examples of new devel-opments in communication tools. In addition, social book marking and social searching have come to the fore, where information streams can be shared and connected to those of others, thus creating networked information.

Blogs are interactive online diaries and offer the opportunity to post comments to which, in turn, reactions can be made. A blog reflects personal opinions and areas of interest of the 'blogger' and can be personal, although numerous journal-istic, political and subject specific blogs have emerged. Communication with others is at the centre of the blog, which makes it more than an individual diary.

Most bloggers have a blog-roll showing a list of links to their favourite sites, which has resulted in the quick growth of communities of interest, further aided by aggregators (RSS feeds) that filter a number of blogs for areas of interest. The developments have contributed to the formation of a steadily growing web of interest-driven, inter-related searchable sites in which people participate and collaborate.

Wikis are quite different. They are websites that offer people the opportunity to add documents and individuals are encouraged to edit entries from other people if they think they have any knowledge to add. One or more people are responsible for the venture, but the aim is to develop a project collaboratively. Most commentators see their strength in offering a collaborative framework for knowledge creation, some even see them as the ultimate in democratic creation as they encourage participation by providing opportunities for anybody to add anything, which at the same time is seen as their downfall as what has been created today could be destructed tomorrow. If we look at the best-known open content wiki, the Wikipedia, surprisingly enough, 'what seems to create chaos, has actually produced increasingly respected content which has been evaluated and revised by the thousands to visit the site over time' (Lih 2004: 3). Wikis come very close to what Sir Tim Berners-Lee (1999: 1) looked for when starting the World Wide Web:

> The basic idea of the Web was that of an information space through which people can communicate, but communicate in a special way: communicate by sharing their knowledge in a pool. The idea was not just that it should be a big browsing medium. The idea was that everybody would be putting their ideas in, as well as taking them out. This [the internet] is not supposed to be a glorified television channel.

Communication and participation are at the heart of all peer-to-peer tools and a number of academics have shown an interest in blogs and wikis and have seen their potential in an educational environment (Downes 2004; Halavais, in Glaser 2004; Lankshear and Knobel 2006). Comments from lecturers about the use of blogs in their classes include: 'the push into critical thinking, critical reading and reflection' (McIntire-Strasbourg 2004: 1); 'the ability to achieve active back-and-forth discussions outside the classroom' (Martin and Taylor 2004: 1); 'Students are blogging about topics that are important to them. Students direct their own learning while receiving input and feedback from others' (Ferdig and Trammell 2004: 5). Lamb (2004) also notes the openness of the wiki environment. He sees a number of possibilities to use wikis in an educational context: as spaces for brainstorming; as collaborative areas for teams to work on projects, outlining and managing activities or research; and as repositories of shared knowledge. Additionally, James (2004) and Lamb (2004) indicate the need for teachers to hand over control over content in using wikis to ensure successful knowledge-building. The role of the tutor would lie in 'setting the scene' and thinking up problems related to the subject being taught, while allowing students to develop the wiki to their own liking.

Most lecturers who have used blogs and wikis in adult education have seen opportunities to improve the traditional learning environment, particularly as a means for communication, collaboration, reflection, ordering thought and knowledge. They appear to have all been enthusiastic bloggers and participants in wikis themselves and are generally keen users of technology. No surprise, then, not to find many critical publications about these tools and developments.

Some educationalists and learning technologists (Arina 2006; Lankshear and Knobel 2006; Wilson et al. 2006) see how they can be used to move from a hierarchical teaching approach, that is, structured in courses, controlled by the institution using a lecturing model in an enclosed environment, creating individual knowledge, to a networked approach, that is, adaptive to learners' needs, that uses an aggregation model in a personalised open learning environment, that is a fluid extension of the wider informal personal space and that facilitates collective knowledge creation. A transition to the latter model could clearly lead to an undermining of the authority of the knowledge-keepers of the past as people can communicate and find knowledgeable others on a global scale, can collaborate on knowledge creation projects such as wikis, and discuss topics of interest with others, while at the same time connect this to information that is readily available. They can bypass academia altogether. Social tools are already called disruptive technologies as they are changing the work practices of journalists and broadcasters. Learning technologists expect them to also disrupt and change education. It is very much up to the academy to take up the challenge to ensure that students engage critically with the internet, by the framing of questions, working with the learners on developing intellectual depth and a critical analysis of source material found on the internet, and by fitting this learning process into the institutional structure.

The way the gatekeepers of knowledge in the past engage with the new developments varies; a number of academics and librarians have noted the bias and unreliability of some written material in blogs, wikis and personal spaces and don't want any engagement with the new developments, while others have embraced blogs and wikis as tools for debate and found out that they work differently from a traditional academic environment. Pike (quoted in North 2006: 6):

> The sites are no respecter of status. You don't get any deference to professors or to people who say: 'research shows . . .'. People reply: 'Post a hyperlink to the research then, and we will see for ourselves.' That is a virtuous kind of Socratic dialogue model. You don't know anything about the person you are having an argument with, and what's at stake is the argument itself.

Walker (in Glaser 2004: 1) notes:

> Blogging alongside other academics in my field . . . is a form of indirect collaboration. . . . There is an openness and a willingness to share in blogging

. . . that means I know more about many of my fellow bloggers' research than I do about a colleague whose office is down the corridor.

Power and control

The new technological development has been driven by technology, but also by youth culture. Young people use technology as the older generations use books, paper and pen, and we can no longer avoid the way in which learners have fundamentally changed. Marc Prenski (2001) argues that current institutions were not designed for the students of today and tomorrow. He makes distinctions between 'digital natives', who have been immersed in technology all their lives, who are used to these immediate forms of communication with peers, and who use technology in a very different way from 'digital immigrants'. Most adult learners and tutors would fall in this latter category and have to adapt to each new emerging technology. As more and more digital natives enter adult education and university classrooms, the tension will grow between the technologies used at home and in the educational setting. Consequently, the learning strategies used will no longer be relevant to the expectations and experiences of the learners.

'Digital immigrant' teachers, who might be struggling to keep up with the new technological developments, might assume that their students are the same as before, but according to Prenski, they no longer are:

> They are used to the instantaneity of hypertext, downloaded music, phones in their pockets, a library on laptops, beamed messages and instant messaging. They've been networked most of their lives. They have little patience for lectures, step-by-step logic, and 'tell-test' instruction.
>
> (2001: 3)

Major changes in pedagogy are envisaged through the new tools, but also because of a new generation of students with potentially different needs and expectations from earlier generations related to their 'connected' lifestyles. Research by Kvavik (2005) shows that 72 per cent of young students prefer moderate or extensive ICT in the classroom, while 2.2 per cent prefer entirely online teaching and only 2.9 per cent classes without ICT at all, which indicates that teaching strategies will need to be adapted to make more use of interconnecting technology.

So far these potentially liberating and creative tools have inspired innovation in a number of areas outside education, including journalism, commerce and political lobbying. Their fast development and uptake has made it impossible for governments and institutions to impose control over their use. The control has been in the hands of the users and a number of observers (James 2004; Lamb 2004) see their application in an educational context work most powerfully if the learner remains in charge.

If the tools work best while the learners are in control, it is time for tutors to relinquish some power and trust their students to get on with the activity of blogging or wiki-writing on the internet and be satisfied with the organic growth of knowledge made possible by wikis and blogs, which would also allow for learning from others. They might have to be happy with a change in their role of provider of content to one of supervisor, currently used for post-graduate research students. Ronald Barnett (2002: 9) points out that in this world of 'super-complexity' the world of work is changing: 'Work, communication, identity, self, knowing and even life: the meaning of fundamental concepts are no longer clear in a world of change.' It becomes increasingly important for tutors to learn on the job and in the job and professional development will be key to the development of our educational institutions to ensure that they adapt within this changing environment.

Arina (2006) indicates that the learner motivation is higher if she is in control rather than the institution, as apart from control over the content the learner would also be in charge of the purpose of the learning and of the process itself. This could be added to possible affective (Picard et al. 2004) advantages of participating in networks of interest.

The hardest part when the control moves from institution to learner will be the validation of knowledge. If the learner finds information on the World Wide Web and communicates in the 'blogosphere' to make sense of that information according to his own interests and experiences and constructs knowledge away from the institution, the institution will still have to have structures in place to fit the learning into its quality systems. It is a paradox that technology has facilitated a closer control on assessment and validation of knowledge, while what will be required to use the new technologies effectively is flexibility and a willingness to adapt to a new assessment practice. There will be an important negotiating and facilitating role for the local tutor in linking the knowledge constructed online to a local community of practice and accreditation structure.

Educational and institutional change: revolution or evolution?

> A wave of young people empowered to create knowledge, not merely absorb it, now flows in and out of the classroom, calling into question the convictions and processes that have served as the foundation of traditional higher education. It remains to be seen whether traditional higher education will adjust sufficiently to truly engage the Net Generation.
>
> (Barone 2005: 14)

The way in which global networks and communities of interest are currently being formed through emerging technologies is encouraging young people in particular to develop new and different forms of communication and knowledge creation outside formal education. By creating a personalised learning space, linked to a local learner group, or possibly to a global network of people and supported by a knowledgeable tutor, the learning space is very open. It seems likely that digital natives will thrive in this environment, as it is what they have been accustomed to outside education for the past years. For the digital immigrants, particularly older learners and people from social classes IV and V (from a partly skilled and unskilled background), who traditionally have a low participation rate in adult education, it might be a step too fast and too far. They might have problems keeping up with the change and would need training in digital literacy and a more traditional learning space, structured by the tutor to gain confidence and knowledge.

How can institutions make the most of the new technological developments? Government funding has enabled ICT infrastructure and Virtual Learning Environments (VLEs) to become an integral part of institutional life. It is clear that there is a large discrepancy between the rate of change at which the academy evolves and the rate at which technological innovations are emerging. It could invigorate education if institutions were able to harness the innovative potential of these new tools. In the words of McLuhan and Fiore (1967): 'Our time is a time for crossing barriers, for erasing old categories, for probing around. When two seemingly disparate elements are imaginatively poised, put in apposition in new and unique ways, startling discoveries often result.'

As communication is an important aspect of constructivist and 'community of practice' approaches, the biggest challenge for online tutors has been to intrinsically motivate the learners to use the tools. The integration of a variety of learning tools within one VLE has been the start of making them accessible to the learner and easy to use for the tutor. However, these systems are very much part of formal and institutionalised structures derived from traditional face-to-face teaching strategies. The emergence of online social tools, personalised learning spaces, availability of broadband, and the exponential growth in their use has shown that interest-driven and user-controlled communication tools are attractive to millions of people outside an educational setting. Their potential as tools for learning has not yet been extensively tested, but early use by enthusiasts shows their potential for communication in communities of interest, also in an educational setting. Learners can make their voices heard while communicating and interacting with a global audience with links to information, while developing thoughts and knowledge.

The use of communication in VLEs has had the problem that in message-based discussion structures communication will work best if used between 20 and 50 people (Palme 1995). The Web 2.0 equivalent, where the networked interconnectedness means that knowledge is no longer solely created through messages, but also through the aggregation of communications in blogs, wikis and information, will offer the potential for interaction with many more people, but still avoid 'communication overload'.

No research is yet available to show if the communication and network forming taking place through social tools would be of the same value for education purposes as the traditional two-way communication.

Conclusion

The value of emerging technologies in adult education needs careful consideration as their introduction requires very different teaching and learning strategies from current practice.

It would not make sense for educators to 'rush to become providers of instant messaging, blogs, wikis, computer games, social networking sites [. . .] The real opportunity lies in observing and talking to today's students to learn more about how they conceptualize and use these new tools. With this knowledge institutions can create contexts for technology use to enhance learning, improve student services and enrich students' social lives' (Oblinger and Oblinger 2005: 6). Social tools support collaboration and student-centred knowledge creation and could enhance traditional study by offering informal, interest-driven communication.

The challenges lie in the integration of the tools in a formal educational setting and how best to adjust to a more open learning environment. Currently, people are experimenting with social tools in education and researching the effect they have on the learning process, sometimes linked to e-portfolios and personalised spaces which are very different to more traditional VLEs. They are not centred around institutional requirements, such as courses, timetables and assessments, but use tags to connect to other learners with similar interests, and thus create networks and communities of interest. Early indications are that social tools will initially be used in combination with VLEs. Although this would help digital immigrants to adapt, it might lead the tools to lose their potential for innovation and creativity (Wilson et al. 2006). The tools could be disruptive or energising to formal education, but as Lamb (2004: 44) states: 'Change is happening. What remains unknown is whether educators, institutions, and developers will join (or coexist with) the revolutionary forces or whether they'll stand their ground and simply be overrun.'

References

Arina, T. (2006) *Social Web in Support of Informal Learning*, EU eLearning 2006 conference, Espoo, at: http://tarina.blogging.fi.

Barnett, R. (2002) 'Learning to work and working to learn', in F. Reeve et al. (eds) *Supporting Lifelong Learning, Volume 2. Organising Learning*, London: RoutledgeFalmer.

Barone, C. (2005) 'The new academy', in D. G. Oblinger and J. L. Oblinger (eds) *Educating the Net Generation*, Educause, at: www.educause.edu/educatingthenetgen.

Bereiter, C. (2002) *Education and Mind in the Knowledge Age*, Makwah, NL: Erlbaum Associates.

Berners-Lee, T. (1999) *talk*, at MIT Laboratory for Computer Sciences 35th celebrations, Cambridge, Massachusetts, USA, 14 April 1999, at: http://www.w3.org/1999/04/13-tbl.html.

Cobb, P. (1999) 'Where is the mind?', in P. Murphey (ed.) *Learners, Learning and Assessment*, London: Paul Chapman Publishing, pp. 135–150.

Downes, S. (2003) 'What do we know about knowledge?', Learnscope, Australian Flexible Learning Framework, at: http://www.downes.ca/cgi-bin/xml/papers.cgi? format=full& id=13.

Downes, S. (2004) 'Educational blogging', *EDUCAUSE Review*, 39(5): 14–26

Ferdig, R. and Trammell, K. (2004) 'Content delivery in the "Blogosphere"', *Technological Horizons in Education Journal*, at: www.thejournal.com.

Glaser, M. (2004) 'Scholars discover weblogs pass test as mode of communication', *Online Journalism Review*, USC Annanberg, 11 May, at: http://ojr.org/ojr/glaser/1084 325287.php.

Glaser, R. (1999) 'Expert knowledge and processes of thinking', in R. McCormick and C. Paechter (eds) *Learning and Knowledge*, London: Paul Chapman Publishing, pp. 88–102.

Gulati, S. (2004) *Constructivism and emerging online learning pedagogy: a discussion for formal to acknowledge and promote the informal*, Annual Conference of the Universities Association for Continuing Education, University of Glamorgan, April.

Guy, T. (2004) 'Guess who's coming to dinner: a discussion on knowledge, power, and presence', *A Symposium, Adult Education Quarterly*, 54(2): 140–144.

James, H. (2004) *My Brilliant Failure: Wikis in Classrooms*, Kairosnews, weblog for discussing Rhetoric, Technology and Pedagogy, at: http://kairosnews.org/node/ 3794.

Kvavik, R. (2005) 'Convenience, communications, and control: how students use technology', in D. Oblinger and J. Oblinger (eds) *Educating the Net Generation*, Educause, at: www.educause.edu/educatingthenetgen.

Laferriere, T. (2006) 'Learning communities networks: learning to participate, participation to Learn', keynote speech at Collaborative Construction of Knowledge via Internet seminar, Barcelona, January.

Lamb, B. (2004) 'Wide open spaces: wikis, ready or not', *EDUCAUSE Review*, 39(5): 36–48.

Lankshear, C. and Knobel, M. (2003) 'Planning pedagogy for i-mode: from flogging to blogging via wi-fi', International Federation for the Teaching of English Conference, Melbourne, 7 July.

Lankshear, C. and Knobel, M. (2006) 'Blogging as participation: the active sociality of a new literacy', American Educational Research Association Conference, San Fancisco, April.

Lankshear, C., Peters, M. and Knobel, M. (2000) 'Information, knowledge and learning: some issues facing epistemology and education in a digital age', *Journal of Philosophy of Education*, 34(1): 17–39.

Lave, J. and Wenger, E. (2002) 'Legitimate peripheral participation in communities of practice', in R. Harrison et al. (eds) *Supporting Lifelong Learning, Volume 1: Perspectives on Learning*, London: RoutledgeFalmer, pp. 111–126.

Lee, M. (2000) *Chaotic Learning: The Learning Style of the 'Net' Generation?*, in globaled.com, at: http://www.globaled.com.

Lewis, T. (1999) 'Valid knowledge and the problem of practical arts curricula', in B. Moon and P. Murphy (eds) *Curriculum in Context*, London: Paul Chapman Publishing, pp. 130–137.

Lih, A. (2004) 'Wikipedia as participatory journalism: reliable sources? Metrics for evaluating collaborative media as a news resource', 5th International Symposium on Online Journalism, University of Texas, April.

Lyotard, J. (1984) *The Postmodern Condition: A Report on Knowledge*, Manchester: Manchester University Press.

MacCallum-Stewart (2004) 'Inside the Ivory Tower', *The Guardian*, 23 September, p. 19.

MacIntire-Strasborg, J. (2004) 'Blogging back to basics', *Lore: An E-journal for Teachers of Writing*, Fall, at: http://www.bedfordstmartins.com/lore/digressions/index.htm.

McLuhan, M. and Fiore, Q. (1967) *The Medium is the Message*, New York: Bantam Books.

Martin, C. and Taylor, L. (2004) 'Practicing what we teach: collaborative writing and teaching teachers to blog', *Lore: An e-journal for Teachers of Writing*, Fall, at: http://www.bedfordstmartins.com/lore/digressions/index.htm.

Mayes, T. (2002) 'The technology of learning in a social world', in R. Harrison et al. (eds) *Supporting Lifelong Learning, Volume 1: Perspectives on Learning*, London: RoutledgeFalmer, pp. 163–175.

North, M. (2006) 'Political debate is thriving as academics blog on', *Times Higher Education Supplement*, 22 September.

Oblinger, D. and Oblinger, J. (2005) 'Is it age or IT: first steps towards understanding the net generation', in *Educating the Net Generation*, Educause, at: www.educause.edu/educatingthenetgen.

O'Hara, K. (2002) *Plato and the Internet: Postmodern Encounters*, Cambridge: Icon Books.

Palme, J. (1995) *Electronic Mail*, Boston and London: Artech House Publisher.

Picard, R., Papert, S., Bender, W., Blumberg, B., Breazeal, C., Cavallo, D., Machover, T., Resnick, M., Roy, D. and Strohecker, C. (2004) 'Affective learning – a manifesto', *BT Technology Journal*, 22(4): 253–269.

Prenski, M. (2001) 'Digital natives, digital immigrants', *On the Horizon*, 9(5): 1–6.

Salmon, G. (2004) *E-moderating: The Key to Teaching and Learning Online*, London: RoutledgeFalmer.

Scardamalia, M. and Bereiter, C. (1994) 'Computer support for knowledge-building communities', *Journal of the Learning Sciences*, 3(3): 265–283.

Selwyn, N. and Gorard, S. (2004) *How People Learn to Use Computers*, Occasional paper series, Paper 58, Cardiff: University of Cardiff.

Wilson, S., Johnson, O., Beauvoir, P., Sharples, P. and Milligan, C. (2006) 'Personal learning environments: challenging the dominant design of educational systems', draft paper to be presented at ECTEL conference in Crete, at: http://www.cetis.ac.uk/members/scott.

Chapter 17

The pedagogy of confession
Exploring identity and the online self

Dianne Conrad

Society's rush into cyberspace has far surpassed what innovative educators once easily classified as distance education. Not only has the use of technology stretched through as many as five generations (Bernard et al. 2004), ranging from the introduction of print-based correspondence courses to completely interactive internet and multi-media communication technologies, but accompanying shifts in our interaction with technological products have resonated through all aspects of society. Although our adaptation to technology for educational purposes is of foremost importance to us, as educators we cannot forget to consider the developments in our own field against the broader societal spectrum in which we live. In the way that innovators were once encouraged to 'think outside the box', it is today's commonplace knowledge that we now live, learn, and communicate outside most traditional boxes – in increasingly novel and diverse ways.

Modern society has witnessed many types of response to the realities of the new electronic age in which we live (de Kerckhove 1997; Feenberg and Barney 2004). Within the education sector, online learning, or e-learning, has created for learners an intriguing medium for connecting though self-revelation. Within e-learning platforms, online learners engage in interactive activities through acts of intimate self-disclosure – acts similar to the act of confession. This chapter will explore and position the related phenomena of 'confession' and identity as emergent e-learning trends, drawing upon the literatures of adult, lifelong, and distance learning; communication theory; and communities of practice. The 'beyond the gate' learning discussion that follows also raises the pedagogical issues of online participation, motivation, assessment and best practices within the larger framework of space, self and social presence.

Space, self and social presence: Alice and the wonderland of the looking glass

In Lewis Carroll's famous tale, Alice confronts issues of identity when she confesses to the Caterpillar that she is not quite herself (Jones 2005). Carroll's classic motifs that include mysterious spaces, lost identities, and confusion and revelation have been re-born into modern mythology in the cyber-worlds that we currently experience as part of our society's internet and online usage. The complex phenomenon of our relationship with Turkle's (1997) 'screen' intrigues educators, communicators, psychologists and sociologists alike; and while the educational realms of e-learning differ markedly from the more fantastic worlds of gaming and avatars, there are similarities that bear on the discussion of identity.

Jones, describing the gaming world, declared that the spaces of computer-networked environments do not constitute fixed entities. Rather, 'space is an arena for human agency and intentionality' (Jones 2005: 416). The constructivist view sees learning spaces in the same way. Following this view, 'presence is viewed as social accomplishment, and individuals are part of social settings which they actively constitute with others, who are also actively being present in an environment' (ibid.).

Social learning theorists have long been aware of the importance of social ambience on both the formation of learners' behaviours and on their ability to learn (Bandura 1971, 1986). On the theoretical side of the equation, social learning theory combines with constructivism and with the adult education philosophy of andragogy to shape the conceptual understanding of the online learning space and the activities that unfold there (Rourke et al. 1999). On the technological side of the equation, the recent evolution of social software – which 'enables people to rendezvous, connect or collaborate through computer-mediated communication and to form online communities' (*Wikipedia* 2007) – gives form to the reality of the demands of the learning space. Social software provides a ready-made form, and forum, for participants to give voice to their sense of self. In this way, they are exercising their sense of social presence, an aspect of online learning that has been characterised as one of the three central domains of online learning, along with instructional presence and cognitive presence (Garrison et al. 2000). It is within the realm of social presence that the cyber-self seeks connection and expression through behaviours that I label here 'acts of confession'.

The need for identity, online: connecting through confession

There are many types of confession. Most commonly, confession occurs in religious and legal environments. The recent rise in popularity of e-learning activity, however, in giving voice to a new type of pedagogical interaction among learners – participation by confession – pushes the boundaries of educational exchange. 'Confessional' types of display by learners may give rise to a variety of responses from other learners: alarm, dismay, identification or even kinship. Confessional behaviours by learners may require or inspire a variety of responses from instructors. Whoever the audience and whatever reciprocal actions are taken, confession-as-pedagogy presents opportunities for fresh insights into online learning behaviour.

The occasion of confessional behaviours can be linked conceptually to issues of identity and learners' sense of self. Building on the work of Goffman (1959), whose seminal work on self and the discomfort of adjustment to a multiplicity of roles has contributed to our current understanding of roles and role behaviour, post-modern thinkers promote the notion of identity as a process that is continually evolving. Hence, two important considerations of self are 'perpetual mobility and incompletion' (Sarup 1996: xvi). As the thrust of media and communications into modern lifestyles creates fertile ground for the multiplicity of self, so too do e-learning platforms provide rich opportunities for the creating of 'self' while at the same time providing 'new opportunities for reflection, perception, and social experience' (Marshall 1998). Echoing the communications work of McLuhan and de Kerckhove, Burnett and Marshall (2003: Chapter 4) extended communication theory into a timely cyber-iteration:

> Information and communication technology shapes our perceptions, distributes our pictures of the world to one another, and constructs different forms of control over the cultural stories that shape our sense of who we are and our world. The instant we develop a new technology of communication – talking drums, papyrus scrolls, books, telegraph, radios, televisions, computers, mobile phones – we at least partially reconstruct the self and its world, creating new opportunities for reflection, perception, and social experience.

In exploring communication technologies for their relationship to the concepts of confession and identity, Marshall (1998) purported that confession is, 'at its base, a revelation of the self. It is marking one's boundaries of identity, particularly in how that identity is publicly displayed'. The public display of identity while learning online, however, is the essence of social presence, a combination of 'the salience of the other in a mediated communication and the consequent salience of [learners'] interpersonal interactions' (Short et al. 1976: 65). Since the work of Rourke et al. (1999), the concept of social presence has been recognised as a major contributor to the more visible and more easily understood concept of online community as learners' sense of social presence precedes the interjection of their sense of self into the larger milieu of the learning environment.

Forming the last piece of a closely entwined causal relationship, however, before there can be social presence, there must be 'self'. And while the creation of self is beyond the purview of this discussion – the stuff of psychology theorists – there exists, between the self and its presentation to others, the notion of identity. How, then, is one's identity brought forward publicly in the online learning environment? What factors constitute its boundaries? Who contributes to its shape, and why?

'Identity refers to who or what one is, to the various meanings attached to oneself by self and others' (Gecas and Burke 1995: 42). The self is aware of its personality and seeks to control its presentation to others through the notion of self-efficacy. Self-efficacy refers to individuals' ability to perceive of themselves as causal agents in their environment' (ibid.). Individuals' natural tendency to strive for this sense of self-control underpins the need to validate, sustain or promote whatever identity they hold for themselves. There is an investment, therefore, in learners being perceived by others to be who they think they are. Individuals also engage in self-monitoring behaviours whereby they observe, regulate and control the ways in which they present themselves to others in social and interpersonal situations (Snyder 1987).

Citing Lewin's work on personality and also drawing on his own research, Snyder (1987) also suggested that while some people may present the same self to the world in many situations, others may in fact present many different selves as different situations arise. The three major strategies that he presents for understanding individuals' differences in social behaviour and personality – dispositional, interactional and situational – are reminiscent of elements of social learning theory that seek to explain the complex interplay of learners' life-worlds with their learning behaviours (Bandura 1971; Wenger 1998).

More recently, communications scholars have worked at re-framing identity in light of modern internet-based realities. Turkle (1997) outlined early attempts for coherence and the consolidation of identity through users' building of home pages on the internet. Post-modernists, however, have adopted the notion of post-self, ceding to Gergen's (1991) 'multiphrenic' self – the result of thinking of 'identity as a process, a constant reinvention, a coming into being' (Ewins 2005: 371). The process of reinvention and the 'no self' moments that occur along the way are troublesome for some, and in learning environments, the struggle for the creation of identity and 'being' emerges in the affective domain, at times in the form of confessional behaviour.

Online learning and adult education as venues for 'being'

As online educators, we facilitate and animate online learning through the use of communication technologies. The rhetoric of social presence and community (Wenger 1998; Rourke et al. 1999; Swan 2002) seeks to explain the complex interplay of the teaching–learning dynamic. Instructional design, appropriate technical support, assessment, interaction, participation and facilitation and teaching skills are all factors in the fabric of online learning dynamics. Similarly, many distinct behaviours constitute online learning's affective domain, shaping the nature of learners' participation and interactions with instructor, colleagues |and content. Learners-as-social-beings who both draw inspiration *from* their learning communities and give commitment and inspiration *to* their communities are also key to the learning dynamic (Wenger 1998). Behind this equation, however, from their origins in psychology and sociology, lie the concepts of learner identity and self.

Online learning lends its format to the expression of self through behaviours that I have labelled confessional. The fact that the elements of online environment nurture confession as pedagogy speaks loudly about the existence of comfort, community and social presence within online communities. Ironically, learners' tendencies to adopt confessional stances are tacitly supported by the adult education and constructivist principles that underlie collaborative online learning environments.

The philosophy of adult education is reflected in Knowles' (1970) foundational principles that emphasised meaningful problem-centred learning and self-direction. Carl Rogers' work on humanism, with its promotion of individuals' autonomy and positive sense of self, underpins Knowles' assumptions. In implementing these principles, adult educators use many strategies in face-to-face classrooms to create comfortable, facilitative adult learning environments (Mackeracher 2004; Renner 2005). Optimal online learning environments rely even more heavily on these principles in order to compensate for and accommodate learners' possible sense of isolation or technical awkwardness. The implementation of adult education principles makes possible the creation of a strong sense of community among online learners. Some of the strategies and activities through which community is built are outlined here.

Community-building

Research has indicated conclusively in recent years that adult learners welcome online learning environments utilising collaborative, constructivist-oriented approaches (Gunawardena 1995; Richardson and Swan 2003). Learners who experience such learning environments report that they value the support, safety and sense of community that result from consistent and sustained interaction with like-minded peers (Conrad 2005).

The building of a strong community among those engaged in online learning involves not only learners but also instructors, programme administrators, guest speakers and, according to some learners, their support systems comprising partners, colleagues, family and friends (ibid.). Casting such a wide net familiarises and personalises online learning terrain; against this setting, adult-oriented instructors can strive to foster a sense of community by constructing break-the-ice orientation activities. Such activities often include self-revelation in structured ways. Learners tell about their learning histories, about their motivation for taking courses, about their hobbies, their families or their pets. Quite often, the first few interactions in online courses fall into this warm-up category. Learners who are new to online technology (although it is not very complicated) use this time to familiarise themselves with the process, while at the same time inserting themselves and their own sense of social presence into the developing group dynamic.

Group activities

There are many practical managerial and pedagogical reasons for using groups in online learning. The formation of groups serves as a community-building device, at times strategically mixing learners and at times allowing them to congregate in groups of their own choosing according to their interests or goals. Cautious adult learners taking comfort in the intimacy of small groups are more likely to engage in substantive reflective activity in a more private domain. Online instructors can focus their energies on managing intensive small-group discussions more constructively than in more rambling and diffuse large-group exchanges.

Group assignments

Similarly, group assignments encourage collaborative knowledge-building efforts among adult learners while providing a practical and pedagogically sound way for online instructors to reduce the size of the workload generally associated with teaching online (Reeves 2002). Learners are encouraged to work together on a product that can be presented in some way individually or collectively, that can precipitate response and input from either the instructor alone or the whole group, or that can serve as an initiation to further study. Whatever the intended outcome, an often *unintended* outcome is the creation of an intimate, sub-community within the larger community of the class.

Authenticity

Adult education philosophies have contributed to the reshaping of teaching–learning roles. As a part of redefining the distribution of power and authority in the classroom and adopting a learning-centred stance that highlights learners and their learning, adult educators have championed the notion of authenticity in teaching and learning (Brookfield 2000; Cranton 2001). Cranton and Carusetta define authenticity as 'the expression of the genuine self in the community' (2004: 7) and note its emphasis on openness, awareness, caring and sharing of self. For teachers, successful authentic teaching can result in both critically examining one's own practice and in inspiring others to authentic practice (ibid.). Examining university teachers' perspectives on authenticity, Cranton and Carusetta (ibid.) found that expressions of authenticity were not always analytical or rational; rather, teachers' critical reflections were often based on their more personal use of intuition, hunches, or feelings.

Autonomy

Like authenticity, autonomy has become critical to the notion of adults learning in self-directed and meaningful ways. Benson (1997) listed five understandings of autonomy, all of which focus on learners' rights and responsibilities as regards directing their own learning. Learners exercising autonomy must find and grasp their sense of self. They must find and raise their authentic voices. They must be a part of, by creating and reciprocating, the energy of a learning community. Additionally, striving for autonomy means taking risks.

Taken together, the conditions described above make it possible to create supportive and personal learning environments for distance learners. At the same time, these conditions can serve as fertile ground for incubation of confessional types of behaviours for learners seeking to find new identities and establish their sense of self in online environments.

Confessing online: what does it look like and why is it important?

Some years ago, a student referred to some of his colleagues' online behaviours as 'birdwalking', by which he meant 'too much information,' stepping over other learners' ideas of reasonable boundaries, and cluttering up the discussion area with overlong and over-personal postings. Research has revealed learners' apprehension, panic and frustration with the 'avalanche' of introductory postings as learners fulfilled the let's-get-acquainted portion of online course start-ups (Conrad 2002).

In short, learners engaging in confessional behaviours online use legitimate opportunities, such as let's-get-acquainted activities, in addition to creating their *own avenues* to impart very personal information about themselves, their lives, their histories, their emotions, their anguishes, their dreams and their fears to their online group. In accounting for these behaviours, Goffman's identity theory is complemented by related understandings from several disciplines. One psychologist accounts for this in this way: 'There is ample research to suggest that disclosing secrets or talking about strong emotions improves physical and psychological health' (Seabol 2005). A writer-researcher who is also a web designer and blogger suggests that 'giving our thoughts a home online helps them to endure' (Ewins 2005).

From the literary world, the writer Milan Kundera coined the term graphomania to describe a writer's manic need 'to impose oneself on others' through already established modes of 'received ideas' and pervasive non-thought' (Napolitano 2005). In commenting on Kundera's assessment of the fact of such emotional expression becoming valuable in and of itself, Napolitano (ibid.) confirms that he finds many online journals frightening in their public-ness. He likens this modern form of communication, which would include many weblogs, at their worst, to 'a new outlet for personal refuge [that] we would otherwise find inane, petty, and grotesquely self-indulgent'.

Emulating Kundera's graphomania, one online learner wrote:

> I have been sitting here at my computer for some time tonight reading all the wonderful stories and messages. There are so many thoughts swimming in my head that I would be here until dawn just writing my comments back to the group.

Many online learners do just that. Stories of childhood, of trauma, of discord, of illness and of workplace unhappiness flood online discussion boards. In another variation of confessional tendencies, learners' stories that want to be told but are judged by their writers as 'too personal' to share with learning colleagues are sometimes directed only to the teacher or tutor. This type of learner–teacher communication creates issues of sensitivity for online instructors in addition to becoming a time-consuming management difficulty. Just as often, stories of an intensely personal nature become the grist of small-group online discussions, where the size of the group and the nature of the group task engender a greater sense of intimacy than in large group settings. Such small-group discussions are often not closely monitored by tutors or instructors; they may even occur outside of the mandated learning system platform. Often, the existence of such confessional acts remains unknown to the course instructor at the time. Knowledge of them eventually surfaces in any number of informal, 'after-the-fact' ways: on course or programme evaluations, in conversation among learners, in casual conversation with other instructors or in programme planning discussions with programme administrators.

The effect of confession on group dynamics has not yet been sifted out qualitatively from the many other factors that characterise online interaction and participation. The issue is still open but anecdotal evidence points to the fact that confessional dialogue alienates and frustrates some learners while providing an emotional home for others. Learners who become alienated as a result of unchecked confessional tirades from peers come to distrust e-learning as a viable pedagogy. From an instructional perspective, confessional dialogue increases and complicates the management and social functions that are so much a part of responsible online teaching (Collins and Berge 1996).

Given the breadth of identity issues that have been described in this chapter, the recent introduction and adoption of social learning software creates a new dimension of intrigue – a double-edged sword, perhaps. Whereas learners previously took licence to create their own learning spaces in order to fulfill their social needs – whatever the dimension of those needs – social software enthusiasts now provide 'technologies to empower students in their self-governed activities' (Dalsgaard 2006). Social software networking systems, developed to foster closer and more collaborative learning opportunities – can include personal web pages, wikis and blogs. Whether regarded separately or taken together, each of these communication devices represents wonderful potential for enhancing discussion among learners. The salient point, however, is this:

> Students' self-governed and problem-solving activities are considered the focal point of a learning process. This conception of a learning process means that it is not possible to structure or pre-determine the students' activities in a learning process – the activities must develop on the basis of the students' own problem-solving.
>
> (Dalsgaard 2006)

In other words, learners create, input to and own their own learning protocols regardless of the amenities that are provided for them. Previous research on learners' construction of community in their learning spaces produced similar constructivist-based findings (Conrad 2005). Our role as teachers, administrators, designers and developers is to encourage, foster, nurture and support, while respecting the rights of learners to self-direct, self-select and self-monitor. The limitations of providers' ability to impose frameworks on learners' voices makes even more important the need to understand the factors – such as identity creation – that shape e-learners' online activities.

Conclusion

In the early days of computer-mediated learning technology, a greater emphasis on the novelty of new learning platforms and hardware-motivated interests often overshadowed discussions of the pedagogy of the new ways of learning. Research at the time was appropriately described as 'philosophically and theoretically barren' (Blanton et al. 1998: 259). From the late 1990s, however, models championing the constructivist and interactive dynamic of online learning presented data to support the potential of powerful learning through participation, communication, and community (Gundawardena 1995; Rourke et al. 1999; Swan 2002).

More recently, as the boundaries of e-learning continue to expand to embrace new discussions on the social and psychological implications of learning technologies, investigating online learning as educational pedagogy has taken researchers into studies of cognition, participation, assessment and, now, 'beyond the gate'. We strive to understand online learning's role as a social fact in our communications-rich society. As the automobile enhanced our ability to communicate and connect, as the telegraph and the telephone enhanced our ability to connect, so too the ease of access to digitised learning is changing our relationship to our learning, to others and to ourselves.

It is the premise of this chapter that the pivotal factor on which the perceived transition hinges is identity. Publicly, identity struggles are currently playing out in the realm of reality shows. If 'privacy has become the greatest privilege in an intrusive society', as has been suggested (Moore 2004: RB3), it is being challenged by western society's fascination with the intimacy of real lives. Online learning environments, in offering what may be understood as a legitimate stage for confessional exchange, present further opportunities for the continued revelation of self.

References

Bandura, A. (1971) *Social Learning Theory*, Morristown, NJ: General Learning Press.
Bandura, A. (1986) *Social Foundations of Thought and Actions*, Englewood Cliffs, NJ: Prentice-Hall.
Benson, P. (1997) 'The philosophy and politics of learner autonomy', in P. Benson and P. Voller (eds) *Autonomy and Independence in Language Learning*, London: Longman, pp. 18–35.

Bernard, R.M., Abrami, P.C., Lou, Y., Borokhovski, E., Wade, A., Wozney, L., Wallet, P.A., Fiset, M. and Huang, B. (2004) 'How does distance education compare with classroom instruction? A meta-analysis of the empirical literature', *Review of Educational Research*, 74(3): 379–439.

Blanton, W.E., Moorman, G. and Trathen, W. (1998) 'Telecommunications and teacher education: a social constructivist review', *Review of Research in Education*, 23: 235–275.

Brookfield. S. D. (2000) *The Skillful Teacher: On Technique, Trust, and Responsiveness in the Classroom*, San Francisco, CA: Jossey-Bass.

Burnett, R. and Marshall, P.D. (2003) 'Webs of identity', in *Web Theory*, at: http://www.tintin.kau.se/webtheory/chapters/chapter4.html.

Collins, M. and Berge, Z.L. (1996) *Facilitating Interaction in Computer Mediated Online Courses*, at: http://www.emoderators.com/moderators/flcc.html.

Conrad, D. (2002) 'Deep in the hearts of learners: insights into the nature of online community', *Journal of Distance Education*, 17(1): 1–19.

Conrad, D. (2005) 'Building and maintaining community in cohort-based online learning', *Journal of Distance Education*, 20(1): 1–22.

Cranton, P. (2001) *Becoming an Authentic Teacher in Higher Education*, Malabar, FL: Krieger.

Cranton, P. and Carusetta, E. (2004) 'Perspectives on authenticity in teaching', *Adult Education Quarterly*, 55(1): 5–22.

Dalsgaard, C. (2006) 'Social software: e-learning beyond learning management systems', *European Journal of Open, Distance and E-Learning*, at: http://www.eurodl.org/materials/contrib/2006/Christian_Dalsgaard.htm.

Ewins, R. (2005) 'Who are you? Weblogs and academic identity', *E-learning*, 2(4): 368–377.

Feenberg, A. and Barney, D. (eds) (2004) *Community in the Digital Age: Philosophy and Practice*, Lanham, MD: Rowman and Littlefield.

Garrison, D.R., Anderson, T. and Archer, W. (2000) 'Critical thinking in a text-based environment: computer conferencing in higher education', *Internet and Higher Education*, 11(2): 1–14.

Gecas, V. and Burke, P. (1995) 'Self and identity', in K. Cook, G. Fine and J. House (eds) *Sociological Perspectives on Social Psychology*, Boston, MA: Allyn and Bacon, pp. 41–67.

Gergen, K.J. (1991) *The Saturated Self: Dilemmas of Identity in Contemporary Life*, New York: Basic Books.

Goffman, E. (1959) *The Presentation of Self in Everyday Life*, Garden City, NY: Doubleday.

Gunawardena, C.N. (1995) 'Social presence theory and implications for interaction and collaborative learning in computer conferences', *International Journal of Educational Telecommunications*, 1(2/3): 147–166.

Jones, C. (2005) 'Who are you? Theorizing from the experience of working through an avatar', *E-learning*, 2(4): 414–425.

de Kerckhove, D. (1997) *Connected Intelligence: The Arrival of the Web Society*, Toronto: Somerville.

Knowles, M. (1970) *The Modern Practice of Adult Education*, Chicago: Follett.

Marshall, P.D. (1998) 'Confession and identity', *M/C: A Journal of Media and Culture*, 1(3). at: http://www.media-culture.org.au/9810/conf.

Mackeracher, D. (2004) *Making Sense of Adult Learning*, second edition, Toronto: University of Toronto Press.

Moore, C. (2004) 'Who is better off – the Prince or the editor?', *National Post*, 13 November, RB3.

Napolitano, T. (2005) 'Of graphomania, confession, and the writing self', at: http://www.electronicbookreview.com/thread/writingpostfeminism/ graphomaniac.

Reeves, T.C. (2002) 'Distance education and the professorate: the issue of productivity', in C. Vrasidas and C. V. Glass (eds) *Distance Education and Distributed Learning*, Greenwich, CT: Information Age Publishing, pp. 135–156.

Renner, P. (2005) *The Art of Teaching Adults: How to Become an Exceptional Instructor and Facilitator*, Vancouver, BC: PFR Training Associates.

Richardson, J.C. and Swan, K. (2003) 'Examining social presence in online courses in relation to students' perceived learning and satisfaction', *Journal of Asynchronous Learning Networks*, 7(1): 68–88, at: http://www.aln.org/publications/jaln/v7n1/v7n1_ richardson.asp.

Rourke, L., Anderson, T., Garrison, D.R. and Archer, W. (1999) 'Assessing social presence in asynchronous text-based computer conferencing', *Journal of Distance Education*, 14(2): 50–71.

Sarup, M. (1996) *Identity, Culture and the Postmodern World*, Edinburgh: Edinburgh University Press.

Seabol, L. (2005) 'Online confessions: a growing number of teens are using their online blogs to express themselves', at: http://www.tuscaloosanews.com/apps/ pbcs.dll/ article? AID=/20051227/PULSE02/512270333/1005.

Short, J., Williams, E. and Christie, B. (1976) *The Social Psychology of Telecommunications*, Toronto: Wiley.

Snyder, M. (1987) *Public Appearances/Private Realities: The Psychology of Self-Monitoring*, New York: W. H. Freeman and Company.

Swan, K. (2002) 'Building communities in online courses: the importance of interaction', *Education, Communication and Information*, 2(1): 23–49.

Turkle, S. (1997) *Life on the Screen: Identity in the Age of the Internet*, London: Phoenix.

Wenger, E. (1998) *Communities of Practice: Learning, Meaning and Identity*, New York: Cambridge University Press.

Wikipedia (2007) 'Social software', at: http://en.wikipedia/org/wiki/Socialsoftware.

Chapter 18

Concluding remarks

Michael Osborne

This book has selected contributions that lean towards pedagogical models that stress the social aspects of lifelong learning. It has been structured around three themes of concern to the pedagogy of lifelong learning. First, those chapters by Malcolm and Zukas, Weedon and Riddell, Stevenson, Findsen and Carvalho, and Field and Malcolm deal variously with questions of learning identity, learning careers and trajectories, and the making of meaning in a range of different locational contexts. Second, the chapters by Dymock, Carmichael et al., Göranssen, Solomon, Wheelahan, and Edmunds et al. consider the role of pedagogy in developing learning culture and the ways in which cultures of organisations and communities facilitate, prescribe and determine learning, and once again consider these issues within different sites of post-compulsory learning. The third section, with chapters by Renkema, Ouellet et al., Grek, Kop, and Conrad, develops the theme of sites of learning, but focuses specifically on pedagogies of lifelong learning beyond traditional face-to-face teaching in institutional settings. Naturally these categorisations are broad generalisations developed to aid the reader and structure this rich set of contributions, and there are a number of themes that cross sections.

It is a truism to say that it has been a long-held view of those working in post-compulsory education that the development of a capacity to learn extends and, although changing in character, scarcely diminishes through life – the endeavours of thousands around the world would be rather hollow without such a belief. However, until relatively recently this view tended to be an article of faith, rather than something based on a raft of scientific evidence, and contrary arguments have tended to be postulated by some psychologists working in the area of cognition. The dominant strands of thinking in the field of adult intellectual development for much of the twentieth century had been those of stability and decrement, albeit carrying less credence in recent decades. Stability models have assumed that it is via cognitive processes in childhood that forms of reasoning and thinking in adulthood are established and that these forms change neither qualitatively nor quantitatively thereafter. Decrement models have suggested that biological deterioration sets in as we reach our fourth decade, leading to irrevocable decline in cognitive function (Tennant and Pogson 1995). There have been silver linings to these models; researchers working within the psychometric tradition have also postulated a best case scenario of decrement and compensation, with the decline in capacity to utilise and organise information as the brain deteriorates compensated by the effect of accumulated experience (Baltes 1987).

From a different perspective, cognitive psychologists operating within Piagean and post-Piagean frameworks have concerned themselves with the qualitatively different types of thinking that manifest themselves during stages of cognitive development, and it is researchers working within these traditions who have provided greatest support to lifelong pedagogical approaches. Whilst influenced by Piaget, a number of theorists have both argued against the limitations that his model imposes on development and built upon it. As stability and decrement has declined in popularity, the significance of learner experience and the learner as a constructor of knowledge have developed strongly as an influence on practice. A number of writers (e.g. Riegel 1973; Labouvie-Vief 1980) have argued against the limitations of Piagean models, and proposed post-formal models of thinking that move beyond the narrow range of problems proposed in Piaget's formal operations of adolescence. It is the greater emphasis given to post-Piagean constructivist approaches, within which it is argued that an individual constructs knowledge through interaction with their environment throughout life , and to social constructivism based on Vygotsky's (1962, 1978) model of social cognition that have come to dominate thinking amongst those concerned with the pedagogy of lifelong learning. The predominant Vygotskian idea concerns the effect of culture on individual development; it provides both the source of knowledge and the tools of intellectual adaptation. As often is the case when a persuasive and appealing theoretical perspective appears, it can assume a dominance in practice. In her chapter in this book, Wheelahan points out that there is a considerable consensus that 'constructivist theories of curriculum [. . .] downplay the importance of knowledge in the curriculum and increasingly emphasise knowledge that is contextual, situational and immediately applicable'. Whilst accepting her further contention that such criticism tends to underplay contextual and situational knowledge, it may be worth reflecting on evidence from the experiences of those engaged in online learning where the predominant paradigm has been constructivism. For example, the preference to 'lurk', rather than engage in active communication, in virtual learning environments (VLEs) (Postle et al. 2003) would seem to be a legitimate choice for the autonomous self-directed lifelong learner as described by Caffarella (1993). Contrary arguments concerning the benefits of the cognitive dissonance engendered by deliberate exposure to the uncomfortable also of course merit examination. Furthermore, whilst the democratic and self-constructed world of wikis and blogs described by Kop provides the technical infrastructure for student-led learning, it also provides the capacity for individuals to drown in a world of infinitely relativistic knowledge.

In this book it is Stevenson's chapter that deals most closely with the ideas of Piaget and Vygotsky, situating a number of studies from vocational and higher education within the frameworks that these pre-eminent theorists have provided.

He provides a number of implications for practice, most notably that teachers would benefit from recognising that learners have different ways of knowing and will not automatically recognise the meaningfulness of other ways. He suggests that 'the role of the teacher is to involve learners in activities that are accessible and meaningful; but which press them into accommodation through the inter-connection of different ways of knowing appropriate and significant at that point in their life journey', and this is perhaps a significant and distinguishing feature of the lifelong learning pedagogue. In Carmichael et al.'s account of literacy practices in UK further education colleges, it is the relationship between practices within and outwith college that impacts significantly upon the making of meaning for the two students whose cases are described. It is argued that for some students the boundaries are sharp between domains, and that there appears to be a need to create 'border crossings'. This perhaps provides further support for Stevenson's assertions. The making of meaning is also central to Grek's study of adult learning within the context of museum education. She makes the important point that without an examination of the socio-historical context of that making of meaning, any research endeavour would be taking a partial approach to analysis.

The idea that learning occurs through participation in social communities and in constructing and developing identity within these communities is associated most closely with the notion of membership of a *community of practice*, a term made popular by Lave and Wenger (1991). Communities of practice are frequently related to specific occupational contexts and are the foundation of workplace learning models (see Allan and Lewis 2006). In this book we are introduced to a number of such workplace models in the chapters by Stevenson and Goransson. They are also used in connection with many and various others sites of formal and non-formal learning, including notably those connected with the use of information and communications technologies (ICTs) (see Hung and Chen 2001), and in this book we see such contexts described in Conrad's chapter. As we indicated in the introduction, many of the principles of design for e-learning, which are based on notions of *commonality, situatedness, interdependency* and *infrastructure*, draw heavily on communities of practice. Whilst commonality refers to shared contexts and interests, situatedness suggests that a valuable learning environment is one that situates learning within authentic practices and engagements with others in the community that participates in these practices. Learning thereby has a real context within which existing knowledge is tested and new knowledge emerges. Interdependency refers to participants within a learning group taking advantage of the different strengths of individuals, using diversity in a positive manner. Infrastructure refers to 'rules and processes, accountability mechanisms and facilitating structures' (Hung and Chen 2001: 9).

Solomon draws our attention to a key feature of situatedness, authenticity, in her account of a vocational school operating as a hotel, and the view of educators in that establishment that 'pedagogy can/should replicate the "real"'. As with Goransson's firefighters in another chapter, there is a certain dissatisfaction amongst Solomon's hotel workers, in this case because of the unrealistic nature of simulations to which they had been subjected. It is clear that contingency inevitably reigns in most teaching and learning situations, even those associated with a workplace context. Indeed it might be argued that a simulated environment is a quantum leap in authenticity by comparison to the majority of formal learning experiences. Nonetheless even the best simulations and hyper-realities where the real and unreal are blurred have clear limitations. Solomon, however, provides us with a positive pedagogical prospect for lifelong learning, that of developing reflexive learners. Rather than viewing simulation as an attempt to duplicate the 'real' world, it might be treated as 'a discursive practice which produces its own world, which is a hybrid of work and learning and whose conditions and problematics are peculiar to itself'.

In previous work, reported in part in this book by Edmunds et al. and previously by others (Brennan and Jary 2005; Brennan and Osborne 2006; Houston and Lebeau 2006), the concepts of *social mediation* and *organisational mediation* in the context of what is learned in higher education have been used. These mediations carry resonance for a range of work reported in this book. In the SOMUL project described in the Edmunds et al. chapter, the initial conceptualisation of social mediation was as follows:

> By social mediation, we refer to the life situations of the students on a particular programme of study – individually and collectively – and including the social and educational backgrounds of the students as well as features of the student culture within the particular institution or programme – together providing the 'social context of study'.
>
> (Brennan and Osborne 2006)

This description seeks to draw attention to three forms of social difference, in the case of higher education students, but equally applicable in other formal environments. First, there are differences that are *imported* into education and that arise from the social and educational backgrounds of the students which determine their initial competences, expectations and ambitions (the student 'habitus' in Bourdieu and Passeron's (1977) terms). Second, there are differences in the student experience during education that are *externally generated* and which determine student lifestyle choices and necessities (for example, where to live, whether to take a part-time job, domestic commitments, etc.). Third, there are differences in the student experience that are *internally generated* and which determine both the level and nature of the student's engagement with his or her studies and the level and nature of the student's engagement with other aspects of educational life, for example clubs, sport and other forms of social behaviour. All three forms of social difference are inter-related and are also related to the SOMUL project's other key concept of 'organisational mediation'. As Houston and Lebeau (2006: 1) suggest, social mediation of learning refers to the 'life situations of the students on a particular programme of study – individually and collectively – and including the social and educational backgrounds of the students as well as features of the student culture within the particular institution'. In short, they argue that context is a key determining factor of the learning process, and suggest that some of the most established and influential research strands concerned with learning in HE, specifically those concerned with 'approaches to learning' (Marton and Säljö 1976; Entwistle and Ramsden 1983; Biggs 1987) appear to avoid 'any real engagement with the complexities of location and context' (Haggis 2003: 101).

A number of chapters in this book, both those dealing with HE and those concerned with other locations of learning, formal and non-formal, are concerned with social mediation. The interplay between the range of individual social and cultural backgrounds of students, and the increasing diversity of institutional environments is played out in the individualisation of student trajectories. Weedon and Riddell report in their chapter on the experiences of students with dyslexia in UK higher education institutions and suggest that learning careers of those diagnosed as dyslexic may depend on such an interplay between their own backgrounds and the particular institution that they attend. For Field and Malcolm, social mediation is presented within a broader canvas when considering lifelong learning trajectories. In their biographical studies of adult learners in Scotland, it is different historical and generational contexts that influence perceptions of and values and behaviours in relation to learning. In Findsen and Carvalho's study of adult learners in New Zealand, a social context seems particularly strong as a mediator for learning. Motivation for participation in learning as an adult has received considerable attention over the years since Houle's (1961) formative qualitative work and the many subsequent quantitative scales and related typologies that have been created (e.g. Morstain and Smart 1974; Boshier and Collins 1983). Citing Morstain and Smart's study, Findsen and Carvalho suggest that amongst six clusters of motivation for learning it is *social relationships*, *social welfare*, *escape/stimulation* and *cognitive interest* that predominate amongst older adults. The need to develop and sustain social relationships does not diminish with age, and the social context of the group appears particularly important.

The other main conceptualisation within the project described by Edmunds et al. is 'organisational mediation' and has been described as follows:

> By organisational mediation, we refer to the ways in which curriculum knowledge is organised, including the influences of modularity, extended student choice and different modes of study – together providing the 'principles of curriculum organisation'.
>
> (Brennan and Osborne 2006)

This is an important, albeit only one, perspective of organisational mediation[1] strongly influenced by Bernstein's ideas of *classification* and *framing*. Despite having originated from and being contextualised within the domain of school education, Bernstein's framework is potentially transferable to other domains. In his work, classification refers to *relations between categories* (e.g. academic subjects, occupations, social classes). Strongly classified categories are insulated from others and according to Bernstein (1996: 21), each 'has its unique identity, its unique voice, its own specialised rules of internal relations'; power preserves the strength of the insulation. Framing refers to control or regulation within a context (or category). Where provision is strongly framed, the 'transmitter' has explicit control over the 'acquirer' through both regulating social order ('hierarchical relations' in the pedagogic relationship) and discursive order (selection of communication, its sequence and pacing and criteria of knowledge). Strong framing produces *visible pedagogic practice* where the rules and requirements are explicit, and may be observed in the ways in which curricula, students, staff, space and time are organised. Similar arguments are put forward by Nespor (1994), who is concerned with the ways in which individuals become enmeshed in fields of practice in higher education which localise space, pattern time, standardise curricula, define interests and allow particular identities.

We see an example of strong framing in one of Malcolm and Zukas' cases, Sarah, whose initial conception of being a teacher was that of a transmitter of knowledge and where her identity was constructed around knowing more than her students and through her knowing being separated in time and space. But these authors also report a weakening of the hierarchy within the pedagogical relationship with the realisation that learners may be co-constructers of knowledge in the Vygotskian sense.

It is in work-based learning that one might expect there to be a high propensity for weaker framing, and for learners to exert greater control over learning. But this does not necessarily lead to positive outcomes. Goransson's account of the work-based learning of Swedish firefighters illustrates the challenges intrinsic to engagement with experienced practitioners. The strength of bonds between individuals and the culture of the collective in an organisation means that the group can as a whole either accept or reject the challenge of new learning methods. A number of the accounts in other chapters could also be analysed using Bernstein's notion of framing, with Kop's online social learning tools most clearly demonstrating another manifestation of weak framing and potentially a spectrum of classifications.

Clearly the social and the organisational are not dichotomous. Organisation mediations have a social component, and are both a function of social structures and act upon these structures. Renkema's chapter illustrates the relative weakness of social interventions mediated via organisational structures and incentives in his account of ILAs in the Netherlands. He suggests that 'subjective norms, educational attitude, perceived self-efficacy, and situational factors such as prior learning experiences and the influence of others' are difficult to influence through such interventions. Whilst learning may be mediated by structures, individuals, groups and communities may (cf. Giddens (1984) theory of structuration) use their agency to exert their influence in refining these. Further, the agenda may be set by individuals and groups. Dymock reports on studies of learning communities in Australia, making links to the work of Faris in Canada, who has utilised the concept in a number of different ways. It can refer to 'a community within a classroom or educational institution, a virtual global learning community, communities of practice, or those of place' (Faris and Wheeler 2006), and suggests these are part of a Russian doll of nested social learning environments of ever increasing scale, collectively termed *Learning Communities of Place*. Dymock reports on learning regions and communities in a largely rural setting where there are considerable difficulties in developing a learning culture. Nonetheless his work points towards the considerable educational resources that individuals themselves possess and which could be capitalised upon within the range of organisational structures encompassed by the learning community. This work also directs us towards considering the role of a range of social actors within the lifelong learning enterprise (see Longworth 2006), the role of experience in learning and the forms of two-way or multiple social interactivity between individuals and groups that might be facilitated. The theme of regionalism and multiple actors is also taken up by Ouellet et al.'s report of the plurality of representations of essential skills training between sectors and between actors in Canada. Whilst pointing out the potential relative roles of national, provincial and local government, businesses, training organisations and individuals, their account reminds us of the lack of homogeneity both within and between categories that we might construct.

Faris and many others have also described the ways in which learning communities can be manifested in virtual form using ICTs and in this book Conrad uses social constructivism combined with Knowles' andragogical philosophy (itself derived from a variety of theoretical traditions) as a background to her account of adults' online learning and communication. Conrad is also one of a number of contributors who places identity at the core of her pedagogical considerations. Her account suggests that online learning environments lend themselves to the expression of self, and in her case through what she describes as the 'confessional'. She provides strong arguments in favour of there being a place for fostering this component of interactive communication within online learning environments, though also points out the challenges. Kop's account of the recent phenomenon of wikis and blogs also points out the opportunities afforded by social tools to support student-driven construction of knowledge through informal and interest-driven communication. These and the other emerging tools of the MySpace generation will no doubt present considerable opportunities for pedagogical practice in lifelong learning. However, we might also consider the freedom that these environments provide for individuals to experiment with the presentation of self and to create identity, some of the dangers therein having recently been explored by Timms (2007). We have stressed identity as a key theme within this book and in Edmunds et al.'s chapter; we are also provided with an account with this theme as a central element. In their work from a HE context, identity is interpreted both in the context of academic and professional development; and as personal development and conception of self. Explicitly, these identities are argued as key components of *what* is learned alongside traditional conceptions in the cognitive domain.

Conrad's references to Knowles' (1970) work may also be helpful, particularly as a reminder of strands of thinking from previous decades that he utilised (e.g. Rogers' (1969) teacher as facilitator, Tough's (1971) independent learner, Dewey's (1938) experiential learner, Bruner's (1961, 1966) inquiry and problem-based discovery method and self-directed learning, and Postman and Weingartner's (1969) subversive teacher). Although Knowles' andragogical model has been challenged over the years for the broad generalisations that it makes, particularly concerning the distinctions that he originally made between children and adults across dimensions including 'needing to know', 'self-concept', 'experience', 'readiness to learn', 'orientation to study' and 'motivation', it will be interesting to see how his assertions stand up to testing within the realms of the new evidence from modern neuroscience described later in this chapter.

This leads to some final thoughts about the future research agenda for the pedagogy of lifelong learning. Terenzini and Pascarella (1994), in the context of undergraduate education in the US, spoke about at least five myths; and on the basis of a review of over 2,600 pieces of research, provided compelling contrary evidence to the following:

Institutional prestige and reputation reflect educational quality

Traditional methods of instruction provide proven, effective ways of teaching undergraduate students

Good teachers are good researchers

Faculty members influence student learning only in the classroom

Students' academic and non-academic experiences are separate and unrelated areas of influence on learning.

(Terenzini and Pascarella 1994)

We can no doubt construct a series of myths concerning teaching and learning more generally across sites of post-compulsory education, but one set above all seems most pertinent to de-bunk. Early in this chapter, it was the faith of pedagogues in the enterprise of lifelong learning that introduced a very brief history of perspectives on the robustness of human learning over time. This faith may now be testable against emerging evidence from neuroscience. The set of myths that are being challenged are those that concern the brain and learning, the *neuro-myths* (OECD 2002: 69–73). As Wolff (2003: 8) has argued, the implication of neuroscience research using methods such as magnetic resonance imaging (MRI) and positron emission tomography (PET) is that 'life-long learning is not a dream since it is embedded in the capacity of the brain to respond throughout life to environmental demands'. Except in the cases of particular diseases of the brain, the neurons which process information do not as previously thought decline during life, but for the main part remain healthy. Furthermore, the plasticity of the brain, its capacity to develop, once thought to be a phenomenon of the early years of life, is now considered to be a lifetime occurrence. As de Magalhães and Sandberg (2005: 1031) report, 'not all cognitive and memory functions decline with age and different functions change at different paces with age' (Craik and Salthouse 1992; Kausler 1994; Gopnik et al. 2000). Knowledge and learning depends on neural connectivity, which occurs via the synapses, and these grow rapidly in the first three years of life, ending their growth around the time of biological adulthood. The further neuro-myth is that the greatest potential for learning occurs during the period of synaptogenesis, but this does not take into account the role of the selective pruning of synapses thought now to be a normal part of development, and part of the acquisition of some skills.

We have emphasised research with a strong social context within this book and there can be little doubt of the importance of context at both the micro and macro scale to pedagogical interventions. A future agenda, however, may be a marriage between this tradition and that of neuroscience. Already the OECD in meetings of its Learning Sciences and Brain Research project has brought together the neuroscientific and education community, including those with backgrounds in post-compulsory education (see Tippelt 2005: 37–39), to discuss what could be expected from neuroscience research in relation to lifelong learning. Questions being posed include:

- What is the brain's flexibility for learning capacity over the lifespan?
- Is there a timeframe for optimal learning?
- Can we expect investments in learning for senior adults to effect a 'seven-fold' health saving?
- Is there evidence from neuroscience regarding the level of involvement in social networks and brain functional activity?
- Is there an alignment between the psychological measures used in education research and the measures of brain activity in neuroscience?
- How can neuroscience inform with regards to the transfer of learning?

There certainly is a substantial future interdisciplinary research enterprise within this domain for the future.

Note

1 See Brennan and Osborne (2006) for a fuller account, including a discussion of higher level organisational mediations. Referring to the literature of, amongst others, Baldridge (1983), Cohen and March (1991) and Bourgeois and Frenay (2001), they argue that higher level organisational factors concerned with such factors as quality assurance mechanisms, social justice initiatives to widen participation and the need to prioritise research, have considerable impact on pedagogical practice over and above the influences upon classification and framing exerted by disciplines.

References

Allan, B. and Lewis, D. (2006) 'Virtual communities as a vehicle for workforce development: a case study', *Journal of Workplace Learning*, 18(6): 367–383.

Baldridge, J.V. (1983) 'Organisational characteristics of colleges and universities'. in J.V. Baldridge and T. Deal (eds) *The Dynamics of Organizational Change in Education*, Berkeley, CA: McCutchan Publishing Corporation.

Baltes, P.B. (1987) 'Theoretical propositions of life-span developmental psychology: On the dynamics between growth and decline', *Developmental Psychology*, 23: 611–626.

Bernstein, B. (1996) *Pedagogy, Symbolic Control and Identity: Theory, Research and Critique*, London: Taylor and Francis.

Biggs, J.B. (1987) *Student Approaches to Learning and Studying*, Hawthorn, Victoria: Australian Council for Educational Research.

Boshier, R. & Collins, J. (1983) 'Education participation scale factor structure and sociodemographic correlates of 12000 learners', *International Journal of Lifelong Education*, 2(2): 163–177.

Bourdieu, P. and Passeron, J.C. (1977) *Reproduction in Education, Society and Culture*, Beverly Hills, CA: Sage.

Bourgeois, E. and Frenay, M. (2001) *University Adult Access Policies and Practices across the European Union and their Consequences for the Participation of Non-traditional Adults*, final report to European Commission of the TSER Project, SOE2-CT97-2021.

Brennan, J. and Jary, D. (2005) *What is Learned at University? The Social and Organisational Mediation of University Learning: A Research Project*, York: Higher Education Academy.

Brennan, J. and Osborne, M. (2006) *The Organisational Mediation of University Learning*, York: Higher Education Academy.

Bruner, J. (1961) *The Process of Education*, Cambridge, MA: Harvard University Press.

Bruner, J. (1966) *Toward a Theory of Instruction*, Cambridge, MA: Harvard University Press.

Caffarella, R. (1993) 'Self-directed learning', *New Directions for Adult and Continuing Education*, 57: 25–35.

Cohen, J. & March, J. (1991) 'The processes of choice', in M. Peterson, E. Chaffee and T. White (eds) *Organisation and Governance in Higher Education, an ASHE Reader*, Needham Heights, MA: Simon & Schuster.

Craik, F.I.M. and Salthouse, T.A. (1992) *Handbook of Aging and Cognition*, Hillsdale, NJ: Lawrence Erlbaum.

Dewey, J. (1938) *Experience and Education*, New York: Macmillan.

Entwistle, N. and Ramsden, P. (1983) *Understanding Student Learning*, London: Croom Helm.

Faris, R. and Wheeler, L. (2006) 'Learning communities of place: situating learning towns within a nested concept of social learning environments', paper presented at Australian Learning Communities Network (ALCN) National Conference 2006 25–27 September, Brisbane.

Giddens, A. (1984) *The Constitution of Society: Outline of the Theory of Structuration*, Cambridge: Polity Press.

Gopnik, A., Meltzoff, A. and Kuhl, P. (2000) *The Scientist in the Crib: What Early Learning Tells Us about the Mind*, New York: HarperCollins.

Haggis, T. (2003) 'Constructing images of ourselves? A critical investigation into "approaches to learning" research in higher education', *British Educational Research Journal*, 29(1): 89–104.

Houle, C. (1961) *The Inquiring Mind*, Madison: University of Wisconsin Press.

Houston, M. and Lebeau, Y. (2006) *The Social Mediation of University Learning*, York: Higher Education Academy.

Hung, D.W.L. and Chen, D.-T. (2001) 'Situation cognition, Vygotskian thought and learning from the communities of practice perspective: implications for web-based e-learning', *Educational Media International*, 38(1): 3–12.

Kausler, D.H. (1994) *Learning and Memory in Normal Aging*, San Diego, CA: Academic Press.

Knowles, M. (1970) *The Modern Practice of Adult Education*, Chicago: Follett.

Labouvie-Vief, G. (1980) 'Beyond formal operations: uses and limits of pure logic in life span development', *Human Development*, 23: 141–161.

Lave, J. and Wenger, E. (1991) *Situated Learning: Legitimate Peripheral Participation*, Cambridge: Cambridge University Press.

Longworth, N. (2006) *Learning Cities, Learning Regions, Learning Communities: Lifelong Learning and Local Government*, London: Routledge.

de Magalhães, J.P. and Sandberg, A. (2005) 'Cognitive aging as an extension of brain development: a model linking learning, brain plasticity, and neurodegeneration', *Mechanisms of Ageing and Development*, 126: 1026–1033.

Marton, F. and Säljö, R. (1976) 'On qualitative differences in learning: I – outcome and process', *British Journal of Educational Psychology*, 46(4): 11.

Morstain, B. and Smart, J. (1974) 'Reasons for participation in adult education course: a multivariate analysis of group differences', *Adult Education*, 24(2): 83–98.

Nespor, J. (1994) *Knowledge in Motion: Space, Time and Curriculum in Undergraduate Physics and Management*, Philadelphia, PA: Falmer Press.

OECD (2002) *Understanding the Brain: Towards a New Learning Science*, Paris: OECD.

Postle, G., Sturman, A., Mangubhai, F., Cronk, P., Carmichael, A., McDonald, J., Reushle, S., Richardson, L. and Vickery, B. (2003) *Online Teaching and Learning in Higher Education: A Case Study*, Canberra: Department of Education, Training and Youth Affairs.

Postman, N. and Weingartner, C. (1969) *Teaching as a Subversive Activity*, New York: Dell.

Riegel, K. (1973) 'Dialectics: the final period of cognitive development', *Human Development*, 16: 346–370.

Rogers, C. (1969) *Freedom to Learn*, Columbus, OH: Merrill.

Tennant, M. and Pogson, P. (1995) *Learning and Change in the Adult Years*, San Francisco, CA: Jossey-Bass.

Terenzini, P.T. and Pascarella, E.T. (1994) 'Living with myths: undergraduate education in America', *Change*, 26(1): 28–33.

Timms, D. (2007) 'Identity, local community and the Internet', in M. Osborne, K. Sankey and B. Wilson (eds) *Social Capital, Lifelong Learning and the Management of Place: An International Perspective*, London: Routledge.

Tippelt, R. (2005) 'Proposition notes – key issues in lifelong learning', 3rd meeting of OECD/CERI Lifelong Learning Network, Riken, Wako, Japan, 20–22 January, at: http://www.oecd.org/dataoecd/3/9/34391230.pdf.

Tough, A. (1971) *The Adult's Learning Projects: A Fresh Approach to Theory and Practice in Adult Learning*, Toronto: OISE, at: http://ieti.org/tough/books/alp.htm.

Vygotsky, L.S. (1962) *Thought and Language*, Cambridge, MA: MIT Press (originally published in 1934).

Vygotsky, L.S. (1978) *Mind in Society: The Development of Higher Psychological Processes*, Cambridge, MA: Harvard University Press.

Wolff, L. (2003) 'Brain research, learning, and technology', *TechKnowLogia*, 5(1): 7–9.

Index